IFAC

International Federation of Automatic Control

ARTIFICIAL INTELLIGENCE IN REAL-TIME CONTROL 1989

IFAC Workshop Series, 1990. Number 4

IFAC WORKSHOP SERIES

Editor-in-Chief
Pieter Eykhoff, University of Technology, NL-5600 MB Eindhoven, The Netherlands

---

CHESTNUT *et al.*: International Conflict Resolution Using System Engineering (*1990, No. 1*)
SIGUERDIDJANE & BERNHARD: Control Applications of Nonlinear Programming and Optimization (*1990, No. 2*)
VILLA & MURARI: Decisional Structures in Automated Manufacturing (*1990, No. 3*)
RODD *et al.*: Artificial Intelligence in Real Time Control (*1990, No. 4*)
NARITA & MOTUS: Distributed Computer Control Systems (DCCS'89) (*1990, No. 5*)
KNUTH & RODD: Distributed Databases in Real Time Control (*1990, No. 6*)
LOTOTSKY: Evaluation of Adaptive Control Strategies in Industrial Applications (*1990, No. 7*)
MEYER: Real Time Programming (1990, No. 8)
MOWLE: Experience with the Management of Software Products (*1990, No.9*)
TAKAMATSU & O'SHIMA: Production Control in Process Industry (*1990, No. 10*)

RODD: Distributed Computer Control Systems (*1989*)
CRESPO & DE LA PUENTE: Real Time Programming (*1989*)
McAVOY: Model Based Process Control (*1989*)
RODD & SUSKI: Artificial Intellligence in Real Time Control (*1989*)
BOULLART *et al.*: Industrial Process Control Systems (*1989*)
SOMMER: Applied Measurements in Mineral and Metallurgical Processing (*1989*)
GOODWIN: Robust Adaptive Control (*1989*)
MILOVANOVIC & ELZER: Experience with the Management of Software Projects (*1989*)
GENSER *et al.*: Safety of Computer Control Systems (SAFECOMP'89) (*1989*)

Other IFAC Publications

AUTOMATICA
the journal of IFAC, the International Federation of Automatic Control
Editor-in-Chief: G. S. Axelby, 211 Coronet Drive, North Linthicum, Maryland 21090, USA

IFAC SYMPOSIA SERIES
Editor-in-Chief: Janos Gertler, Department of Electrical Engineering, George Mason University, Fairfax, Virginia 22030, USA

Full list of IFAC Publications appears at the end of this volume

ARTIFICIAL INTELLIGENCE IN REAL-TIME CONTROL 1989

Proceedings of the IFAC Workshop, Shenyang, People's Republic of China, 19–21 September 1989

Edited by

M. G. RODD

Institute for Industrial Information Technology, University of Wales, Swansea, UK

HUA-TIAN LI

Northeast University of Technology, Shenyang, PRC

and

SHI-QUAN SU

Northeast University of Technology, Shenyang, PRC

Published for the

INTERNATIONAL FEDERATION OF AUTOMATIC CONTROL

by

PERGAMON PRESS

Member of Maxwell Macmillan Pergamon Publishing Corporation

OXFORD · NEW YORK · BEIJING · FRANKFURT

SÃO PAULO · SYDNEY · TOKYO · TORONTO

U.K.	Pergamon Press plc, Headington Hill Hall, Oxford OX3 0BW, England
U.S.A.	Pergamon Press, Inc., Maxwell House, Fairview Park, Elmsford, New York 10523, U.S.A.
PEOPLE'S REPUBLIC OF CHINA	Pergamon Press, Room 4037, Qianmen Hotel, Beijing, People's Republic of China
FEDERAL REPUBLIC OF GERMANY	Pergamon Press GmbH, Hammerweg 6, D-6242 Kronberg, Federal Republic of Germany
BRAZIL	Pergamon Editora Ltda, Rua Eça de Queiros, 346, CEP 04011, Paraiso, São Paulo, Brazil
AUSTRALIA	Pergamon Press Australia Pty Ltd., P.O. Box 544, Potts Point, N.S.W. 2011, Australia
JAPAN	Pergamon Press, 5th Floor, Matsuoka Central Building, 1-7-1 Nishishinjuku, Shinjuku-ku, Tokyo 160, Japan
CANADA	Pergamon Press Canada Ltd., Suite No. 271, 253 College Street, Toronto, Ontario, Canada M5T 1R5

First edition 1990

British Library Cataloguing in Publication Data

Artificial intelligence in real-time control 1989.
1. Control systems. Applications of computer systems
I. Rodd, M. G. II. Li, Hua-Tian III. Su, Shi-Quan
IV. International Federation of Automatic Control V. Series
629.8312

ISBN 0-08-040185-6

These proceedings were reproduced by means of the photo-offset process using the manuscripts supplied by the authors of the different papers. The manuscripts have been typed using different typewriters and typefaces. The lay-out, figures and tables of some papers did not agree completely with the standard requirements: consequently the reproduction does not display complete uniformity. To ensure rapid publication this discrepancy could not be changed: nor could the English be checked completely. Therefore, the readers are asked to excuse any deficiencies of this publication which may be due to the above mentioned reasons.

The Editors

Printed in Great Britain by BPCC Wheatons Ltd, Exeter

IFAC WORKSHOP ON ARTIFICIAL INTELLIGENCE IN REAL-TIME CONTROL 1989

Sponsored by
The International Federation of Automatic Control Technical Committee on Computers

Co-sponsored by IFAC Technical Committees on:
Manufacturing Technology
Applications
Social Effects of Automation

Organized by
Chinese Association of Automation
Northeast University of Technology, PRC
Shenyang International Conference Center for Science and Technology, PRC

Supported by
National Natural Science Foundation of China

PREFACE

The IFAC Workshop on Artificial Intelligence in Real-Time Control has rapidly established itself as a key event in the IFAC series of Workshops and Symposiums. The large number of papers submitted to the first Workshop, which was held in Swansea, Wales, United Kingdom, encouraged the organisers to proceed to arrange subsequent events. The Workshop in Shenyang was notable for its high number of papers submitted and the International Programme Committee was faced with a tremendously difficult job in selecting those to be actually presented, while still maintaining a highly interactive Workshop atmosphere. These Proceedings contain papers which were considered by the IPC to be representative of the state-of-the-art of AI in Real-Time Control. The Workshop itself was extremely well supported and twelve IFAC countries were represented.

The scope of the Workshop included the use of AI methods in the design, implementation, testing, maintenance and operation of real-time control systems. The workshop series focuses on the fundamental aspects of the methodologies and technologies rather than on specific applications. However, a selection of application papers is always accepted, in order to put the emerging theories into perspective. A feature, also of the Workshop series, is the continual and active participation of the International Programme Committee in keeping a balanced programme. Of particular importance is the selection of Keynote Addresses in order to provide lead-ins to specific areas.

In these Proceedings, Professor Henk Verbruggen of the Netherlands, together with his colleague, Professor Karl Åström of Sweden, describe a range of possible applications of AI methods in control engineering. Their paper discusses, in particular, the use of fuzzy control in neural network-based systems and the paper provides an exceptionally broad and comprehensive review of the state-of-the-art. In the second keynote paper, Professor Mike Rodd of the United Kingdom, takes a user-oriented view of knowledge-based computer vision systems used specifically as components of real-time control systems. In this paper he notes that potential industrial users require solutions which can co-exist in industrial environments, and ones which must react at speeds which are acceptable so that the vision systems can form part of the closed loop. He indicates in this paper that we must strive towards highly integrated but flexible explicit knowledge-based solutions which are capable of fast deterministic performance, but which also have inherent learning capabilities.

In a third invited paper, Professor Chris Harris of the United Kingdom addresses the question of a multi-level approach to sensory integration, particularly for automatic-guided vehicles. In this paper, considering reviewing the rich data sources which are available, the author reviews fuzzy logic, evidential theories and non-monotonic AI methods, such as endorsements or explanation-based reasoning, for dealing with symbolic fusion.

The Proceedings are broadly divided into five areas, starting with the fundamental architectural issues necessary to consider when creating AI-based real-time control sytems. This is followed by the question of knowledge-acquisition and learning, and leads into a series of papers reviewing new techniques or validating proposed ones particularly in the real-time control environment. The question of scheduling, monitoring and management of both manufacturing and process control is reviewed through three papers with particular industrial experience, and finally, in the traditions of the IFAC Workshops, a series of papers review specific application of various AI techniques.

A key feature of the IFAC Workshops is the on-going discussion which occurs amongst the delegates present. It was clear from various discussions, particularly one chaired by Professor Joh-han Pao of Case Western University, on the topic of "The Challenge of AI in Real-Time Control", that traditional AI technologies are facing the challenge posed by the need to integrate complex systems in real-time control. It was pointed out that the AI technology which is currently available, however, tends to be static, and that speeds of execution are not acceptable in many on-line situations. As these Proceedings graphically show, many methods from software to hardware, have been suggested for implementation of AI in real-time control - including such techniques as knowledge-based parallel processing, dynamic modelling of knowledge, etc. Although it must be admitted that many of these techniques are still at a laboratory stage, it is clear that the dawn of the application of AI technology in real-time control is upon us.

CONTENTS

ARTIFICIAL INTELLIGENCE AND FEEDBACK CONTROL

H. B. Verbruggen* and K. J. Åström**

**Delft University of Technology, Faculty of Electrical Engineering, Control Laboratory, P.O. Box 5031, 2600 GA Delft, The Netherlands*
***Lund Institute of Technology, Department of Automatic Control, Lund, Sweden*

Abstract

This paper describes some possible applications of Artificial Intelligence methods in control engineering. Due to the restriction of AI methods to well-defined knowledge domains (expert systems), the growing interest in fuzzy control methods and the possible application of simple neural networks, a large number of applications in all areas of technical science came into consideration. The recent availability of adequate software and lately also of special purpose hardware tools has accelerated this development.

1 Introduction

In process automation there is a tendency to use Plant-wide Control systems which combine in one system tactical, managerial, scheduling, operational and control tasks for production and process control. A multilayered information processing system is defined based on the various levels of decision making. An increasing number of people from different disciplines are involved in the operation of these systems, each with their own background and expertise and their different demands and requirements concerning the overall system behavior. The system should provide the various users with advisory and consultancy possibilities, based on the different kinds of specialized knowledge. It is clear that a lot of quantitative information is processed within and between the various levels of automation, but there is also a growing need for concentrated and qualitative information. In the expert systems used at these levels the main emphasis is on explanation facilities and knowledge translation, highlighting the key functions and parameters on each decision level. There is a need for a distributed expert and intelligent system, passing global information to the various levels of automation and inferencing on the specialized and more detailed information at the given level. This system should be coupled to the distributed computer control system or incorporated in the existing hard- and software. When we classifiy the application areas of expert sytems in automation systems we can distinguish systems which are based mainly on static or on dynamic information. Another division could be based on classification requirements or design and control problems. It is clear that because of the time critical situation the highest demands are put on the use of expert and other intelligent systems on the supervisory and control level. In these systems the expertise of process operators and control systems designers is mixed with the time-varying information obtained directly from the process by the measurements.

This paper is concerned with the lower levels of automation at which the knowledge-based and intelligent system should be implemented in a real-time environment. The most promising applications are found in the areas of:
- alarm monitoring, diagnosis and handling
- supervisory and adaptive control
- modeling of the operator
- intelligent and direct expert control

The application of expert systems in modeling and system identification and in control system design will only be touched on in this paper, because of their mainly off-line character and their emphasis on explanation and user-guidance facilities. However, the development of a combination of a real-time control system which automatically asks for advice and initiates a design and identification session is a most challenging prospect.

The paper is organized as follows. Some general reflections on feedback control and artificial intelligence are given in Section 2, where different ways to use AI methods in feedback control are reviewed. Section 3 deals with the case when an expert system is used to supervise different control strategies, this is called indirect expert control because there is a weak coupling between the control system and the expert system. In Section 4 we discuss direct real-time expert control where the expert system is more tightly coupled to the control system. There is a special class of direct real-time expert control systems that have been used in industry for some time. They are based on modeling the actions of a good operator by rules. Such systems are discussed in Section 5. Section 6 gives a brief treatment of learning systems, which appear to be a very promising area both from the research and the application point of view.

2 Feedback Control and Artificial Intelligence

Historically, feedback control and artificial intelligence have common roots in early cybernetics. After the initial development stage the fields, however, evolved in different directions. A major difference is that AI has almost exclusively focused on static problems while dynamics is the key issue in feedback control. Today, however, there is a growing awareness that AI techniques may be useful in control systems. This is manifested by manufacturers of control systems that are exploring AI and by vendors of AI systems who are looking into process control applications. See Kawakita et al (1988), Moore et al (1987), Oyen et al (1988), Reynolds (1988) and Sachs et al (1986). Among the applications considered we find monitoring, diagnosis, alarm handling, quality control, design, planning and scheduling and control. It is, however, less clear precisely where the advantages may lie. In this section we present an overview of the different application areas. Some of them will be treated in more detail in the following sections.

Algorithms and Heuristics

The development of control theory has for a long time been characterized by algorithm development, both algorithms for on-line control and algorithms to design control systems. In control engineering practice there are, however, many problem areas that are not handled by algorithms alone. It is, for example, necessary to have a good knowledge of a control problem: including the dynamics of the process and the disturbances, specifications and implementation constraints to be able to choose a particular algorithm. This knowledge is difficult to represent in algorithms but it can conveniently be represented in rules or semantic networks. Because of the focus on algorithms the other aspects of control system design have also largely been disregarded in the control research community. The possibilities of representing the design knowledge using AI techniques may refocus the interest.

Supervision Logic

In the actual practical implementation of control systems the algorithms are only a minor part of the code in a control system. Apart from the man-machine interface the major part of the code in a control system is actually the logic that surrounds the control algorithm. This logic takes care of switches between manual and automatic control, bumpless parameter changes and anti-windup in simple controllers. In more complex controllers it also handles the supervision of automatic tuning and adaptation. It is also a common experience that the effort required to implement and debug this code is significant. Since the supervision code is easily expressed in logic it is a natural candidate for use in an expert system.

Merger of PLC and DDC

In process control there are two types of automation systems, the continuous time control executed by the control algorithm (DDC) and the discrete logic and sequencing (PLC). It is a clear trend that these systems are merging. Suppliers of DDC systems are adding logic and sequencing, and suppliers of PLC systems are adding PID algorithms. An expert system can be used as an alternative to logic and sequencing or as an extension.

Merger of MIS and DCCS

In Plant-wide Control there is a merging between Management Information Systems (MIS) and Distributed Digital Control Systems (DCCS). Suppliers of both systems are developing software and network facilities in order to to realize an information processing system for the complete framework of operational and control tasks. At various levels of automation expert systems are introduced. It is clear that these systems should process knowledge related to the demands of their respective automation level, but also should pass, receive and distribute knowledge to their neighboring levels in a concentrated form. A distributed expert system can be used to guide and supervise the shut-down and start-up procedures and the transients between different modes of operations in a multi-product plant under various load conditions.

Modeling and System Identification

Modeling and system identification are important elements in solving a control problem. Conventional static and dynamic models contain a wealth of knowledge which can be exploited in many ways. There are, however, also situations where the models are not known with sufficient accuracy or where they are too complex. Qualitative physics and qualitative modeling developed in the AI community may be an interesting complement. See Bobrow and Hayes (1984), de Kleer and Brown (1984), Forbus (1986) and Kuipers (1986). The field of system identification has developed significantly over the past 30 years. A lot of the knowledge developed has been included in software packages like Idpac and Matlab. Considerable expertise is required to use these packages. Two types of knowledge is required, knowledge about system identification and knowledge about a particular package. It has been shown that both types of knowledge can conveniently be represented using scripts and rules. See Larsson and Persson (1986, 1988a, 1988b).
A challenging feature of these sytems can be experiment planning by the in-line application of system identification and modeling procedures. On the basis of the acquired and required knowledge, a selection of experiments is made, restricted by available or allowed measurement time, allowed signal magnitude, the frequency domain to be excited, etc.

Control System Design

Control system design is an area which requires expertise. Several attempts have been made to capture this expertise in a knowledge based system. See e.g. Taylor, Fredrick, James et al (1987), MacFarlane and Ackermann (1987). In the first experiments the use of conventional expert system shells was attempted. It appears, however, that it would be highly desirable to have tools that can also interact with conventional models of control systems and conventional control design algorithms.

Automatic Tuning Devices

There are several devices on the market that attempt to help a user to tune a controller. Examples are the Supertuner and the Protuner. These devices typically carry out some type of system identification from plant experiments and then give the recommended controller tuning. Related techniques are used in some of the single loop controllers with automatic tuning. See Bristol and Kraus

(1984), Kraus and Myron (1984) and Åström and Hägglund (1988). Although these devices are useful it is clear that the tuning of a controller is not always uniquely determined by the process dynamics. It also depends on the purpose of control. A typical example is level control where the purpose can be tight level control as well as surge tank operation when it is desired that the level swings over the full range. From this viewpoint it appears reasonable to have a more sophisticated system for tuning advice that can also can take the purpose of control into account. It would also be highly desirable to have design data in such a system because sometimes good tuning parameters can be computed from design data. It is also clear that applications in control system design and in automatic tuning are closely related.

In sophisticated controllers such as adaptive and predictive control algorithms a number of parameters have to be preset by a control engineer and to be tuned or supervised by an intelligent system. A few parameters are, however, strongly related to the system requirements and should be tuned by the operator or control engineer. These parameters represent the key parameters in a control loop design, like bandwidth, overshoot and noise reduction. These parameters are the controller knobs of the controller and are translated to parameters inside the controller algorithm which can be completely irrelevant for the user. An example of the tuning of a self-tuning adaptive controller is given in Krijgsman et al. (1988). A knowledge-based system forms the natural link between the idea of the control system designer as to how the system should behave, and the mathematical description of the process. Using the correct calculations and heuristics it sets the right parameters of a controller or chooses the right controller configuration. An example is the choice of the different controller configurations using the Unified Predictive Controller, see Soeterboek et al (1989). Many parameters should be chosen during the design phase, and a number of parameters, related to the given system behaviour, adapted during operation. A rule base is set up to manage this task in an efficient way. Rules can be added when more experience of the controller or the process has been gained. The number of rules is relatively low and to speed up the procedure the knowledge-based system can be translated into conventional software.

Learning Systems

Learning control is perhaps the most interesting point of tangency between control and AI. There are strong similarities between the learning algorithmns of AI systems and adaptive control algorithms. There are also marked differences. Adaptive control systems are often more structured and they use more apriori data. The typical learning algorithms are more general and less structured. It would be an interesting task to attempt a merger of the ideas.

3 Indirect Expert Control

Perhaps the most direct way of using a knowledge-based system for feedback control is to realize that any controller contains algorithms and logic. A natural separation is then to stucture the system in algorithms and logic, possibly in a hierarchical structure as indicated in the introduction. At the lowest level we would then have simple control algorithms of the PID type, possibly with automatic tuning and scheduling and supervision. The heuristic knowledge of how the system should be run in different modes is then implemented in terms of rules. An advantage of such a system is that it gives a clean separation of algorithms and heuristics. Systems of this type have also been used to prototype PID controller with scheduling, tuning and adaptation although the systems have been hardcoded for production.

Supervision and Tuning of PID Controllers

Most industrial control problems are today solved by PID control. Because of the benefits of good tuning, several attempts have been made to tune regulators automatically. One idea based on pattern recognition was developed at Foxboro, see Bristol (1977), Bristol and Kraus (1984) and Kraus and Myron (1984). Another successful approach is based on relay feedback, see Åström and Hägglund (1984, 1988a).

In the pattern recognition approach a PID controller is connected to the process. The response to step changes or disturbances is observed and the controller parameters are adjusted, based on the response pattern. The procedure mimics the procedure used by an experienced process engineer. It requires that reasonable controller settings are known prior to the experiment and it can be implemented as a rule based expert system. This expert system is composed of a transient analyser that determines the damping and the frequency of the closed loop system based on a transient, and a PID designer which is a collection of empirical tuning rules.

The relay auto-tuner is based on the idea that knowledge of the ultimate frequency, i.e., the frequency where the phase lag of the open loop is 180 degrees, the crucial information for tuning a PID controller. The ultimate frequency can be determined from an experiment with relay feedback. When tuning a loop the process is first brought to steady state operation under manual control. When tuning is desired the process is then connected to relay feedback. A limit cycle oscillation is then obtained. The controller setting is calculated from the amplitude and the period of the limit cycle and the controller is automatically switched to PID control. It is practical to introduce hysteresis in the relay to avoid chattering due to noise, and a feedback so that the limit cycle oscillation is kept within specified limits. The ultimate frequency is determined from zero crossings and the ultimate gain from the peak amplitude of the oscillation. The measurements of separate half-periods of the oscillation can be compared to establish that a steady state oscillation is obtained. The only prior information that has to be provided is the initial relay amplitude. The hysteresis of the relay is determined by measuring the noise level.

A system with relay auto-tuning can conveniently be described in terms of algorithms and logic. The algorithms will cover relay feedback, noise analysis, limit cycle analysis, computation of PID parameter, and PID control. The logic will cover the mode switches and the tests for switching between the operating modes. The operation of the system is conveniently described using a script. See Shank (1986).

Gain Scheduling

Gain scheduling is a powerful technique to handle variations in process dynamics when there are measurable signals that correlate well with the changes in dynamics. With automatic tuning it is easy to obtain gain schedules automatically simply by having a table for different operating conditions and to save the parameters obtained when tuning for different operating conditions. The implementation of such a system can also be straightforwardly expressed in terms of scripts, rules and algorithms. These ideas have been incorporated in simple single loop controllers. See Hägglund and Åström (1989).

Assessment of Control Performance

Automatic tuning and adaptation are now well established for simple PID controllers. These controllers can be said to automate those tuning functions normally performed by instrument engineers. To achieve a higher level of automation it is useful to have systems that can also reason about specifications and achievable performance and guides in the selection of controllers. Eexpert systems are well suited to the solving of these problems. Applications are discussed in Åström (1988) and Åström et al (1989).

Supervision of an Adaptive Controller

The key elements of an adaptive controller are a control algorithm, a recursive parameter algorithm and a control parameter calculation. Since an adaptive controller is more complex than a PID controller it also requires more supervision. It is also natural to have a simple PID controller as a backup controller. The supervision of and the adaptive controller itself can be structured as follows:

Main Monitor	Stability and control quality supervisor
Estimation Monitor	Excitation.
	Estimates and covariances.
	Drift and jump detection.
	Perturbation signal generation.
Back-up Control	PID control. Automatic tuning.
Design Supervision	Controllability and observability tests.
	Specification supervisor
Scheduling Supervisor	Scheduling tables. Quality test.

More details are given in Åström et al (1986) and Årzén (1987, 1989).

Example - Expert Control

It is natural to consider a controller which consists of several different algorithms orchestrated by an expert system as was suggested in Åström et. al. (1986) and further elaborated in Årzen (1988, 1989). We call such a system an *expert control system.* The architecture of the system is shown in Figure 1. The system consists of several algorithms for control and estimation, for example a PID controller, a PID tuner, a gain scheduling table, a least squares recursive estimator and a pole-placement self-tuner. The system also has other algorithms for supervision and analysis and signal

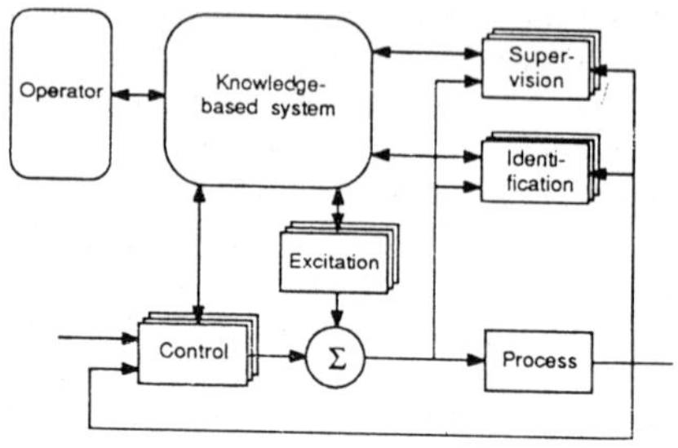

Figure 1: Block diagram of an expert control system.

generation algorithms to improve identifiability. All the algorithms are coordinated by the expert system that decides when to use a particular algorithm. The expert system architecture separates the control algorithms from the logic and it supplies a convenient way to interact with the system. The architecture also forces a disciplined structure. A blackboard structure has been found to be very useful. Such a system which has forward chaining and backward chaining as well as procedural knowledge sources has been implemented by Årzén (1987, 1989).

It is interesting to compare an expert control system with an auto-tuner. The systems are similar in the sense that they both can provide reasonable parameters for a PID regulator. However, the expert control system can also interact with the user in a much more effective way. It can provide answers to queries like, Is the system running normally? List all loops that have been tuned last week. List all regulators where derivative action is used. List all loops where dead-time compensation seems to be required. List the 10 loops with the poorest performance. A functionality like this is certainly useful both for operators and for instrument engineers.

Strategy Switching

Depending on the system requirements and the actual behavior of the system it can be very useful to change the controller configuration. Especially in a MIMO system it can be advantageous to reconsider the connection between controlled variables and controller actions. Due to the mode of operation, the production level and the properties of the raw materials to be processed, an adaptation of the control strategy can be advantageous. In a SISO system the strategy switching can be related to the dynamic selection of a control algorithm (bang-bang controller, P, PI or PID controller). In Baars et al (1987) an example of strategy switching using an expert system in the temperature control system of large buldings is described.

4 Direct Real-Time Expert Control

In a conventional or sophisticated control system the controller design is based on fundamental knowledge, described by mathematical equations (state equations, transfer functions, etc), deduced from physical laws and experimental data. This knowledge can be divided into structural knowledge (order of the process, noise characteristics, etc) and in parametrized and numerical knowledge (i.e. parameter values of the transfer function, value of the delay time, etc). In direct expert control (d.e.c.) a knowledge-based system using qualitatives replaces a controller based on fundamental knowledge, see Figure 2. D.e.c. is based on the experience of the operator and control engineer as well as on the observations of the process and control variables. Relationships among variables may be known or assessed in qualitative terms. Usually the knowledge-based system contains a mixture of qualitative and fundamental knowledge. A d.e.c. approach is less useful for linear systems with well known parameters, but can be applied succesfully in those cases where the process is highly nonlinear or hard to describe while existing theories do not cover the analysis and design of those systems. Because of their very nature d.e.c. systems lack conventional characteristics such as guaranteed stability of the contol loop, consistency and desired prescribed performance. However, by careful supervision also based on an expert system, acceptable control behavior and a certain amount of learning capability can be realized.

It is obvious that in d.e.c. guaranteed response times are crucial and high demands are put on the processing speed of the system. In industrially distributed digital control systems it is crucial that an expert system is embedded in the original automation hierarchy. A good allocation of tasks between the real-time monitoring and control environment and the expert system is necessary. It is very important that the expert system can be embedded in real-time software.
Most of the knowledge-based systems known today have been developed for diagnosis and classification purposes. The main emphasis is on explanation facilities and the handling of a large number of rules and not on time-critical behavior. In a real-time knowledge-based system (the possibility of dividing the knowledge into a multi-layer configuration is very interesting). Each layer has its own kind of knowledge and therefore its own rule base. This kind of reasoning is called progressive reasoning. The inference engine starts with the lowest layer. When a conclusion is obtained in this layer, this conclusion is stored and the "reasoning" continues in the next upper layer. This reasoning/conclusion storage cycle continues upwards to the next layers. As soon as the system is interrupted because a time-critical action should be performed (at the sampling time for example) the 'best' conclusion up to then is taken and the related control action executed.

Example: EXPERT-3

To make real-time experiments possible, a real-time knowledge-based system EXPERT-3 was developed at our laboratory. It is written in FORTH as an extension of EXPERT-2, see Broeders (1988). It contains a backward and forward chaining inference mechanism and a rule compiler to guarantee fast inferencing. The knowledge representation is based on production rules. An agenda-driven scheduling mechanism has been added to the backward chaining mechanism. There are facilities to compile more than one rule base.

EXPERT-3 operates on a 68000 system (ATARI ST) under Real-Time Forth (RTF) which is a small comprehensive development environment for the design, implementation, testing and debugging of microsystems. RTF offers multi-tasking; synchronization and communication between tasks can be performed by the use of semaphores and queues. The real-time facilities include timer and delay statements.

The controller consists of five hierarchically ordered layers. The first three layers classify the the process in an area of the phase plane, spanned by the error signal and its first difference. Experiments were performed with different shapes of the areas dividing the phase plane. The best results were obtained by using elliptically shaped areas. Successively the system is classified by:
- the signs of the error and its first difference (first layer, 4 rules)
- the size of the error (second layer, 6 rules)
- the size of the difference of the error (third layer, 2 rules)
resulting in 48 areas in the phase plane.
Each layer classifies the system and calculates a proper control action. Then the next layer is initiated and the conclusion about the control signal is overruled as soon this layer comes to a conclusion and has calculated the related control signal. In the areas far from the origin, this will be the maximum or minimum control signal U_{max} or U_{min} or a fraction of U_{max} or U_{min}; in the areas near to the origin, the control action is calculated by:

$$u[k] = \alpha u[k-1] + (\beta U_{min} + \gamma(U_{max} - U_{min}))$$

The weighing factors α, β and γ are different for the several areas ($0 \leq \alpha \leq 1$, $0 \leq \beta \leq 1$ and $0 \leq \gamma \leq 1$).
The areas we use are elliptical shapes around the origin of the phase plane. They cross the $\Delta e(k) = 0$ axis in fixed points, while the radius on the $e(k) = 0$ axis can be varied by a factor ρ, where $\rho = 1$ means a circle. When this factor is very large the phase plane is almost completely filled by the outer areas, so the process is controlled using maximum and minimum output signals. The variation of ρ is obtained by some heuristic rules which express that the maximum or minimum controller output must be used for large setpoint changes.
Note that the controller actions could be compared to a proportional + reset action in the neighborhood of the origin of the phase plane. When the distance to the origin is large the controller is similar to bang-bang control.
The overall aim of our controller is to bring the system to the origin of the phase plane in a cautious way without any overshoot. To realize this goal a fourth layer has been implemented. This layer is based on what is called a Model Reference Expert Controller (MREC). When the system enters a new area in the phase plane a first-order model refence trajectory is calculated (a straight line to the origin from the point reached by the system at the given sampling instant). A one sampling time ahead prediction is made of the next point in the phase plane along this reference trajectory. The position of this point is influenced by the time constant of the reference model and the sampling period and can be set by the control engineer or a supervisory controller. Also a one sampling time ahead prediction is made of the next point of the actual system, based on a linear or quadratic extrapolation. The prediction error between the predicted reference trajectory and the predicted trajectory of the actual system serves as the basis for the calculation of the control signal. The angle Φ between the two trajectories is used to realize MREC. Some simple rules were implemented, such as: when $\Phi > 0$ the control signal is increased and when $\Phi < 0$ the control signal is decreased, depending on the length of the error vector.

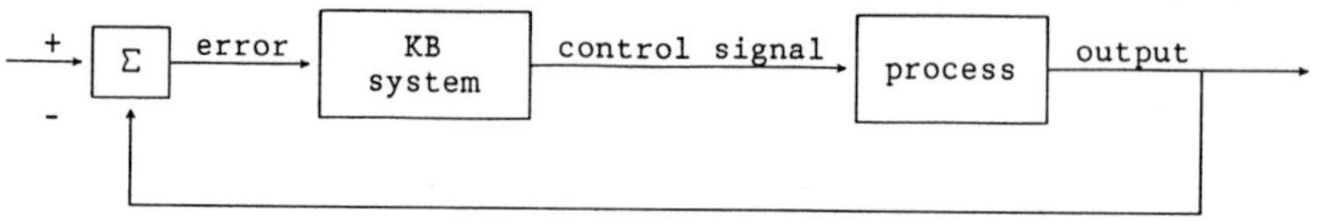

Figure 2: Block diagram of a direct real-time expert control system.

Only the rule sets that belong to areas at a distance not too close to the origin will use this kind of MREC knowledge. Other rule sets contain specialized knowledge such as: how the d.e.c. should act as a regulating controller. In this case it is important to keep the controlled process as close as possible to the origin, instead of steering it fast and secure to the origin. Thus, in the areas surrounding the origin MREC is not useful.

The task of the fifth layer is to supervise the performance of the lower layers. For example, observing the trajectory in the phase plane during the very first samples, allows the determination of whether the controlled system is a "fast" or a "slow" system and provides useful knowledge about the choice of the reference model time constant. These conclusions have a specific effect on the performance of the lower layers; e.g. in the case of a "fast" process, they start calculating the control signals in a more cautious way. Another example of the influence of the supervisor on the lower level knowledge layers is the adaptation of boundaries used to classify the controlled system in the phase plane.
The third function of this layer is to recognize the entry of the steady state area in the phase plane. In this case, the fourth knowledge layer is switched off and all boundaries, α's, β's and γ's that are used in the first three layers are decreased by a scaling factor. In effect, the whole phase plane zooms in on the steady state area positioned around the origin. This zoom function should ensure a zero steady state error.

The forward chaining mechanism is used for the reasoning in the first four layers while the backward chaining mechanism is used in the fifth layer. Observing the knowledge trees in these layers, it can be shown that this is the fastest way to achieve a solution for the respective layers. An agenda control algorithm within the backward chaining inference engine not only assures that the most likely to be concluded hypothesis will be investigated as soon as possible (heuristic search), and that the most important hypothesis will be searched for first, but also that the hypotheses which can never be proved at a specific moment are not investigated. To achieve this last possibility, meta-knowledge has been added to the fifth layer.
To summarize, it can be stated that this supervisory layer does not provide a control signal but helps the lower level layers (and itself) to perform their job in a better way. It contains a number of heuristic rules based on general system behavior, provided by the operator and control engineer in order to enable a choice between different strategies and to set parameters in the lower level layers of the d.e.c. system.

To give an idea of the response time of this system we carried out many experiments. The absolute minimal sample time for d.e.c. with EXPERT-3 on the ATARI-ST is 55 ms. The system requires 430 ms to assure a response matching a first-order trajectory and a zero steady state error for processes that have time constants greater than 2 seconds. The fifth knowledge layer adds about 50 ms to the calculation time. We performed the same type of experiments on real-time systems using the commercially available expert shell NEXPERT embedded in our real-time environment MUSIC on a VAX-station. This combination is an excellent tool for the prototyping of dedicated expert systems. A much higher performance in terms of real-time reaction time could be obtained by implementing the final rule-based system in the conventional programming language C.

Currently, we are investigating processes controlled by a d.e.c. system with non-uniform sampling. While linear digital control design is based on uniform sampling there is no reason for uniform sampling in a d.e.c. system. That means adaptive sampling, based on the measured state of the system, can be used by applying some heuristic rules. It is also possible to use predicted error signals to influence the parameters of the given control laws or to introduce additional terms in this control law, introducing a kind of derivative action in the d.e.c.

Figure 3 gives the results of an experiment with a second-order nonlinear system controlled by this direct expert controller. The process

$$H(s) = \frac{2}{(10s+1)(25s+1)}$$

is preceded by a dead zone from -3 to 3. In spite of this nonlinearity the process is controlled in an acceptable way, without having any exact information about the system (unknown order, time constants, gain and no knowledge about the existence and type of the nonlineairity) ; only the sample period is chosen beforehand.

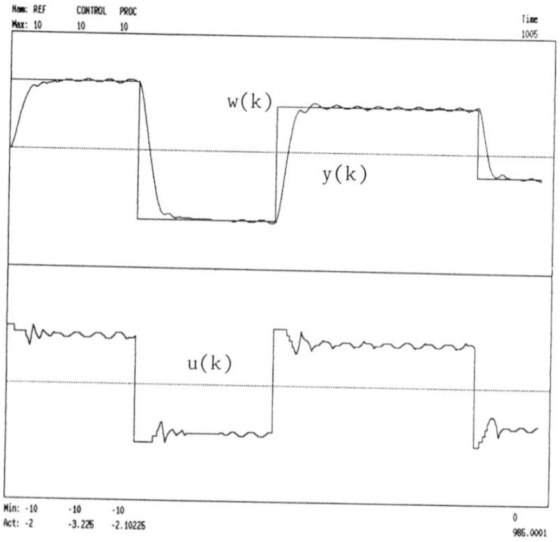

Figure 3: Experiments using EXPERT-3 to control a second order nonlinear plant

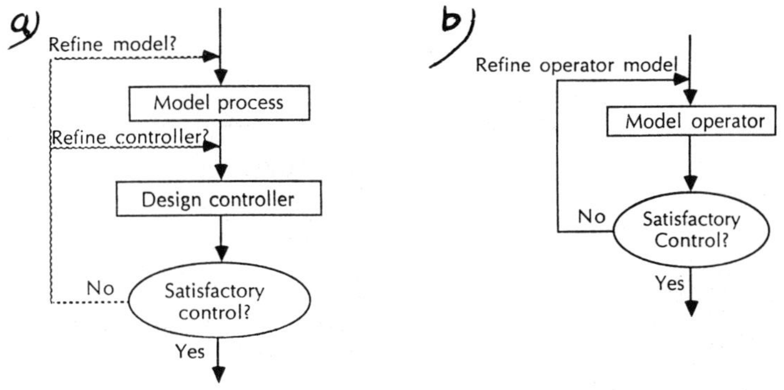

Figure 4: A comparison between a) conventional control and b) control based on modeling of the operator

5 Modeling of the Operator

For some difficult control tasks it has proven very difficult to follow the conventional path of modeling and control design. The main reason for the failure is that the processes are poorly understood. In spite of this it has been demonstrated that human operators are able to control the plants well when they wish to do so. Because the operation is manual there is, however, a significant variation in performance in time and between different shifts of operators. A typical example of this is control of cement kilns, whose dynamics are typically nonlinear and multivariable with long process delays. A different approach to control design has been developed for this class of problem, it is based on the idea of trying to make an automatic system that imitates the actions of the operator. The difference between conventional control and this approach is illustrated in Figure 4. In the conventional approach, the tuning effort consists of modifying both the model of the plant and the controller; in the operator modeling approach the controller is a direct modeling of the operator's decision processes. Successful applications of control based on operator modeling applied to cement kiln control have been reported by F.L. Smith in Denmark (Holmblad and Ostergaard, 1982) and by Blue Cirle Cement in the UK (Haspel et al, 1987). The Danish approach is called fuzzy control and the UK approach linguistic control.

Fuzzy Control

The idea of fuzzy sets is due to Zadeh (1965). The first control applications are described in Mamdami (1974). A system for controlling a cement kiln based on fuzzy control is described in Holmbland and Ostergaard (1982). The key idea is to make a crude quantization of the variables e.g. into five levels *very low*, *low*, *about right*, *high* and *very high*. The fuzzy controller then calculates the output using fuzzy logic. This fuzzy variable is then mapped into a real variable, representing the quantized change in control signal, which is fed to an integrator which drives the control signal. The resulting controller may be viewed as a multivariable, nonlinear integrating controller where the nonlinear function is represented by logic. It has proven very easy to develop the required logic from prior data, operator experiences and minimal experimentation.

Fuzzy control has recently received a significant amount of interest because the calculations required lend themselves very well to parallel computing. Chips for fuzzy control have been developed both in USA and Japan.

Linguistic Control

The lingusitic controller is also a constituent of a nonlinear controller with integral action. The controller is a nonlinear function which gives the changes in control as a function of measurements and command signals. The nonlinear function is described in terms of rules like:

> If the temperature of the furnace is a little high and the combustion gas oxygen level is on the low side, then reduce the kiln fuel rate by a small amount.

This description clearly indicates a crude quantization of the state and the control variables. The approach is therefore also called **linguistic control**. A more concise description of the rule above is:

> **IF** kiln temperature **high** and O_2 **low THEN** +5% feed and 0% fuel

A system called LINKman (Haspel et. al. 1987) has been developed which makes it very easy to implement the system. The system also runs efficiently. In contrast with a normal expert system, the system lacks the power of explanation.

Experiences

Fuzzy control and linguistic control are very similar. Experience from several installations indicates that it is possible to mimic the actions of good operators using rules. In practice, the operator's knowledge is also combined with the knowledge of process engineers, process designers and R&D departments into a coherent strategy. Significant performance increases have been noticed. It is claimed that they derive from using the same strategy consistently. The deviations due to delay and the overreaction of human operators to disturbances and perturbations due to shift changes are avoided. Compared to PID control, the major difference is that the control strategy obtained is nonlinear and multivariable. The rule based systems are also claimed to be easy to commission.

6 Learning Systems

It has been a longstanding goal of control engineers to develop control systems that can learn more and more about the process and its environment as they operate. Devices for automatic tuning and adaptive controllers (Åström 1988) are simple examples of such systems. Much higher levels of learning do, however, occur in biological systems.

The way biological systems are controlled and the learning abilities of rational living beings, based upon experience and observations, has always fascinated control engineers and researchers in Artificial Intelligence. In most cases, the control and learning behavior seems not to be based on fundamental knowledge, but is build up by performing many experiments and applying the gained knowledge to speed up learned actions or to react in a rather similar way in comparable circumstances. This behaviour stimulated the research on neural networks, describing in a certain sense the functioning of the brains of rational beings. Control engineers are, however, not primarily interested in a possible description of the internal structure of the information processing of the brain. They are mainly interested in algorithms that, using a simple black box model, describe reasonably well some of the learning capabilities of the brain.

Neural Networks

Both fuzzy control and linguistic control can be described as nonlinear functions which compute the changes in the control signals. The structure is thus a nonlinear integrating controller. The nonlinear function is derived from the knowledge of operators and process engineers. A neural network is an alternative way of implementing the system. This has the advantage that the nonlinear function can be learned automatically from the actions of an experienced operator. Early attempts in this direction are the experiments with Adaline by Widrow (1963) and BOXES by Chambers and Michie (1968).

A Learning Fuzzy Controller

Another way to introduce learning in a fuzzy controller will now be discussed.

At Delft University, a system has been developed which uses a pattern recognition mechanism and fuzzy decision making, see Van Der Rhee (1988). The fuzzy system uses a data structure built up with cells. The data is stored in cells representing the input and output data at one sampling period; it is represented as a 2-tuple (u_k,y_k) of a single-input single-output process at time $t = kT$, T is the sample time.

The system is used in two phases:

- A learning phase, in which the knowledge about the system is learned and stored in a data structure (a data base of stored input and output data).
- An application phase, in which this knowledge is used by retrieving data from the data structure.

The search algorithm used to find the correct data in the proposed data structure substantiately determines the succesful application of the system. The data structure is organized according to two types of relations:

- Relations in time: with the 2-tuples (u_k,y_k), $k = 0,1,...,n$, these relations represent information about the process behavior (time responses).
- Relations in signal magnitudes representing the information about similar (parts of) responses.

An item (2-tuple) stored in the data structure is called a basic cell. Of course, other types of cells can be used to store data in a different way.

The learning phase is used to store input and output data in the data structure, activating the process by a well-suited learning signal. A number of responses of different length can be stored in the data structure. No actions are performed to check the consistency or the redundancy of the responses stored in the data structure. Actually there is no processing of data during the learning phase.

During the application phase a number of algorithms can be applied to the data of a process stored in the data structure during the learning phase. At this moment the system can be used as a predictor and as a controller. Both algorithms evaluate time responses in the data structure: pattern recognition methods are used to compare responses stored in the data structure with the actual behavior of the process based on fuzzy reasoning.

A search algorithm is used to find the relevant data in the data structure in a particular situation. It is obvious that the efficiency of the search algorithm determines the minimum sampling time of the fuzzy system.
When we look at possible industrial application of this system we must think of systems that are very hard to model in a mathematical way. The process may not vary too much in time. At this moment the application as a fuzzy controller takes too much time to be useful in the majority of real-time applications. Research is going on in order to improve the efficiency of the method through findeing a different way to store and retrieve information through efficient hashing schemes and by defining other cell concepts (meta-cells) which can contain more information through compressing parts of the responses.

Albus Cerebellar Model Articulation Controller

The algorithm treated in this section is a very simple representative of a neural network, called CMAC (Cerebellar Model Articulation Controller), and was proposed by Albus (1975). It is based on ideas about the possible functioning of a particular area of the brain called the cerebellum, which area controls the trained movements of the muscles. The application of CMACs are described by Miller (1987), Betz (1988), Handelman (1988) and Vlothuizen (1988).
The method is based on a table lookup technique, different from a classical table lookup. The algorithm produces output values related by this table to multiple input variables. When the CMAC is used as a modeling device it predicts the output of the process based on previous process inputs and outputs, called the input state. When the

CMAC is used as a controller an adequate process input signal should be produced. Depending on the input values fed to the CMAC several table locations are selected and an output value is obtained by a summation of of all values stored in the selected table locations. The main problem is how the table should be filled in and build up.
When we first look at one input the following procedure is performed: the value of the input is quantized using a number of "quantizing functions". Each quantizing function maps the input value in exactly one address of an associated table. By applying a number of quantizing functions, each with a small offset in the active range of the input values, two effects will be produced: several addresses in the table will be selected in parallel (situated in completely different locations) and the resolution of the input variable will be enhanced.

If there are several inputs to the CMAC (i.e. inputs and outputs of a process at different sampling instances) each input is quantized by a number of quantizing functions. Thus, each input produces a number of addresses in the associated table. When we look at all possible combinations of quantized input variables, the size of the necessary memory could be very high and is related to the number of inputs, N, the number of quantizing functions, K, and the number of addresses produced by the quantizing function, Q.
The memory space needed comprises KQ^N addresses. When we call this memory the virtual memory we have to map this virtual memory to a much smaller memory, called physical memory, by a number of transformations. It is clear that the reduction in memory can lead to what is called collisions, i.e. several different inputs are mapped to the same memory location. To minimize the probability of collisions between distant input values, a uniform and pseudo-random mapping should be used. The mapping must be deterministic because the same input value must always select the same memory locations. Attention has to be paid to the problem of finding such a mapping (hashing scheme), see Venema (1989). The effect of a collision depends on the number of memory locations which are common for two different inputs. Note that collisions between nearby input values will not deteriorate the behavior of the CMAC very much. After restricting the number of memory locations to a manageable proportion, we focus our attention on the last step in the algorithm: the generation of the output value of the CMAC. The output due to a given input vector is generated by summing the weights stored in the assigned physical memory locations. The number of weights depends on the number of quantizing functions and determines the generalization effect of the CMAC. When a CMAC is used as a modeling device, the CMAC should first learn about the process by looking at the process in- and outputs. In the learning phase the weights are updated by comparing the output of the CMAC with the real output of the process. Only a limited number of points have to be learned by the CMAC due to the generalization effect. Because nearby inputs influence each other, not all possible points have to be learned. Interpolation between two learned points is used if the distance is equal to the number of quantizing functions. Figure 5 shows the result of an example using CMAC to predict the output of a second-order process. After a certain learning period the output of the process is predicted very well. Successively the input signal to the process, the process output and the output predicted by CMAC are shown.

To use CMAC as a controller of a dynamic process it should be noted that it does not exhibit memory for former input values. Therefore, the dimension of the input vector should be chosen high enough. Initially CMAC can be learned, while the process is controlled in a more or less conventional way. CMAC observes the response of the process and the inputs applied. If similar behavior is desired in the future, CMAC will remember what input signal should be applied to the process. After a certain period of training, CMAC can control the system, although it might keep on learning for further improvements or be able to respond to changes in the process.
It is interesting to note the analogy to the way movements are learned by the brain. Initially, movement is jerky and slow and needs the full attention of the brain. After training, movements are controlled subconsciously by the cerebellum in a kind of play-back mode. After a learning phase which could be short if the right parameters are chosen [Venema], a very fast method for predicting output signals or producing process input signals is obtained due to the table lookup principle. CMAC is capable of controlling nonlinear processes and processes which are difficult to model with a speed independent of the complexity of the process. A problem is the validity of the table lookup. If some of the parameters of the process change, the stored information which is not explicitely related to the process parameters can not be adapted immediately, while the information about the process, due to the mapping procedure, is spread all over the table. Therefore questions arise as to the validity of data, although by a so-called learning factor continuous updating of the table can be performed.

7 Conclusions

In this paper an attempt has been made to review some of the current attempts to introduce ideas from artificial intelligence into feedback control systems. Expert systems seems well suited for the supervison of different control algorithms They offer a good way to structure the systems in such a way that the supervison logic is well separated from the control algorithms. There are also interesting possiblities to introduce knowledge as to when a particular control algorithm can be applied in the feedback system, hence offering control systems with a higher level of automation. A key difficulty which has not been solved properly is the finding of suitable mechanisms for reasoning about time.

Knowledge-based and intelligent systems can be used for direct and indirect control. In the latter case they are able to control unknown, nonlinear or time-varying systems provided that they are supervised. A supervisory layer is necessary to guarantee the stability and consistency of the control system. The most useful features of Learning Systems are the speed of operation and the possibility to control non-linear processes and processes that are difficult to model. A combination with knowledge-based systems can be used to ameliorate the system behavior by checking the consistency of gathered information and tuning some of the learning parameters of the learning system. Intelligent systems will penetrate into all levels of a multi-layered information and control system. Provisions should be considered to pass on adequate information between the different levels of automation and to translate this information to key parameters relevant to the given levels. Finally, it should be stated that intelligent control is a very promising

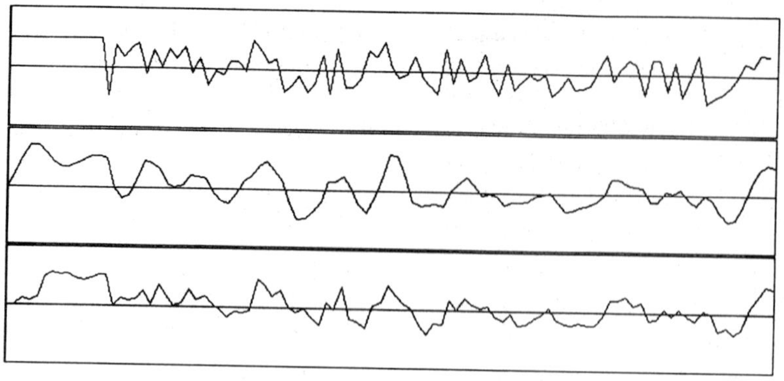

Figure 5: CMAC as a predictor

and challenging field of research, however, in many cases a well-tuned conventional or adaptive controller will perform satisfactorily and should not be replaced by a more sophisticated, intelligent controller as long as there is no evidence that this is necessary because of the possibilities of serious malfunctioning under certain conditions.

Acknowledgement

The research at the Department of Automatic Control of Lund University of Technology has been supported by the Swedish Board of Technical Development (STU) under contract 85/3084T.

The research at the Control Laboratory, Delft University of Technology, was performed in the project "Real-Time Expert Control". Special thanks to Piet Bruijn and Ardjan Krijgsman for their support in writing sections 5 and 6.

References

[1] Albus, J.S., *A New Approach to Manipulator Control: The Cerebellar Model Articulation Controller (CMAC),* Transactions of the ASME, pp. 220-227, September 1975.

[2] Albus, J.S., *Data Storage in the Cerebellar Model Articulation Controller (CMAC),* Transactions of the ASME, pp. 228-233, September 1975.

[3] Åström, K.J. and T. Hägglund (1988), *A New Auto-Tuning Design,* Proceedings IFAC International Symposium on Adaptive Control of Chemical Processes, Copenhagen, Denmark.

[4] Åström, K.J. and B. Wittenmark (1989), *Adaptive Control,* Addison-Wesley, Reading, Ma.

[5] Åström, K.J. (1988), *Assessment of Achievable Performance of Simple Feedback Loops,* 1988 IEEE Decision and Control Conference, Austin, Texas.

[6] Åström, K.J. (1987), *Adaptive Feedback Control,* Proc. IEEE, 75, 185-486.

[7] Åström, K.J. and T. Hägglund (1984), *Automatic Tuning of Simple Regulators with Specification on Phase and Amplitude Margins,* Automatica, 20, 645-651.

[8] Åström, K.J., J.J. Anton, and K-E. Årzén (1986), *Expert Control,* Automatica, vol. 22, no. 3, pp. 277-286

[9] Åström, K.J. and T. Hägglund (1988), *Automatic Tuning of PID Regulators,* Instrument Society of America, Research, Triangle Park, N.C.

[10] Åström, K.J. (1988), *Dominant pole placement design of PI regulators,* Internal Report CODEN: LUTFD2/TFRT-7381, Department of Automatic Control, Lund Institute of Technology, Lund, Sweden.

[11] Åström, K.J., C.C. Hang and P. Persson (1988), *Heuristics for assessment of PID control with Ziegler-Nichols tuning,* Internal report CODEN: LUTFD2/TFRT-7404, Department of Automatic Control, Lund Institute of Technology, Lund, Sweden.

[12] Baars, W., P.M. Bruijn and H.B. Verbruggen (1987), *Some Experiences with Expert Systems for On-Line Control.* Journal A, vol.28, no.3.

[13] Betz, R.E. and others, *An AI Based Controller for Dynamic Systems,* Proceedings of the IFAC Workshop on Artificial Intelligence in Real-Time Control, Swansea, UK, September 1988.

[14] Bobrow, D.G. and P.J. Hayes (Eds) (1984), *Qualitative reasoning about physical systems,* Artificial Intelligence, Special Volume 24, (1-3).

[15] Bristol, E.H. and T.W. Kraus (1984), *Life with Pattern Adaptation,* Proc. 1984 American Control Conference, San Diego, CA, pp.888-892.

[16] Broeders, H.M.T. (1988), *Real-Time Expert Systems,* Report A88.057 (in Dutch), Control Laboratory, Fac. of El. Eng., Delft University of Technology.

[17] Gupta, M.M. (1988), *Design of Cognitive Feedback Controller,* Proceedings of the 27th Conference on Decision and Control, Austin Texas.

[18] Hägglund T. and K.J. Åström (1989), *An Industrial Adaptive PID Controller,* IFAC Symposium on Adaptive Systems in Control and Signal Processing, Glasgow, UK.

[19] Handelman, D.A., S.H. Lane and J.J. Gelfand (1988), *Integration of knowledge-based system and neural network techniques for robotic control,* Proceedings of the IFAC Workshop on Artificial Intelligence in Real-Time Control, Swansea, UK.

[20] Hang, C.C. and K.J. Åström (1988a), *Practical aspects of PID auto-tuners based on relay feedback,* Preprints IFAC Int Symposium on Adaptive Control of Chemical Processes ADCHEM'88, Copenhagen, Denmark.

[21] Hang, C.C. and K.J. Åström (1988b), *Refinements of the Ziegler-Nichols Tuning Formula for PID Autotuners,* Proc. ISA Annual Conference, Houston, USA.

[22] Haspel, D.W, A.D.J. Lormier, C.J. Southan and R.A. Taylor (1987), *High Level Control,* IEEE San Fransisco, May.

[23] Haspel, D.W., C.J. Southan and R.A. Taylor (1987), *The Benefits of Kiln Optimisation using LINKman and High Level Control Strategies,* World Cement 10, No.6.

[24] Holmblad, L.P. and J. Ostergaard (1982), *Control of a Cement Kiln by Fuzzy Logic.* North Holland Publishing, pp. 389-399.

[25] King, P.J. and E.H. Mamdani (1977), *The Application of Fuzzy Control Systems to Industrial Processes,* Automatica, Vol. 13, pp.235-242.

[26] Kraus T.W. and T.J. Myron (1984), *Self-tuning PID controller uses pattern recognition approach,* Control Engineering Magazine, June.

[27] Krijgsman, A.J., P.M. Bruijn and H.B. Verbruggen (1988), *Knowledge-based Real-Time Control,* 1st IFAC Workshop on Artificial Intelligence in real-time control, Swansea, U.K.

[28] Krijgsman, A.J., P.M. Bruijn and H.B. Verbruggen (1988), *Knowledge-Based Control,* 27th IEEE Conference on Decision and Control, Austin, USA.

[29] Larsson, J.E. and P. Persson (1986), *Knowledge Representation by Scripts in an Expert Interface,* Proc. of the 1986 American Control Conference, Seattle, Washington.

[30] Larsson, J.E. and P. Persson (1988), *An Intelligent Help System for Idpac,* Proc. of the 8th European Conference on Artificial Intelligence, Technischen Universität München, München, pp. 119-123.

[31] Larsson, J.E. and P. Persson (1988), *The Knowledge Database Used in an Expert System Interface for Idpac,* Proc. of the IFAC Workshop on Artificial Intelligence in Real-Time Control, Swansea, UK.

[32] Lattimer Wright, M. and co-workers (1986), *An expert system for real-time control,* IEEE Software, pp. 16-24, March.

[33] MacFarlane, A.G.J., G. Gruebel and J. Ackermann (1987), *Future Design environments for Control Engineering,* Proc IFAC World Congress, Vol. 7, pp.363-369.

[34] Mamdani, E.H. (1974), *Application of Fuzzy Algorithms for the Control of Dynamic Plants,* Proc. IEEE No 12, pp 1583-1588.

[35] Miller, W.T. (1987), *Sensor-Based Control of Robotic Manipulators Using a General Learning Algorithm,* IEEE Journal of Robotics and Automation, Vol. RA-3, No. 2, April.

[36] Moore, R.L. and others (1987), *Expert System Methodology for Real-Time Process Control,* Proc. 10th IFAC World Congress, pp. 274-281.

[37] Oven, R.A., M.A. Keyes and M.P. Lukas (1988), *An Expert System Shell embedded in the Control System,* Preprints of the IFAC Workshop on AI in Real-Time Control, Swansea, U.K.

[38] Reynolds, D. (1988), *MUSE: A Toolkit for embedded Real-Time AI,* in R. Engelmore and T. Morgan (Eds.): Blackboard Systems, Addison Wesley.

[39] Rhee, F. van der (1988), *Fuzzy modeling and control based on cell structures,* Ph.D. Thesis, Control Laboratory, Fac. of El. Eng., Delft University of Technology.

[40] Sachs, P.A., A.M. Paterson and M.H.M. Turner (1986), *Escort - an Expert System for Complex Operations in Real Time,* Expert Systems, 3, 1, pp.22-29.

[41] Soeterboek, A.R.M., H.B. Verbruggen and P.P.J. van den Bosch (1989), *Unified Predictive Control - analysis of design parameters,* Proc. of the IASTED International Symposium Modelling, Identification and Control, Grindelwald, Switzerland, pp.164-168.

[42] Taylor, J.H., J.R. James and D.K. Frederick (1987), *Expert-aided Control Engineering Environment for Nonlinear Systems,* Proc IFAC World Congress, Vol. 7, pp.363-369.

[43] Vlothuizen, W.J. (1988), *The CMAC Method,* Report A88.071, Control Laboratory, Fac. of El. Eng., Delft University of Technology.

[44] Widrow, B. and M.E. Hoff (1960), *Adaptive Switching Circuits,* IRE Wescon Connection Record, New York, pp. 96-104.

[45] Zadeh, L.A. (1965), *Fuzzy Sets,* Inform. Contr., Vol.8, pp 330-353.

KNOWLEDGE-BASED VISION SYSTEMS IN REAL-TIME CONTROL

M. G. Rodd and Q. M. Wu

*Institute for Industrial Information Technology,
Department of Electrical & Electronic Engineering, University of Wales,
Swansea, UK*

Abstract: This review paper takes a user-orientated view of knowledge-based computer vision systems – a viewpoint biased towards the practical applications of the technology as a component in a real-time control system. It investigates the characteristics of this area of application and defines the potential role of vision-based systems. On the basis of this, it reviews current progress in fulfilling these roles. It highlights critical areas – especially the need to recognise that the industrial environment requires solutions which can co-exist in those environments, and can react at speeds which are acceptable in the closed-loop control situation of which they form a part. It is argued that simply bringing together well-understood low-level processing systems and currently-available expert systems-based high-level processing, is bound to fail and indeed partially accounts for the many unsuccessful installations. In practice, a total systems-approach must be taken, recognising the realities of the application – including the still-unresolved problems relating to knowledge-acquisition. The paper concludes that low- and high-level processing must be integrated into highly flexible, explicit knowledge-based solutions to produce systems which are capable of fast, deterministic performance, but have inherent learning capabilities to cope with changing applications.

Keywords: Artificial Intelligence in Control, Expert Systems, Computer Vision, Knowledge-Based Computer Vision, AI in Real-Time Control, Image Processing.

1 INTRODUCTION

Computer vision has yet to make its mark in industry – particularly in terms of applications in on-line Real-Time control. Whilst it is undeniable that certain specific problems can be solved using the various commercially-available vision systems, and that in many cases these are, indeed, very successful, it cannot be denied that there is still a whole range of industrial problems which are looking for solutions. According to Rao and Jain (1988), computer vision research seeks to "understand complex visual processes and to construct effective computer-based visual systems". However, what is so often forgotten by researchers in this subject, is the *real world* in which the results of their research are to be applied.

Machine vision (or computer vision) is by no means a new technology, and has been the subject of much effort for many years. It has become a relatively well-established technology – an indication of this is the maturity of some of the texts which have emerged, such as the definitive text by one of the giants of the subjects, Berthold Horn (1986). However, as a control engineer, one must rush to point out that much of the claimed success, particularly as illustrated in the journals, has been in highly theoretical laboratory environments involving problems which, although tough, are simply not true representations of the industrial environment (Rodd, 1987). Huge gulfs still exist in many areas of application. This paper tries to highlight some of the real, practical problems and point the way ahead for future research.

As will become clear there can be no doubt that the vision systems which are required in industrial applications are *all* inherently knowledge-based. We have to analyse a scene, representing some part of our process, which is captured by some form of sensing device, and analyse that information *in its engineering context*. As with the equivalent human observer, we have to call on an extensive amount of *a priori* information about the measurement that we are trying to make. Having used that knowledge to identify the object of our observations, we then have to go to the next level of solution, and actually make process measurements – size, color, shape, etc. *AND* these measurements must be made with an accuracy appropriate to the devices or controllers which are using the information for some subsequent control function.

Underlying many of the problems of utilising vision systems is that very few commercially available systems can operate in *real-time*. For many decades the computer boffin has run amok in the industrial world with wonderful solutions – ranging from complex computing systems to sophisticated process algorithms, all the way through to advanced communication systems, which, in themselves, are magnificent achievements. However, when one looks at the reality of applying many of these techniques, one sees relatively little progress being made. In most cases the answer to the non-acceptance of many solutions lies not only in their inherent high costs, but even more in the *real-time* nature of the very processes that we are required to control.

The point is that any real-world process system, to be controlled, must have its control system designed according to the needs of the process. Unless a computer vision system produces its outputs quickly enough to be fed back to the process which is producing the articles being observed, in time to affect that process, there is little point in making the measurement. A computer vision system, for example, undertaking the measurement of the size of rocks is of no value if it cannot produce measured variables fast enough to provide useful information to the control system. In the case of a vision system looking at the result of a numerically-controlled metal-forming operation, it must react quickly enough to detect, say, that a tool is broken, before the next operation occurs.

Useful, commercially-acceptable solutions have emerged for the industrial user. It must be acknowledged that the problem is extremely difficult - particularly as the actual objectives of computer vision in such environments are often poorly understood by those researchers required to produce the solutions. We therefore have in potentially important areas a mis-match between current computer vision products and their application requirements. Current vision products cannot match the speed or the complexity required in many industrial applications. The answer must lie in developing a new breed of highly flexible, re-configurable, high-speed (but low-cost) vision systems.

2. COMPUTER VISION - A REVIEW

The objective of computer vision is to make "sense" of the images being sensed. From low-level processing we hope to receive a collection of rudimentary "information", not simply expressed as a data array, but with some degree of useful structure - in the way of possible edges, connected edges, regions-of-similarity etc. The object of high-level processing is to use appropriate techniques to deduce *usable information* about the original observed image. It is extremely critical at this point to remember that the context of this paper is in industrial image scenes. This means that the high-level processing has to result in *useful information* for forwarding to a *control system.* This might be in the form of measurements relating, say, to hole sizes, the average size of particles, or the number and position of the objects. It also might require quantitative information, such as the condition of surface finishes, presence of defects, etc. The whole point is that high-level processing is heavily context-dependent, and NO generic, inflexible, implicit knowledge-based solutions will ever be possible, although the tools *used* might, themselves be generic.

In summary, it is important to recognise that to apply vision, a total system is required. Figure 1 indicates the various aspects of such an industrial computer vision system, whose functions will include:

1. Sensing . Here the visual image (not necessarily visible only to the human eye - it could be an infra-red, ultra-sound or X-ray image) is captured by a "camera" and held in store - typically referred to as a *frame store.* This information is then made available to:

2. Pre-processing . Here we attempt to improve the signal, typically by removing irrelevant noise by filtering, edge-detection, thresholding, etc. This set of improved (or enhanced) data is then provided to:

3. Feature extraction . Here we attempt to extract object features which *might* correspond to geometric or critical features of the object being viewed, i.e. moments, perimeters, Fourier descriptors, etc. Essentially, we are compacting the data before sending it to the next stage of vision processing:

4. Feature Interpretation . Here we essentially attempt to take the data and *map* it back to the *real objects* which we, with our human visual systems, would recognise. The output here is in some form of symbolic representation - which we would subsequently pass on to:

5. Post-Processing . This section is used to feed information back to system users or, increasingly, to the overall control system.

It is important to realise that each of these steps is closely inter-related with all the others, and it is normally necessary to feed back information, in a normal control-loop fashion, to assist in any of the preceding processes.

Computer vision has naturally become a major aspect of artificial intelligence research - calling as it does on knowledge of the environment, of the specific nature of the object being observed, and of the required parameters to be assessed. Although extensive work has been carried out in this area, and in some specific cases has proved to be most successful, in general very few useful, commercially-acceptable solutions have emerged for the industrial user. It must be acknowledged that the problem is extremely difficult - particularly as the actual objectives of computer vision in such environments are often poorly understood by those researchers required to produce the solutions.

3. REQUIREMENTS OF INDUSTRIAL VISION SYSTEMS

There are at least two, very different, categories of application-oriented problems which vision systems will face in industrial control. In the first, there is a range of *unstructured* images which occur in applications such as particle size analysis, surface inspection, etc. The differing aspects of these problems are dealt with in (Berger, 1985). Although some of the ideas which are expressed in this paper are applicable, this area will receive relatively little further attention here. It must be pointed out that this is not an inadvertant omission, but an acknowledgement that there is extensive and important work taking place in this area - relating more specifically to medical and topographical imaging. Particularly important work, and a useful illustration of the success which has been achieved using intelligent systems applied to unstructured images, is covered in the paper by Lin et al (1988).

The other common type of industrial application occurs where the images are, to a high degree, well-structured. Much attention was paid in the early days of vision to certain aspects of this, and some successful work will be highlighted later, but many applications are still unfulfilled. We refer here generally to areas in which the objects are relatively regular, and typically formed with well-understood and well-defined geometrical features. In many cases indeed, one of the prime objectives of introducing computer vision systems into these environments is to distinguish *variations from* the idealised geometric properties.

An important fact which is now being increasingly recognized, is that in many cases the objects are themselves not only built with regular geometric features, but have also been developed on computer-aided design (CAD) systems in which *they have to be* based on relatively simple mathematical formulations! For example, in the sheet-metal handling industry, punching and nibbling numerically-controlled machines are used to produce panels, boxes, etc. These very machines are programmed from data originally captured from designs produced using CAD systems. This is an extremely important fact, as it means that a significant amount of knowledge is available in a database - right from the start. This naturally alleviates many of the problems which occur in capturing knowledge about specific objects (see the later discussions on knowledge-acquisition).

It is critical, therefore, in reviewing the problems of applying computer vision systems in the industrial environment, to discuss some of the properties of the objects being observed and the environment in which we will have to operate.

a. Geometric Features:
Here absolute or relative position, orientation, position and condition of edges and corners, width, surface volume, roughness, shape and proximity may have to be considered. We might not only have to recognise any or all of these geometric properties, but also to *measure* their absolute parameters. It is simply insufficient in an inspection task to say *where* the centre of a hole is; we must also know its radius, as well as the *condition* of its boundary.

b. Optical Features:
Again, this is where the laboratory departs from the factory! In an industrial environment it is extremely difficult to control specific lighting levels and conditions. In order to make sense of any acquired images, aspects such as reflectance, chromatic characteristics, color, texture etc., might have to observed and defined.

c. Mechanical Characteristics:
Many an industrial inspection system fails because the general mechanical or inherent material characteristics of the objects being observed have not been considered. A simple illustration is where the heat from the illumination system can result in objects being distorted. Aspects such as acoustic performance, hardness and temperature characteristics of objects being observed must be taken into consideration.

d. Environment:
A nasty shock is in store for laboratory-based vision experts when they venture onto the shop floor! The environment can be dusty, polluted by sizeable particles, smoky, full of electromagnetic interference, oily, dirty, etc. Maintenance is normally done by unskilled or unmotivated technicians - 100-Watt bulbs are replaced by 60-Watt (if at all!), and cameras are adjusted with a large, dirty hammer! Electrical supplies are full of spikes, and power failures occur at regular intervals.

It is also critical to consider the *actual*, *stated* needs of the potential *user* of a computer vision system. Whilst to an engineer this is an obvious statement, so often to those involved in high-technology research it is the most-often-forgotten parameter! It is difficult to generalise this need, but it can be confidently stated that the fundamental *need* in the industrial environment is for inspection, manipulation and process control. The fundamental *requirement* is for a system which works under plant conditions and matches the rest of the system and the operational needs.

In terms of *inspection*, the need is normally to determine whether an article has been correctly manufactured and meets the required tolerances. It is unreasonable to require objects to be well-orientated, so a relatively free environment is inherent. Thus, although one could constrain an object to, say, a conveyor belt, one cannot precisely predict where it will be or which way round it will arrive! (Currently, of course, many of the installed systems require this rigid part-location, and by using various mechanical devices, a certain degree of alignment can take place. However, it can be argued that the cost of this will, in most cases, outweigh the real benefit of having the vision system in the first place!)

In this environment therefore it is essential first to *find*, via the vision system, the objects being inspected, and then to undertake the tasks necessary to ensure that ll the design parameters have been met. This will require not only recognition of the object, and also of any sub-objects within that object, but actual undertaking of precise measurements - relating to size, position, curvature, etc. To be of value, these calculations must be undertaken to an accuracy which is appropriate to the application. It is critical to repeat that not only must a hole be found, but we must be able to calculate its precise position and radius, and also how *good* the edges are. In this case, such information can be used to determine if the correct drill has been used, if the hole is in the correct position, and, finally, whether the drill is sharp, or is broken or worn.

In the second case, that of *manipulation*, it is important to recognise the object, but also to know *precisely* its orientation and position. Since such processes will subsequently be used for picking up the article - say, by a robot - it is critical to match the accuracy of measurement to that of the manipulator.

Here we must return to an underlying aspect of industrial applications, and re-state that the failure of current vision systems is not only that they cannot meet a large number of the above criteria, but that almost without fail, they do not meet the application requirements in terms of the speed of operation. It does not matter how sophisticated the algorithms are or how efficiently they have been coded, if the real-time response is inappropriate, the solution is irrelevant It is critical, also, that a measurement of the average response is not good enough; the *absolute* processing time must be well-defined. This imposes particularly important conditions on the higher levels of processing, where knowledge-based systems appear to hold many answers to the complex recognition problems posed. Whilst one can handle the lower levels in a deterministic fashion, it is extremely difficult, with the current state of technology, to handle the recognition side in a totally deterministic fashion.

In all time-critical processes the actual definition of *real time* is actually a function of the process being controlled. Again this takes us back to defining the *real needs of the user*. If, say, the conveyor belt on which objects are being inspected runs at two meters per second, and we capture an image covering a 0.1m length of belt, then we simply have to accept that we must process 20 images per second, *and provide outputs in time to halt production if necessary, or alternatively to reject articles from the belt - without stopping it!*

This raises one final aspect which must be considered by the designer. Whatever the output from the system, it must be in a form which suits the control application. This might be feedback information to the operator, a control signal to a control loop, or impulses to a series of actuators moving erroneous articles off the inspection site. It is always a case of *completing the control loop - we measure only in order to control!*

4. KNOWLEDGE-BASED COMPUTER VISION SYSTEMS

Whilst we can say that ll software systems which solve problems are essentially knowledge-based, it is important to understand whether we are making use of *explicit* or *implicit* knowledge. The system which uses *explicit knowledge* has the advantage that the user may enhance the system itself, improve the system's performance, or indeed change its whole application, by improving the quality, extent or nature of the knowledge available. Essentially we aim in explicit knowledge-based systems to separate the *knowledge-source* from the *processing* of the knowledge! Systems based on *implicit* knowledge, however - and this is true of most (conventional) sequentially-programmed systems - require extensive system modifications to improve or modify their application or performance. Therefore, implicit knowledge systems are inflexible, and will have to be reprogrammed as the problem they solve changes. However, they do not require the apparently extensive amount of knowledge management of an explicit system. A serious issue is that the more flexible we make a system, the more *it* (the system) is in control of parameters, such as total run-time. Therefore, we have a dilemma - the more flexible we make a system, the more non-deterministic it seems to become, and the less control we have over its performance.

So, in terms of explicit knowledge vision systems, it is essential to embed the description of the objects we are seeking to recognise as efficiently as possible into the system. This should mean that our final system can be faced with a large number of different objects to handle without reconfiguration - *but* we must also strictly control the processing so as to meet the application demands in terms of processing throughput.

The best known form of knowledge-based system is, of course, the ubiquitous *expert system*. However, as has been pointed out in the past, it is not strictly correct to call current vision systems which analyse scenes, expert systems, knowledge-based and rule-driven though they may be; the tasks normally performed do not require access to expertise. This is by no means a mere semantic quibble; expertise in vision is not easy to describe and the problem is not one of simply determining the right rules for an expert system kernel. Expert systems typically solve expert-type problems, i.e. complex problems requiring highly specific knowledge which is used in a specific way. We require a vision system, however, to use relatively poor knowledge, in a poorly defined field, in whichever way *it* chooses, to solve a problem which is not well-understood by human experts!

Typically, an expert system can be described as having two major components - a knowledge-base and an inference engine or knowledge processor. The knowledge-base typically holds information which is used to solve problems presented to the system. The inference engine utilizes this knowledge to solve these specific problems. There are obvious disadvantages to this structure, for example, in complex areas in which the available knowledge is limited. Thus, in the case of vision systems the system cannot itself determine a strategy to solve a problem - necessary when the knowledge is so ill-defined. With current expert systems, therefore, the problem-solving strategy adopted will be that of the system's architect.The expertise available to an expert system is naturally limited by the current problems related to gathering together, and subsequently handling, large quantities of knowledge. Current systems are also normally restricted in having in their knowledge-bases only the initial knowledge available to the system's designer (i.e. no deduced information, etc.). The knowledge base can so easily be considered purely as a *rule-base* - which can cause the system to restrict the power of the available knowledge! We should clearly strive towards knowledge-bases which contain *knowledge-sources* - in which each knowledge-source is of similar format to, and has the same function as, a rule in a conventional expert system! We require, however, a knowledge-based system that it is able to reason about how *it* should *manage knowledge* - it should be able to choose, say, between possibly contradictory knowledge-sources, on the grounds of other evidence. This brief review of the problem of fixed knowledge-bases presents one argument for not using conventional expert systems in solving computer vision problems! Other, more technical reasons, will be discussed later.

Despite some of the expressed reservations, knowledge-based systems are penetrating the image-processing arena and there is much evidence of useful work being carried out. Nazif and Levine (1984) present an application of expert systems techniques to low-level image segmentation, which, according to the paper, gives good results. In a similar way Lin (1988) shows how an expert system can integrate image segmentation and recognition. Niemann (1985) and his group describe another system which uses knowledge to interpret results from a segmented picture. This work appears, however, to use implicit knowledge to segment the picture, and subsequently to extract the information needed for its analysis. Wu (1989) shows how an integrated approach to the use of knowledge-based systems in computer vision may be used with much success for handling real, industrial objects.

One cannot leave this review without referring to the work done in the early days of computer vision, when researchers promoted the idea of using model knowledge. In this they attempted to match image features against features predicted by models. This approach had its origins in simple template matching. Whilst it cannot be denied that template matching, and variations thereof, have met with some success, the approach suffers from rigidity and inflexibility and, in many cases, poor speed-of-processing. A general approach to this area has been referred to as image feature access (Rao and Jain, 1988), which includes the introduction of knowledge of the objects at an early stage to guide interpretation. As discussed in (Rao and Jain, 1988), the approach leads to a classic chicken-and-egg problem - how can we interpret before we segment, and *vice versa!* It is now clearly recognised that image recognition is a cyclic rather than a linear process. This point will be referred to later, since it is part of the feedback necessary in applying intelligent control over each stage in the image-processing chain.

5 KNOWLEDGE-REPRESENTATION AND -ACQUISITION FOR COMPUTER VISION

Essential to any knowledge-based system is the acquisition of the knowledge and the way it is internally represented. In this paper we will not be tackling these aspects in great depth - but it is appropriate to look briefly at them in the context of vision systems, particularly where they have extensive impacts on the computational facilities required in applying the ideas to industrial systems.

Turning first to the question of knowledge-representation, and using the pioneering survey by Brachman and Smith, (1980) we build on definitions which include:

- *Knowledge* being a collection of descriptions, simulations, assimilation-procedures, and problem-solving methods.
- A *representation* of knowledge combines data structures and interpretation procedures that, if used correctly, will lead to a knowledgeable behaviour.

AI researchers have produced many candidate data-structure classes for holding information, and several procedures that enable suitable manipulation of these data structures to draw required inferences.

As has been pointed out previously, knowledge-based systems require good representations of knowledge to assist us to strive towards good solutions. Unfortunately the choice of representation is not normally free, but is constrained by the problem at hand. For this reason, knowledge-representation structures which are applicable in certain applications are not always appropriate in, say, computer vision work. It is also obvious that we have to include *various types* of knowledge for image understanding. We require, for example, to represent knowledge relating to object edges, as well as to an object's total structure. It is also important ultimately to be able to *measure* accurately, aspects of the object. We will also have to define certain performance parameters so that we have some idea of how *efficiently* our analysis is proceeding, to give a quality-of-measurement or -recognition factor. Also, we must have knowledge about the environment - such as how fuzzy our images are likely to be - so as to adjust filtering factors etc.

As has been reviewed in the paper by Rao and Jain (1988), at least knowledge-representation techniques are currently in vogue - semantic networks, frames, rules and first-order logic. One suspects that most work in the field is still relatively *ad hoc* and that decisions as to representation structures are made on an arbitrary basis! It is interesting to note that most application papers propose knowledge-representations that have constituents of two or more of the above approaches. Maybe this is appropriate anyway - thinking of a piece of knowledge, say, as a rule, and thinking of it solely in those terms, does seem to restrict our perception of the potential of knowledge, since it is far too easy to get distracted by the strict implication of the "if - then" construct (particularly when we are still trying to define an ill-defined problem!)

Inherently, the use of semantic networks appears to be a good starting point, as they represent structures in which the knowledge is represented by links of different types between nodes. Nodes themselves usually represent objects and the links describe the relationships that exist between them. Thus, as in the well-documented cases of inspection of printed circuit boards, one could start with the fact that the board consists of chips, resistors, capacitors and tracks.

In turn, each of these consists of sub-components; for example, a chip consists of an object which is essentially a rectangle surrounded by sixteen tiny rectangles. Each of the rectangles is in turn made up of lines. So, one represents the board by a semantic network which has at the lowest levels, some well-defined primitive shapes. Indeed, as we have seen before, the whole concept of primitives is extremely important to consider in the visual field, and could well be the key to recognition and hence a major consideration in representation.

Turning to the widely used production-system architecture approach we find that this knowledge-representation method has become popular in expert-system-based visual systems. This is not unexpected, as indeed it has been proposed by several authors that this is a model of the basic human reasoning process. The concept is simply that a piece of knowledge is expressed in an "*if* (conditions) *then*" (actions) form. Clearly, one can also use such structures to represent a form of semantic network.

The implementation of production-system architecture consists, essentially, of a rule-based system which contains antecedents-consequence pairs: the antecedents usually examine data and the consequences of the rules result in data modification. Normally such production systems have three components - a database, a set of rules and an interpreter, or inference engine. The problem, of course, is to derive the rules for a particular application and this gets us to the problem of *knowledge-acquisition*.
It must be said at this stage that little is coming out of the research world to give us any solid guidelines for knowledge-acquisition. It is important first to note that in many industrial inspection systems it is possible to utilise some information directly from the *CAD system* used to produce the original parts. Indeed, one can also go as far as *scanning* original diagrams of mechanical components in order to acquire their characteristics. An alternative is to acquire the knowledge from a vision system which looks at an idealised picture of the objects to be inspected. Such techniques have been widely explored with some success in application areas such as printed-circuit-board inspection, but little has been reported in applications to mechanical components (possibly because it is extremely difficult to get a "very good" original image).

Naturally, any information gathered as suggested above, represents only part of the story as it ignores environmental factors, changing conditions, materials, etc. It also provides only an ideal version of the object, and ignores any optical effects etc.

It is important to point out that most successful applications of knowledge-based expert systems to computer vision appear to acquire data by observing the human operator at work - not surprising, since this is the stated objective of an expert system! As has been illustrated by Bartlett et al (1988), the very first question to be asked in designing an expert system for, in this case, solder joint inspection is simple - "What visual cues are used by inspectors to classify the solder joints if checking via a camera image?" Essentially, what one is doing is to find out what the human inspector is observing, and to try and match that knowledge by a set of rules. All very obvious - but in practice the task is by no means simple when it is realised that in any particular inspection task, a multiplicity of indications have to be individually weighted to come up with some *reasonable* guess. Thus, when inspecting a particular mechanical component, say an automobile disk brake, much time has to be spent in the actual factory looking at how current inspection is undertaken. In an actual example this required many weeks of work, as it was found that at least 200 different characteristics could exist, and might be used as clues by inspectors to determine whether the surface was acceptable - and this was outside of *mere* mechanical measurements of flatness etc. Slight color variations, observed at different angles of incident light, gave clues as to unacceptable heat treatment, or slight mis-machining, etc. Likewise, very slight shadows could indicate either minute pits, or slight burn marks.

In a similar way, in developing a knowledge-base to assist in the inspection of biscuits, as discussed by Wu (Wu, 1989) it was a question, in the first place, of asking the manufacturers what the ultimate, acceptable parameters were in terms of size, breakages etc. It was also essential to find out, from the human inspectors (who are, anyway, reluctant to impart their know-how!) what conditions they would accept in terms of overcooking, burning etc. All this information has to be fed into the sets of rules which are created for a particular application. (Of course, the knowledge should not be in the rules, but handled as a knowledge source.)

The problem is that the whole problem is starting to look highly application-specific, and indeed the current state-of-the-art illustrates this. One immediately jumps to the conclusion that it is appropriate to use available expert system shells to implement the higher levels of processing required for computer vision. This temptation, however, must be resisted! As has been pointed out in the past by one of the "godfathers" of expert systems, Yoh-Han Pao (1986), important as expert system shells are, they are inherently very generalised structures and tend to be relatively inefficient. (Of course from a realistic, economic point-of-view one can expect this when it is understood where most shells have come from. Typically, they are derived from special-purpose systems which have been produced for well-defined applications. When it was found that the investment could not be recovered in the application area for which they were designed, they were then stripped of application-specific knowledge and marketed as shells!)

One cannot leave the subject of expert systems without referring to the questions of data and real-time compatibility. In attempting to match the low-level image-processing tasks to the upper-end knowledge-based processing area, the question of data compatibility becomes a major problem. Typically, at the lower end, one is working with integers and at the top end, with symbolic manipulation - and never the twain shall meet! This is particularly the case where one is trying to graft an expert system shell on top of a low-level processing system. It is common experience (Wu, et al (1988)) that the only real solution lies in developing special-purpose, "expert-system-like" structures - otherwise extensive data manipulation routines are required, with very alarming and time-consuming overheads.

In summary, much current research is being undertaken in knowledge-acquisition for subsequent scene analysis. The danger is that much of this work is built on existing tools, and tool sets, as used in the more-general knowledge-engineering world. The difficulty is that for most industrial scenes these tools are simply inappropriate. However, the methodologies which are being employed are supplying useful keys to the way ahead. The paper by Tranowski (1988), for example, provides auseful description of a knowledge-acquisition environment which has been developed to aid in the capture of expertise from experts involved in analysing scenes from the aerial imagery world. The work is based on the use of an integrated knowledge-acquisition environment. Its goal is to integrate the various inputs, to translate that acquired knowledge into internal representations, and to provide actual execution of the knowledge, with subsequent feedback to the user. The environment used contains a collection of tools facilitating the viewing and editing of knowledge, both in textural and graphic formats, and supporting testing of the knowledge-base; it also provides a degree of performance analysis. However, it does not provide any indication as to how one captures the knowledge stored in the heads of the inspectors on a factory floor, and this is where the real industrial application problems lie!

The point is that it must be recognised that in any computer-based system we are developing a total system. Thus, a totally-integrated approach must be taken. We have not got anywhere towards truly matching the need for a flexible, knowledge-based approach to the handling of the image recognition problems, but we do see some light ahead. This clearly indicates that the division between high- and low-level processing is an artificial barrier - which, despite the obvious advantages of a layered and modular structure (in terms of validation, testability, maintainability, etc), unless we are very careful, can result in highly inefficient systems. Our knowledge-based systems must be created and integrated into the *whole* processing system - from edge-detection and enhancement right though to advanced recognition. The knowledge must be acquired and represented accordingly.

6 CONCLUSIONS

In this paper we have reviewed various aspects of knowledge-based computer vision systems. It is clear that computer vision is an extremely important area of artificial intelligence - however one might choose to define that term! Clearly, computer vision is itself an area of great fascination for AI researchers, but this paper has attempted to take an extremely pragmatic view of computer vision as an important candidate to solve many unresolved instrumentation problems encountered in the hard, industrial environment in which cost and ruggedness rule the day.

The paper has emphasised that there are many successful applications of computer vision, but that most of these call upon fixed routines, operating either in dedicated hardware or on powerful computers, or at speeds of operation which are only acceptable in off-line applications. However, a wide range of problems still await solutions, and are beyond the comprehension and ability of our current generation of vision equipment. These problems are not currently being solved, primarily because the processing of the complex or unstructured nature of the scenes under observation is too slow or too expensive. There is no doubt that knowledge-based systems are extremely important as a methodology for the future. The question as to how much of the existing knowledge-based technology is immediately transferable requires to be assessed. Hopefully, this paper has given some indication of the problems which lie ahead - paramount amongst which must be the tackling of the multi-faceted problems of knowledge-acquisition and representation.

7 ACKNOWLEDGEMENTS

The authors wish to acknowledge most sincerely the assistance they received in preparing this paper from their colleagues Dr. Farzin Deravi, James Powrie and Cao Xing of the University of Wales, and Professor Bao-Zong Yuan of the Institute of Information Science, Northern Territory University, Beijing, Peoples Republic of China.

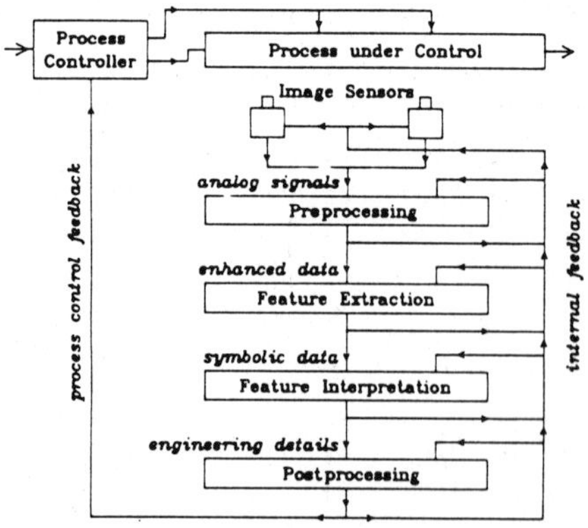

FIGURE 1
Computer vision as part of the control loop.

REFERENCES

1. Bartlet, S.L. et al
"Automatic Solder Joint Inspection", IEEE Trans. PAMI, Vol. 10., No. 1., Jan. 1988, pp 31-34.

2. Berger, G.F.N.
"Software for Particle Size Analyser based on Image Analysis Techniques", Dissertation, University of the Witwatersrand, RSA, Dec. 1985

3. Brachman, R.J. and Smith, B.C. (Eds)
Special Issue on Knowledge Representation, SIGART Newsletter, Feb. 1980.

4. Horn, B.K.P.
"Robot Vision", McGraw-Hill, 1986.

5. Lin, W-C., Weng, Y-T. and Chen, C-T.
"Expert Vision Systems integrating Image Segmentation and Recognition Processes", Int. J. on Eng. Appl. of AI, Vol. 1., No. 4., Dec. 1988, pp. 230-247.

6. Nazif, A.M. and Levine, M.D.
"Low-Level Image Segmentation: an Expert System", IEEE Trans. PAMI, Vol. 5., Sept 1984, pp. 555-577.

7. Niemann, H. et al
"A knowledge-based system for Analysis of Gated Blood Pool Studies", IEEE Trans. PAMI, Vol. 7, No. 3., May 1985, pp. 246-259.

8. Pao, Y-H.
"Summary of Panel Discussions", Proc. IFAC Symp. SOCOCO, Graz, Austria, Pergamon Press, 1986.

9. Rao, A.R. and Jain, R.
"Knowledge Representation and Control in Computer Vision Systems", IEEE Expert, Vol. 3., No. 1., Spring 1988, pp. 64-79.

10. Rodd, M.G. and Deravi, F.
"Image Processing as a Practical Measurement Tool", Proc. Int. Conf. Test & Transducers, London, 1987, Vol. 2., pp. 85-96.

11. Tranowski, D.
"A Knowledge Acquisition Environment for Scene Analysis", Int. J. Man-Machine Studies Vol. 29, No. 2., August 1988, pp. 197-214.

12. Wu, Q-M., Rodd, M.G. and Deravi, F.
"A New Technique for High-Speed On-Line Object Recognition", Proc. IFAC Symp. SOCOCO RSA, Pergamon Press, 1988.

13. Wu, Q-M. et al
"Improved Algorithms for Boundary Segmentation and Curve-Fitting, and their Parallel Implementation on a Transputer Network", Proc. COMPAR '88, Manchester, Sept. 1988.

14. Wu, Q-M.
"Fast Intelligent Boundary Extraction of Touching Objects", Internal Report, University of Wales, Swansea, Image Processing Group, Jan. 1989.

DISTRIBUTED ESTIMATION, INFERENCING AND MULTI-SENSOR DATA FUSION FOR REAL TIME SUPERVISORY CONTROL

C. J. Harris

Department of Aeronautics & Astronautics, University of Southampton, Southampton, Hants, SO9 5NH, UK

Abstract. Fully autonomous or supervisory controlled guided vehicles that utilise on-board intelligent sensing to determine the vehicle's state, the external world, correlate real time events/objects with mapped knowledge, monitor the vehicle's own system health, and compute dynamically its own control strategy, require the use of a wide range of sensors, and the means to fuse or integrate disparate sensor databases when they refer to the same object. In this review paper we consider a multilevel approach to sensory integration for AGVs; level 1 local positional estimation, level 2 sensory consensus, level 3 sensor fusion, level 4 situation assessment. And consider for statistically rich data sources (such as radar, sonar) Bayesian distributed data fusion, whereas for substantialy uncertain events we review fuzzy logic, Dempster-Shafer evidential theories, and finally consider non-monotonic AI methods such as endorsements or explanation based reasoning for dealing with symbolic fusion.

Keywords. Bayesian estimation, sensor integration, multi-sensor data fusion, fuzzy logic, Dempster-Shafer theory, Blackboard IKBS, autonomous guided vehicles, robotics, non-montonic reasoning.

INTRODUCTION

An autonomously guided vehicle (AGV), just as a teleoperated or man controlled vehicle, requires real time perceptual knowledge of its own state (such as inertial position and velocity, orientation, engine conditioning, . .), its immediate enviroment (such as road or surface conditions, weather, traversable regions, position and orientation on known or mapped paths, position, velocity and orientation of obstacles) and environmental conditions in the far field, which are required for future path planning. Any sensor (active or passive) introduces uncertainty about the variable it is measuring, this uncertainty may be introduced through measurement noise, incorrect measurements or through ignorance (or lack of evidence) through say an obscured field of view. To overcome uncertainty (or increase confidence), increase system reliability and hence system survivability, provide enhanced spatial resolution and degree of detection; it is necessary to utilise multiple disparate sensors and data fusion to provide a single integrated 'picture' (with some confidence measure). Sensor integration or multi-sensor data fusion (the continuous process of assembling a model or paradigm of interest from multiple sensors from disparate data sources) is not an end in itself; usually it is an input to higher levels and more abstract levels of situation assessment or perception (ie what does the picture compilation of data fusion mean in the context of the mission plan), and to replaning and control. In the context of say land based road-type autonomously guided vehicles, in a structured urban environment, the vehicle may carry a high level preprocessed map of the obstacle free roadways, and a planned trajectory on it (perhaps including a series of preplanned acceleration, steering and way point commands for anticipatory vehicle motion). A real time estimate of the vehicle's position, velocity and orientation on this pathway is required from deadreckoning (odometry) inertial sensors, GPS, and feature recognition from active/passive sensors (eg recognition of road signs, junctions, specific builidings, by visual sensors or by radio frequency beaons) to correlate 'position with view'. In addition 'risks' or obstacles on a planned pathway need to be detected and assessed for replanning (say local navigation around the obstacle or return to another obstacle free pathway) of for reflexive control is obstacle is risking mission failure through say imminent collision. This simple autonomous guided vehicle scenario illustrates the need for a wide range of real time data rich sensors (inertial, rf, passive and active EO, imaging, acoustical etc) as well as encyclopaedic information such as look up tables for classification, maps, feature models, alternative plans or strategies.

Also other key application reasons for using multi-sensor data fusion in autonomously guided vehicles are the non-repeatability of target/object signatures, competing clutter objects having the same shape as actual objects, and experience with little data information, related to and contained within the image (such as contextual information such as digital maps, range, etc.).

There are many approaches to multi-sensor integration, Henderson et al (1984) introduced the logic sensor and multi sensor kernel system, for vision based systems, Durrant-Whyte (1988) developed sensor integration, sensor models and propagation of geometric sensor observations, and more recently (Rao and Durrant-Whyte (1989) a decentralised Kalman filter for multi-sensory fusion as part of a CEC Esprit II project on sensory perception. Luo et al (1988) introduced a frame or template approach to data fusion, based upon phases related to sensing distances, and a system architecture that is commonly used in perception machines:- a data acquisition or sensor unit, a knowlege data base [including (i) on-board vehicle database of state variables, vehicle control, a priori database of constraint conditions etc (ii) sensor data base], types available, location, sensor characteristics, algorithm set, and an environment database [including the mission goal or task], external sensor processing and data fusion unit, situation assessment unit and a decision making/task execution unit. The Int. J. Robotics Research (Brady 1988) and the SPIE (1988) special issues on 'Sensor Data Fusion' are useful sources of current research in multi-sensor data fusion. A full description of the advantages/disadvantages as well as an application orientated categorisation of data fusion can be found in Harris & Jackson (1989) and Harris (1988).

THE HIERARCHY OF MULTI-SENSOR DATA FUSION: BAYESIAN METHODS

Multi-sensor data fusion is essentially a hypothesis generating process that produces a single real time fused picture (hence the alternative name 'picture compilation') or state vector. The process can be considered as four hierarchical subproblems: assume that there are m sensors, measuring n objects, each with r-state vectors $\mathbf{x}_i = \{x_{i1}, x_{i2}, \ldots x_{ir}\}$ (with elements say position, velocity, orientation. . .); the level 1 problem is:-

(i) Level 1 - Positional Estimation or the Signal Processing Problem

From the jth sensor observation of the ith object $\mathbf{y}_{ij}$, estimate the state vector $\mathbf{x}_{ij}$ at the jth sensor. The methods utilised are primarily analytical (such as Bayesian, Kalman filtering (Harris (1989) etc) since the data sources are statisticaly rich, although parametric methods based upon parameter matching, voting, pairwise track correlation (Harris 1988) have been used. Positional estimation is carried out ususally without the benefit of related identity information, since identity in estimates are either not available at local sensors or are separately processed from the fused positional data.

Let us consider for illustration the static Bayesian case of linear observations;

$$\mathbf{y}_{ij} = \mathbf{H}_{ij}\,\mathbf{x}_i + \mathbf{v}_j \tag{1}$$

where $\mathbf{y}_{ij}$ is the jth observation of the ith object, $\mathbf{H}_{ij}$ is the observation matrix which is usually independent of the 'sensed' object ie $\mathbf{H}_{ij} = \mathbf{H}_j$; the observation noise is such that $E[\mathbf{v}_j\mathbf{v}_j^T] = \mathbf{R}_j$, $E(\mathbf{v}_j, \mathbf{v}_i^T) = 0$ for all $i \neq j$ (assumes independent sensors). If $\mathbf{x}_j$ is completely unknown the Fisher positional estimator is given by

$$\mathbf{x}_{ij} = \Gamma_j\,[\mathbf{H}_j^T\mathbf{R}_j^{-1}]\,\mathbf{y}_{ij} \quad , \quad (j = 1, 2, \ldots m) \tag{2}$$

where

$$\Gamma_j = (\mathbf{H}_j\mathbf{R}_j^{-1}\mathbf{H}_j^{-1})^{-1} \tag{3}$$

(provided that the inverse $(\mathbf{H}\mathbf{R}^{-1}\mathbf{H})^{-1}$ exists); if however there exists an a priori estimated value $E(\mathbf{x}_i) = \mathbf{m}_x$, with covariance

$$\Psi_i = E(\mathbf{x}_i - \mathbf{m}_{x_i})(\mathbf{x}_i - \mathbf{m}_{x_i})^T)$$

then for $j = 1, 2, \ldots m$

$$\hat{\mathbf{x}}_{ij} = \Gamma_j\mathbf{H}_j^T\mathbf{R}_j\mathbf{y}_{ij} + \Gamma_j\Psi_i^{-1}\mathbf{m}_{x_i} \tag{4}$$

$$= \mathbf{m}_{x_i} + \Psi_i\mathbf{H}_j^T[\mathbf{H}_j\Psi_i\mathbf{H}_j^T + \mathbf{R}_j^{-1}]^{-1}(\mathbf{y}_{ij} - \mathbf{H}_j\mathbf{m}_{x_i}) \tag{4a}$$

(which is the minimum covariance positional estimator).

In tracking estimators, not only current positions are required but also predicted next position, for this a dynamic estimator such as a Kalman filter is required (see Rao & Durrant-Whyte (1989)). Owing to lack of space we will not cover dynamic sensor fusion.

(ii) Level 2 - The Association or Contact Problem

Fusing data or positional estimates, which are in conflict or increase the uncertainty in global positional estimates clearly is contrary to the purpose of data fusion. Therefore before assimilating data through sensor integration or fusion, it is necessary to ascertain those sensors (despite differing calibration, spatial and temporal characteristics) which are in consensus. Our association problem is to check if two state estimates from any two sensors relate to the same object. Obvious approaches are nearest neighbour type criteria, or probabilistic distance measures relating to the pairwise (conditional/joint) distributions of sensors - such as J-divergence, Matsusita or Bhattacharyya distances based on the likelihood ratio between two sensor distributions (Ali & Silvery 1966), however in the multi sensor case these approaches are inappropriate. An alternative approach is to consider the individual sensor distributions, and evaluate confidence measures taken by each individually. Consider two sensors (j,k) measuring the same object, i, their respectively one-dimensional conditional probability density functions are assumed to be Gaussian with ($i = 1, \ldots n$).

$$p_{ijk} = p_j(x_{ij}/x_{ik})\,exp\,[-\tfrac{1}{2}[(x_{ij} - x_{ik})/2\sigma_{ij}]^2$$

$$p_{ijk} = p_k(x_{ik}/x_{ij})\,exp\,[-\tfrac{1}{2}[(x_{ik} - x_{ij})/2\sigma_{ik}]^2 \tag{5}$$

$(j, k) = 1, 2, \ldots m$; for $\sigma_{ij} \neq \sigma_{ik}$ the standard deviation of the jth sensor measuring the ith object property. A variety of distance measures based on (5) could be defined, one such confidence measure (Luo et al 1988) is in the case of $x_{ij} > x_{ik}$

$$d_{ijk} = 2\int_{x_{ik}}^{x_{ij}} p_j(x/x_i)\,p(x_i)\,dx$$

$$= \frac{1}{\sqrt{2\pi}\,\sigma_{ij}}\,erf\left(\frac{x_{ij} - x_{ik}}{\sqrt{2}\,\sigma_{ij}}\right) \tag{6}$$

which is zero for sensor total agreement ($x_{ij} = x_{ik}$) and unity for x_{ij} and x_{ik} uncorrelated. In practice we would accept those sensors that agree pairwise for those $\{j,k\}$ for which $d_{ijk} < T_i$, in which T_i is some preseleted threshold value that depends on the specific object property being estimated.

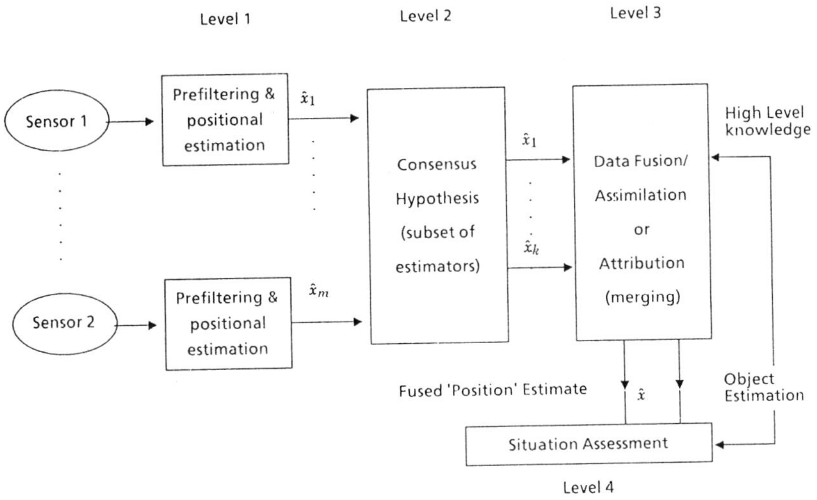

FIG. 1 Hierarchy of multi-sensor data fusion process

The problem with this approach is the need to calibrate and model each sensor, and assume that the measurements are Gaussian distributed. Alternative consensus methods (Harris 1988) rely on hypothesis testing schemata and rely only on the estimated probabilities for a priori support for the hypotheses, and the individual sensors probablity of false detection and false alarms. For example consider two sensors $\{j,k\}$ tracking the same object r-state vector $\mathbf{x}_i$. Consider the positional state error vector between these two sensors

$$\mathbf{z}_{ijk} = \mathbf{x}_{ij} - \mathbf{x}_{ik} \quad , \quad (j,k) \in 1, 2, \ldots m; \tag{7}$$

the problem is to find the largest set of sensors $\Sigma(j,k) \leqq m$ that produce the nearest neighbourhood set of estimates which satisfy the hypothesis:-

$$H_0 : \mathbf{z}_{ijk} = \mathbf{v}_{jk} \tag{8}$$

where $\{v_{jk}\}$ is the estimation error vector, with $E(v_{jk}) = 0$ and $E(v_{jk}\, v_{jk}{}^T) = \mathbf{R}_{jk}$, and pdf $p(z_{ijk}/H_0)$ is $N(0,\mathbf{R}_{jk})$. Also, the sensors are uncorrelated if the hypothesis H_1 is satisfied:-

$$H_1 : \mathbf{z}_{ijk} = \mathbf{m}_{jk} + \mathbf{v}_{jk} \tag{9}$$

where $\mathbf{m}_{jk} \neq 0$ is the vector positional difference between jth and kth sensor; and the conditional pdf:

$$p(\mathbf{z}_{ijk}/H_1) = \frac{1}{\sqrt{2\pi r}\,/R_{jk}} \int_{-\infty}^{\infty} \cdots \int exp[-\tfrac{1}{2}(\mathbf{z}_{ijk} - \mathbf{m})^T$$

$$\times\, (\mathbf{R}_{jk}^{-1}(\mathbf{z}_{ijk} - \mathbf{m}) f(\mathbf{m})\, d\mathbf{m} \tag{10}$$

for $f(\mathbf{m}_{ijk})$ the state spatial density function.

It is assumed that

$$\mathbf{z}_{ijk} = \{z_{ijk}^{(1)}, z_{ijk}^{(2)}, \ldots z_{ijk}^{(r)}\}^T$$

is an individually independent distributed process, thence the conditional pdf can be written as

$$p(\mathbf{z}_{ijk}/H_s) = \prod_{l=1}^{r} p_l(z_{ijk}{}^{(l)}/H_s) \quad ; \quad (s = 0, 1) \tag{11}$$

and the likelihood ratio can be written as

$$L_i(\mathbf{z}_{ijk}) = p(\mathbf{z}_{ijk}/H_1) / p(\mathbf{z}_{ijk}/H_0)$$

$$= \Big(\prod_{l=1}^{r} p_l(z_{ijk}{}^{(l)}/H_1)\Big) / \Big(\prod_{l=1}^{r} p_l(z_{ijk}{}^{(l)}/H_0)\Big)$$

$$= \prod_{l=1}^{r} L_l(z_{ijk}{}^{(l)}) \tag{12}$$

If the a priori hypothesis probabilities are known as $p_i(H_0) = p_0{}^{(i)}$ and $p_i(H_1) = p_1{}^{(i)}$, then the sensor consensus condition becomes

$$\prod_{l=1}^{r} L_l(z_{ijk}{}^{(l)}) \underset{H_0}{\overset{H_1}{\gtrless}} T_i \tag{13}$$

where for Bayes optimum $T_i = (p_0/p_1)_i$ and taking logs of (13) gives the condition:-

$$\sum_{l=1}^{r} log\, L_i(z_{ijk}^{(l)}) - log\,(P_0/P_1)_i \underset{H_0}{\overset{H_1}{\gtrless}} 0 \tag{14}$$

(iii) <u>Level 3 - The Attribution or Assimilation data fusion problem</u>

Given that several state estimates $\hat{x}_{ij}$ ($j \in m$) relate to the same object i, the problem is now to merge or fuse them to give a consensus or improved co-operative estimate. Various numerial methods exist for data fusion including pairwise correlation, voting or endorsements, ranking methods (Harris 1988a) as well as probability/possibility methods such as statistical methods (Bayesian), Dempster-Shafer (Harris 1988b), and fuzzy logic. Non-numeric or symbolic methods (Hirst 1989) such as explanation based reasoning, truth maintenance and feature mapping are usually used for top-down or the high level feature or identity type estimation processes, such as identifying a perceived object within a class of specified modelled objects/features (eg tree within the class of cross-country scene obstacles of {trees, rocks, ditches, bushes, holes, fences, walls, . . }). The complete hierarchical process of data fusion is shown in Fig. 1.

Returning to our statistical positional estimation problem of level 1, having determined by consensus evaluation (level 2) a subset of estimators $\hat{x}_{ij}$ (j = 1, . . l; $l \leqq m$); assuming that the sensor observations are separable then an overall or combined observer process can be written as

$$\mathbf{y}_i = \mathbf{H}^T(i)\, \mathbf{x}_i + \mathbf{v}(i) \tag{15}$$

where $\mathbf{y}_i$, $\mathbf{H}(i)$ and $\mathbf{v}(i)$ can be partitioned as

$$\mathbf{H}^T(i) = (\mathbf{H}_1, \mathbf{H}_2, \dots \mathbf{H}_l) \quad , \quad \mathbf{y}_i^T = (\mathbf{y}_{i1}, \mathbf{y}_{i2}, \dots, \mathbf{y}_{il})$$

$$\mathbf{v}^T(i) = (\mathbf{v}_1, \mathbf{v}_2, \dots \mathbf{v}_l) \; for\, E(\mathbf{v}(i), \mathbf{v}(i)^T) = diag\,(\mathbf{R}_j) = \mathbf{R}(i)$$

From the above partitioning, the composite or assimilation process:-

$$\mathbf{H}^T(i)\, \mathbf{R}^{-1}(i)\, \mathbf{H}(i) = \sum_{j=1}^{l} \mathbf{H}_j^T \mathbf{R}_j^{-1} \mathbf{H}_j$$

Hence

$$\Gamma(i) = (\mathbf{H}^T(i)\, \mathbf{R}(i)^{-1}\, \mathbf{H}(i) + \psi(i)^{-1})^{-1}$$

$$= \left(\sum_{j=1}^{l} H_j^T R_j^{-1} H_j + \psi(i)^{-1} \right)^{-1}$$

$$= \left(\sum_{j=1}^{l} \Gamma_j^{-1} + \psi(i)^{-1} \right)^{-1} \tag{16}$$

Also

$$= \Gamma(i) H^T(i) R(i)^{-1} \mathbf{y}_i = \Gamma(i) (H_1^T R_1^{-1} y_{il} + \dots H_l^T R_l^{-1} \mathbf{y}_{il})$$

$$= \Gamma(i) \sum_{j=1}^{l} \Gamma_j \mathbf{x}_{ij} \tag{17}$$

where $\hat{\mathbf{x}}_{ij} = \Gamma_j (\mathbf{H}_j R_j^{-1} \mathbf{y}_{ij})$ is the individual static Fisher positional state estimate of $\mathbf{x}_i$ from the jth sensor assuming no a priori knowledge of $\mathbf{x}_i$). Clearly

$$E(\mathbf{x}_i) = E(\mathbf{x}_i) = \frac{1}{l} \sum_{j=1}^{l} \mathbf{x}_{il} \tag{18}$$

Then from equations (4a), (16) - (18), the joint/fused or assimilated positional state estimate is given by

$$\mathbf{x}_i = \Gamma(i)\, \mathbf{H}^T(I)\, \mathbf{R}(i)\, \mathbf{y}(i) + \Gamma(i)\, \psi(i)^{-1} E(\mathbf{x}_i)$$

$$= \Gamma(i) \left\{ \sum_{j=1}^{l} \Gamma_j^{-1} \mathbf{x}_{ij} + \psi(i) l)^{-1}(i)\; \mathbf{x}_{ji} \right\}$$

$$= \left(\Gamma_j^{-1} + \psi_l^{-1} \right)^{-1} \left(\sum_{j=1}^{l} \Gamma_j^{-1} + (l\, \psi(i))^{-1} \right) \mathbf{x}_{ij} \tag{19}$$

Note

(i) The fused estimate is not just the raw average across the consensus estimates; a weighting by the various estimator covariances matrices Γ_j is used - biasing those estimates for which there is high confidence.

(ii) If the a priori covariance matrix $\psi(i)$ is unknown, then (19) simplifies to:-

$$x_i = \left(\sum_{j=1}^{l} \Gamma_j^{-1} \right)^{-1} \left(\sum_{j=1}^{l} \Gamma_j^{-1} \mathbf{x}_{ij} \right) \tag{20}$$

- a result already established (Brady (1988), Harris (1989)) for use in AGV multi-sensor data fusion.

Fig. 1 illustrates a fourth level - situation assessment - this is not really part of the prime data fusion process, but rather the interpretation of the results of data fusion. Situation assessment is the process of evaluating fused positional state estimates (levels 1 - 3) in the context of higher level or contextual information (such as a terrain feature database - eg topological, hydrological, vegetation, industrial, agricultural and road features, weather, local plans or other expectational knowledge). However, this interpretation or perception process may also involve the fusion or association of high level expectational knowledge with 'low level' sensory based data knowledge, this 'top-down' process essentially requires symbolic or non-numeric data fusion with at most measures of confidence or belief in the result (see next section).

POSSIBILITY, EVALUATION AND NON-NUMERIC METHODS FOR DATA FUSION

Statistical methods are appropriate for data sources that are information rich and the generated individual estimates can be algorithmically fused; however some knowledge sources may include non-statistical sources of evidence, such as intelligence reports (human statements as to the presence or absence of an object), encyclopaedic or look up tables, algorithms or expert views. Generally the AGV perception unit will have to reason in an intelligent manner from uncertain, incomplete, and sometimes inaccurate information. This information is limited by sensor capabilities (temporal and spatial coverage, resolution, ambiguity rejection, portion of the em specturm selected, feature diversity, etc) and is inherently evidential. Bayesian methods deal well with uncertain evidence, (say noisy environments) however are incapable of dealing with either incomplete evidence (ie ignorance about the environmental possibilities) or incorrect evidence (or in conflict) - especially those bodies of information which are correct about some things but incorrect, to varying degrees, about others. Incompleteness of evidence is coped with in the the Dempster-Shafer belief function theory (Shafer (1976), Harris (1988b)) - for a mathematical description) by assigning upper and lower probabilities to represent belief (or support) and disbelief (plausability) in a proposition; the evidential intervals - the difference between such limits, effectively represents ignorance (or incompleteness) in the support of the proposition. The resulting theory is a set of theorems for the combination (data fusion) or decomposition of evidential intervals for propositions from a set of independent knowledge sources. Probabilities are assigned to propositions (thus reducing ignorance) only when supporting information becomes available. There is a natural transitional relationship between probabilistic and deterministic propositional calculus via Dempster-Shafer belief functions and the associated propositional inference rules. Also in the presence of sufficient statistics, as the evidential interval vanishes, Dempster-Shafer becomes Bayesian, whilst entirely deterministic it becomes ordinary predicate calculus.

The primary advantage of the partial belief method of representing knowledge in autonomous guided vehicles, is that each knowledge source (eg radar sensor or mapped feature) can express itself at the most appropriate level, allowing decisons over one proposition or another to be suspended until further data is available. Each knowledge source can represent exactly what it believes (together with confidence measures) without eliciting unsupported statements about which it has little or no supportive data. Dempster's consensus rule (Harris 1988b) combines multiple bodies of information such as to increase the belief in propositions that are supported by the various bodies of evidence and away from all others; this fusion rule is both commutative and associative, therefore grouping and order of sensor data are immaterial. This allows parallelised results to be obtained from the combinations of the vairious levels of data fusion, albeit partial. The consensus rule also represents the degree of conflict between any two sensors. Finally, the method readily supports hierarchical data fusion of disparate sensor sources, forward and backward chaining, real time control, and plausible reasoning in the presence of uncertain, incomplete and inaccurate information, all within an overall real time blackboard distributed architecture (Harris 1988a and Harris & Jackson 1989) for AGVs. A major difficulty with the Dempster-Shafer reasoning is that the algorithm's complexity increases geometrically as the number of sensors increases, as all the original sensor declarations are forever utilised. Dempster-Shafer data fusion has found widespread applications in command and control (Harris 1988a), air traffic control and target identification (Bogler, 1987), in AGV sensor integration (EEC Esprit I SKIDS project 1560), and in real time supervisory control and fault diagnostics (Silverman, 1987).

A similar approach is to use fuzzy logic (Harris 1988a) whereby ignorance is mapped into a set rather than into line (the evidential interval) in Dempster-Shafer, the connections between both approaches have been identified mathematically by Yager (1982). Fuzzy logic allows the uncertainty in multi-sensor fusion to be directly reflected in the fusion/inference process by weighting the implication operator and the proposition by a confidence or belief measure betwen 0 and 1. The advantage of fuzzy logic is that it has a relatively advanced mathematical structure, adapts well to production rule representation and linguistic descriptions, allows ready sensor management (or ignorance control) to reduce uncertainty, and recently (Harris & Moore, 1990) has been shown to be self-organising ie can be 'taught' to write its own rules for control or sensor management through the minimisation of some linguistic performance index. Applications of fuzzy logic in AGVs include data fusion for scene analysis and object recognition (Huntsberger 1987), real-time self-learning control and system identification (Harris & Moore 1990). An advantage of fuzzy algorithms is computational efficiency and ease of parallelisation tor real time use and ready extension to heuristic based production type rules (see Kamat (1985) for object recognition using multi-sensor fusion). The problem with using rule based methods (unless they are self-organising) for sensor fusion is their monotonicity, causing difficulties in making inferences when conditions change.

Monotonic reasoning does not allow for the retraction of beliefs or change in conditions of production rules that reflect changes in environment or learning. Non-monotonic reasoning systems for AGVs must be capable of contradiction resolution revison in the light of data acquisition, and reason about uncertainty. One such non-numeric approach is the method of endorsements (Hirst, 1989) which reasons about uncertainty and is able to express reasons for believing or disbelieving a hypothesis. The endorsements (evidence for or against a proposition) are the explicit marking of factors relating to one's certainty; they are of three types (i) data (source, type and accuracy) (ii) rules (conditions, inferences - models, causal and correlational) and (iii) conclusions (corroboration, conflict, redundant). A real limitation with this approach to AGVs is an inability to resolve conflict between various sensors and high level expectational knowledge; an approach that does, is explanation based reasoning (Harmon 1986), which produces a network of propositions connected by links representing explanatory links between them, in which reasoning can be regarded as maximising the explanatory connectivity or coherence of beliefs. Such a method readily allows default reasoning, whereby additional information can act as an inhibitor to the inference, and includes uncertainty through plausibility measures ie ascribes some measure or weight (a penalty) to an explanation. When evidence is in conflict, one or more default explanation must be in error and an appropriate competing explanation must be invoked in its place. Ambiguities may be resolved by invoking further levels of explanation to distinguish between competing structures. Non-numeric or symbolic non-monotonic reasoning systems for multi-sensor data fusion in autonomously guided vehicles, are primarliy utilised for 'top down' fusion at the perception level, associated with the functions of 'find' or 'identify' an object in the vehicle's field of view: examples might include 'find safe corridor between obstacles; 'find doorway in wall'; 'identify' obstacle/road sign/navigation beacon etc.

REFERENCES

Ali, S.M and Silvey, S.D. (1986). A general class of coefficients of divergence of one distribution from another. J. Royal Stat. Soc. Ser. B, Vol. 28, p.138-142.

Bogler, P.L. (1987). Shafer Dempster reasoning with applications to multi-sensor target identification systems. IEEE Trans. SMC-17, No. 6, p.968-977.

Brady, M. (Ed.) (1988). Special Issue on 'Sensor Data Fusion'. Int. J. Robotics Research. Vol. 7, No. 6, MIT Press.

Harmon, S.Y. (1986). Sensory data fusion through a distributed blackboard. Proc. IEEE Conf. Robotics & Automation, p.1449-1454.

Harris, C.J. (1988a). Applications of artificial intelligence to command and control systems,. IEE Computing Series, No. 13, Peter Peregrinus.

Harris, C.J. (1988b). Some aspects of the mathematical theory of evidence in multi-sensor data fusion. 5th IMA Conference Control Theory, Strathclyde University, September 1988. (To appear Oxford Univ. Press, 1989).

Harris, C.J. & Jackson, J.V. (1989). Techniques for intelligent multi-sensor data fusion for application to autonomously guided vehicles. IMA Conf. Robotics. Loughborough. July 1989. Proc. OUP.

Harris, C.J. & ,Moore, C. (19). Sub. 11th IFAC World Congress on Control, Tallinn, USSR. Aug. 1990.

Henderson, T.C. & Shilcrat, E. (1984). Logical sensor systems. J. Robotics Systems, Vol. 1, No. 2, p.169-193.

Hirst, R. (1989). Uncertainty in knowledge based command systems. M.Sc. thesis. Manchester University, Computer Science Dept.

Huntsberger, T.L. & Jayaramamurthy, S.N. (1987). A framework for multi sensor fusion in the presence of uncertainty. Proc. Workshop on spatial reasoning and multisensor fusion. St. Charles, Ill. p.345-350.

Kamat, S.J. (1985). Value function struture of mulitple sensor integration. Proc. SPIE. 579. Robotics and Computer Vision, p.432-435.
Luo, R.C., Lin, M-H. & Scherp, R.S. (1988). Dynamic multiple sensor data fusion systems for intelligent robots. IEE Trans. Robotics & Automation. Vol. 4, No. 4, p.386-396.
Rao, B. & Durrant-Whyte, H. (1989). A fully decentralised algorithm for multi-sensory Kalman filtring. SKIDS Esprit I, No. 11560. TN. Oxford Univ. Eng. Sci. Dept.
Shafer, G. (1976). A mathematical theory of evidence. Princeton, U.P.
Silverman, B.G. (1987). Distributed inference and fusion algorithms for real time supervisory control positions. IEEE. SMC-17, p.230-241.
Special Issue of SPIE on 'Sensor Fusion'. Proc. SPIE Vol. 931, 1988.
Yager, R.R. (1982). Generalised probabilities of fuzzy events from fuzzy belief structures. Info. Sciences, 28, p.45-62.

DISTRIBUTED INTELLIGENT OBJECTS IN AN ARCHITECTURE FOR REAL-TIME MONITORING AND CONTROL

V. Lun and I. M. MacLeod

Department of Electrical Engineering, University of the Witwatersrand, Republic of South Africa

Abstract. Knowledge systems exhibit flexibility and potential in a growing number of engineering applications. The key to successful application of knowledge systems in real-time monitoring and control environments is in the management of time, knowledge and system distribution. These three important topics are pivotal in ensuring that knowledge systems will function successfully on a long term basis in real-time applications. The notion of a distributed intelligent object (DIO) is introduced to incorporate and integrate the necessary concepts. The preliminary development of a distributed software testbed to show the viability of such an architecture is briefly described.

Keywords. Knowledge systems, real-time control, distributed computing.

INTRODUCTION

The nature of engineering is such that the engineer must call on both his theoretical and empirical engineering backgrounds in order to solve the problems related to his industry and discipline. As production plants increase in size and complexity, it is becoming increasingly difficult to maintain efficient daily operation of the plant, applying new technology where appropriate and dealing with unexpected events in the plant.

It has been proposed (Lun and MacLeod, 1988) that knowledge systems can play a vital role in ensuring effective and consistent plant operation. One major attribute of knowledge systems that make them attractive and applicable is their ability to assimilate heuristic, qualitative and quantitative information to perform decision-making processes. The relative ease with which they can be developed and maintained also implies that their knowledge bases can easily be kept current with plant operation strategies. We are attempting to identify potential areas where knowledge systems can complement conventional engineering techniques to achieve a balance between intelligence and functionality.

Knowledge system research for engineering applications can be divided into two areas, domain-specific research and system-specific research. Domain-specific research is by far the most popular since it is concerned with finding solutions to current problems that are localized and well-defined. System-specific research is concerned with finding software and hardware architectures that provide flexible and generalized mechanisms to support individual domain-specific systems in order to achieve global system objectives. We believe that the latter approach is important because there is an urgent need to find such architectures to support knowledge systems of the future.

This paper addresses the requirements of future knowledge systems for real-time environments. We discuss the management of three important attributes, 1) time, 2) knowledge and 3) system distribution. The concepts introduced are then embodied into a knowledge entity called a distributed intelligent object. Finally, a distributed software testbed is described to illustrate our initial efforts.

In our research, we use the term *knowledge system* to refer to any system that uses AI techniques such that its performance and operation reflects a greater degree of intelligence than what is normally expected from a piece of conventional software. We foresee the use of both expert system and neural network technology in our quest to create intelligent systems. The question is not whether expert systems are more powerful than neural networks or vice versa, but rather which is more appropriate to the problem at hand.

THE REQUIREMENTS OF FUTURE REAL-TIME KNOWLEDGE SYSTEMS

Large engineering environments such as process plants dictate a number of important and unique criteria. Firstly, such systems operate in real-time. The data that is used for control changes continuously and at different rates. A fundamental requirement of real-time knowledge systems is that their response must both be correct and timely i.e. data validity is dependent on both the correctness of the value and the currency of the data. There are many other issues on the handling of real-time data such as the conversion of measurements into engineering units, the historical logging, data granularity, qualitative mapping etc. (Lun and MacLeod, 1988; Leitch, 1987; Milne, 1987; Bennett, 1987). Suffice it to say that the handling of real-time data is non-trivial and should demand careful attention.

Secondly, there exist a varied number of functions and generic problem solving tasks. Hayes-Roth et al. (1983), describe some of these tasks e.g. interpretation, prediction, diagnosis, design, planning, monitoring, control etc. Correspondingly, there is a set of inference and representational techniques and mechanisms that will be more appropriate for a particular task than others. It is therefore important to identify and select the knowledge system tool that best suits the problem. Chandrasekaran (1986), poses the caveat that often the available paradigms force the problem to fit the tool rather than allow the tool to be fashioned to reflect the problem structure.

Thirdly, several factors motivate the need for knowledge system distribution. The geographical layout of the plant may demand decentralized control. A network of computers may be required because computational and storage resources required may exceed the capability of any single computer. Distributed computer control also has some favourable characteristics pertaining to maintainability, active redundancy, parallel computation, etc. Correspondingly, the need for distribution implies a need for distributed experts. This gives rise to the notion of independent specialists, which are primarily autonomous agents that interact or cooperate with one another to achieve some global objective through various levels of distributed problem-solving.

THE MANAGEMENT OF TIME

Stankovic (1988) states that the real-time systems of the next generation will be even more complex, distributed and capable of exhibiting intelligent, adaptive and highly dynamic behavior. However, there are still many misconceptions about real-time design. Brute force techniques, supercomputer hardware, fast computing, assembly coding all help in meeting the challenge of building real-time systems, but they themselves do not constitute the solution. We concur with these observations. In order to guarantee that time constraints are met, it is necessary to make the time attribute the principle design parameter in the system rather than treating it as an afterthought.

There are three levels at which the time attribute can be addressed, the operating system level, the programming level and the application level. From the application developer's point of view, since the operating system is often dictated by the type of computers that are used, it is possibly the most inflexible of the three levels. Therefore we will concentrate on the latter two levels. We refer to the dealing with time at the programming level as the micro view and dealing with time at the application level as the macro view. Our approach to real-time is to provide a sound set of primitives on the micro level. Meaningful macro primitives can be subsequently built on these micro primitive building blocks.

A Micro View of Time

To develop real-time applications, we maintain that programming constructs are required that deal directly with time. Kopetz (1983) and MacLeod (1983) both propose the need for validity time stamps on all time-varying data. Although we differ slightly from their proposals, their work has inspired many of our current concepts regarding the handling of time. We have created a set of functions/primitives in the C language to deal with real-time. Together with the C preprocessor, these functions enable the programmer to write a program that takes into account the timeliness and correctness of time-varying data. Our system also assumes and makes use of a global physical time base. Many of the time-primitives that are presented here could easily be incorporated at the operating system level which would be more efficient, robust and general at the expense of being less portable.

Each time-based variable is declared as a state variable. In our view, each state variable is associated with a specific real-time 'bucket'. The contents of the bucket is dependent on the type of variable declared. The bucket also has a start and end validity time associated with it. The current global physical time must be between the start and end validity time in order for the contents to be valid. If we wish to support such a bucket in a distributed environment, a naming scheme is required to identify it uniquely. The main attributes of a real-time bucket can be represented as a record that consists of the following attributes:

- system name
- group name
- owner name
- tag name
- type
- size of variable
- version
- start validity
- end validity
- contents/value

The system name is used to identify the physical computer system while the group name specifies the logical function group or cluster i.e. alarming. It follows that a logical cluster of knowledge systems can span one or more physical systems. The owner name is the knowledge system/program that controls the variable. The tag name is the name of the variable itself. The type and size of the variable indicate the kind of variable and its size in bytes, e.g. it may be a floating point number occupying 4 bytes or a complex record structure occupying 50 or more bytes. The version shows the current version of the variable, which may be useful if a history is required.

The start and end validity of the variable changes as the value of the variable is updated. The importance of the validity time cannot be understated because it gives response context to each real-time variable. This allows process variables such as temperatures to have longer validity times because they tend to change very slowly e.g. in the order of minutes and flowrates to have shorter validity times because they may change quickly. Although, the start validity time must always be less than or equal to the end validity time, this does not preclude the possibility that the start time can be greater than the current global physical time. This implies that future values of variables can be asserted in advance.

Rich (1983) discusses the use and difficulties with non-monotonic reasoning (i.e. the addition or assertion of a piece of information may invalidate another). Clearly, in real-time systems, this is a continual condition since variables change as the process progresses in time. Generally, the method used to handle non-monotonicity is to implement schemes such as dependency-directed backtracking, (Doyle, 1979), which try to maintain consistency in the system. The task of propagating changes through the system is non-trivial and time-consuming. Validity intervals can be used to maintain consistency. Because of the state-based approach and validity time intervals, information is automatically and remotely invalidated through the passage of time. There is no need for tree-pruning or information deletion. The key is to select validity intervals that are not too short to require constant and unnecessary undating and not too long such that the information is valid longer than they should be. However, in real-time environments, many of these validity intervals are already dictated by scan times and response requirements.

In our opinion, the above real-time bucket structure is the minimum requirement for real-time data handling on the micro level. Appendix A presents some examples of statements that can be written in a conventional C program to deal with these real-time buckets. The statements allow the programmer to :

- associate variables to real-time buckets
- set the default naming system
- copy local variables to real-time buckets with a validity interval
- copy the contents of real-time buckets to local variables provided they are time valid.
- process a particular program block only if certain variables are time valid and the specified condition filters are true
- allow some default mechanism if a particular program block fails to execute after a specified timeout period
- allow a program to wait a predefined interval
- allow a program block to execute at regular intervals

At the macro level, we implement a macro state variable called a 'bulletin'. A bulletin corresponds to a real-time bucket on the micro level. In fact, bulletins are implemented using buckets. The fundamental difference is that although a bulletin must adhere to the same bucket attribute structure as described earlier, it has the additional constraint that the contents of the bucket must be syntactically and semantically correct. We are presently investigating what these syntax and semantic requirements should be. The term 'bulletin' is appropriate because it signifies a summary of some information that is of public interest. It is usually broadcast to all interested parties and is generally both topical and timely.

Qualitative or macro time primitives are hard to define. Future applications will show the usefulness of the ones proposed and and the need for additional primitives. Using micro-primitives of time, the macro primitives can be easily built and incorporated into any inference engine and knowledge representation. Although such macro abstractions of time may be implemented differently, e.g. rules, frames etc., they are consistent because of the commonality of the micro-level building blocks.

A Macro View of Time

Although the micro specification and handling of time discussed in the previous section can be a powerful technique, there is a need for greater abstraction at the level of the knowledge system tool i.e. inference mechanisms and representational schemes. While the micro-primitives can be viewed as the quantitative handling of time, the macro-primitives emphasise the qualitative aspects.

Arlabosse (1985) gives a synopsis of some of the current temporal logic models proposed. These models range from formal models to qualitative models. Formal models such as the one proposed by Dean and McDermott (1987) appear to be exhaustive but difficult to implement fully and practically. Qualitative models like the one proposed by Allen (1981, 1983) are both expressive and computable. Vere (1985) claims that all these models are computationally expensive and highly inefficient and proposes an alternative using the concept of a time window. At the moment, we are investigating Allen's model because it is sufficiently expressive and intuitive. Some of its inefficiencies could possibly be offset by providing micro-level support in building these macro primitives.

Any temporal reasoning model should provide constructs for inter-interval relationships as well as interval-action relationships. Allen lists thirteen possible relationships between two intervals. These are BEFORE, EQUAL, MEETS, OVERLAPS, DURING, START, FINISHES. These primitive time descriptors are sufficient to describe the relationship between any two time intervals. On the other hand, it is also important to describe the relationships between intervals and actions. Oyen, et.al. (1988) describes some of these relationships which pertain to sustained conditions and actions or delayed conditions and actions. These statements are generally of the form (FOR x SECONDS condition), (FOR x SECONDS action), (AFTER x SECONDS condition), (AFTER x SECONDS action). The FOR statement specifies that a condition must remain true for the time duration specified for it to be viewed as true or that an action must be sustained for that time duration. The AFTER statement enforces a predetermined delay before a condition is tested or an action is completed.

THE MANAGEMENT OF KNOWLEDGE

There are many artificial intelligence techniques that can be used to develop intelligent systems, (Gevarter, 1987). It is not the scope of this paper to discuss them in detail. To deal with these generic tasks such as diagnosis or control, various inference and representational schemes are available e.g. forward and backward chaining, rules, frames. Where learning is important, neural networks may prove to be more appropriate. Given this diversity of techniques to cope with the myriad of tasks, it is often difficult to select the correct paradigm to suit the problem. This has given rise to large flexible tools which offer many different inference strategies and representational schemes.

We maintain that most of the tools currently available are not suited to real-time applications. They do not provide sufficient mechanisms, if any, to handle the time attribute. They tend to be large, monolithic systems often requiring specialized workstations. They generally do not provide adequate communication interfaces with other knowledge systems and programming languages, bringing to bear issues pertaining to the lack of system integration (Eliot, 1988). We propose an alternative methodology which is to allow each problem to be addressed on an individual basis without presuming an a priori model or paradigm. The final implementation of each knowledge system may in fact be written using different languages, developed using different tools or sourced from various vendors. What must be adhered to is some universal communication interface and a well-defined set of micro-level primitives that will allow a loose coupling between all the systems with specific protocols to achieve global coherency and cooperation.

This approach promotes that use of object-oriented design techniques. Note that we should stress that object-oriented design does not automatically assume or demand the use of object-oriented programming languages, although this may be ultimately desirable. Ramamoorthy and Sheu, (1988) show the benefits of using object-oriented systems. Some attractive features provided by object-oriented systems are data abstraction, modularity, encapuslation and inherent concurrency. By viewing each knowledge system as an intelligent object, we can take advantage of these features.

Each intelligent object will contain its own set of inference mechanisms and representational schemes which it deems the most appropriate to achieve its purpose. Although it may operate on data that is quantitative in nature, it may communicate on a qualitative or heuristic basis thus exhibiting the characteristic of data abstraction. Its local autonomy also implies that it has total control over its own data allowing for modular design and implementation. The granularity of each intelligent object is important because it dictates the extent to which it is dependent on other objects. As inter-system dependence increases, the degree of concurrency achievable will invariably decrease. The message interface to each object can be viewed as its window to the real-world. Provided each object provides a compatible message interface, a system can developed consisting of intelligent objects, (each very different internally), communicating and cooperating on a global basis.

The above discussion shows that the object-oriented approach is equally valid at the system design level as it is on the programming level. Given a collection of intelligent objects, it is now necessary to coordinate them and define a universal messaging mechanism. This is a problem of distribution management.

THE MANAGEMENT OF DISTRIBUTION

Distribution is in many instances a necessity in real-time environments. Reasons for this include the geographical layout of the computer system, the need to achieve specific levels of reliability by separating and if necessary, replicating generic functions such as alarming, control and protection and the sheer volume of process monitoring points (Leinweber and Gidwani, 1986). Distribution management is concerned with the coordination and cooperation between several knowledge systems. This coordination involves the seamless transfer of knowledge and information through appropriate syntactic and semantic protocols.

Currently, one of the most popular mediums for distributed artificial intelligence is the blackboard architecture (Huhns, 1987). A blackboard is a centralized point that collates multiple knowledge sources and concurrent contexts. However, despite its inherent flexibility, traditional blackboard models suffer from a few shortcomings. Firstly, they generally have one control mechanism or scheduler which decides what is most important task at hand. Distributed real-time blackboards require the blackboard data to be time-based. They must allow asynchronous and concurrent update of their contents due to multiple independent control modules. They must support the notion of a virtual blackboard, i.e. a global blackboard that stretches across numerous computer systems transparently as far as each knowledge system is concerned. In line with our macro-level bulletins, we refer to these real-time blackboards as 'bulletin boards' since the validity of the information changes with time.

Our current distribution management philosophy defines any system or program to be viewed as a distributed intelligent object. Each object may address its own variables on the bulletin board through real-time buckets. To allow for minimal coordination and loose coupling, we apply the convention that each bucket may only have one writer (the owner), but may have many readers. A voter scheme is employed to simulate a multi-writer condition should the need arise. The bulletin board should be extendable to include a history of selected variables if required. In order to minimise bulletin board traffic especially between systems, a subscription protocol is used, i.e. a bulletin is updated as long as there is a demand/subscription from one or more readers, otherwise updating ceases when the longest subscription expires. Virtual bulletin boards are implemented by bulletin board interface tasks that communicate via networks to other bulletin boards. Remote subscriptions are honoured by broadcasting values to bulletin board interface tasks who then create local proxy bulletins.

Our proposed architecture encompasses the concepts of real-time, knowledge and distribution management. It is a platform from which multi-paradigm knowledge systems can be tested and implemented. The blackboard/bulletin board approach to distribution management is favoured because it specifies some universal interface, it can be extremely efficient and it allows the network interface to be transparent to the knowledge system. One immediate research direction is to examine the type of semantic protocols such as negotiation etc.

ADROIT - A DISTRIBUTED REAL-TIME OBJECT-ORIENTED INTELLIGENT TESTBED

ADROIT is a software testbed that we have implemented on a personal computer (Figure 1). Each distributed intelligent object may have different internal knowledge system architectures. A distributed intelligent object may be an interface to the real-world, an expert system, a neural-network, a simulator etc. The distributed intelligent objects adhere strictly to the concepts discussed thus far. They can be built using the micro-level time primitives or the macro-level time primitives. Each DIO is built using the inference mechanisms and knowledge representations most suited for its intended mission. They access the bulletin board via subscription calls. All real-time data is subject to time validation through its validity intervals.

The capability of the testbed is limited at this preliminary stage of development. There is an interface to a process simulator and a supervisory control and data acquisition system. Some of the DIOs implemented include a forward-chaining monitoring expert system, a backward-chaining diagnostic expert system, a back-propagation multi-layer neural network (supervized learning), a regularity detection neural-network (unsupervized learning). These systems are used to test coordination and cooperation strategies between the DIOs as well as the feasibility of neural networks for real-time control. One of the lessons learnt so far is that such a testbed is invaluable because it tests whether the concepts and theories are practical, efficient and feasible. It also lends further insight to real-time knowledge system requirements demanded by the real-world.

We hope to extend this testbed to incorporate a number of personal computers on a Novell network, some HP 9000 series 300 workstations and 2 PDP-11 computers running under DECNET. This expansion will hopefully achieve three objectives. Firstly, it will test the universality and portability of concept. Secondly, it will expose the testbed to more real-world applications and environments. Thirdly, it provides a basis to test multiple knowledge system paradigms on different applications which inturn should steer this research towards meaningful future directions.

CONCLUSION

Our initial experience with ADROIT shows that an architecture based on the notion of distributed intelligent objects is a promising one. It has allowed us to focus on the problem domain and find the best techniques to deal with it. In addition, the resulting solutions also tend to reflect the structure of the problems. The ability to communicate between systems enables the integration of knowledge systems with themselves and with more conventional software such as simulators and supervisory systems. It is evident that in order to tackle issues relating to real-time control, a bi-directional (i.e. top-down and bottom-up) approach to system design is required which demands the development and use of both micro and macro primitives. Further investigations and case studies will allow us to understand the benefits and shortcomings of such an architecture.

In conclusion, this paper has focussed on three urgent criteria which we believe are necessary to ensure the successful deployment of intelligent systems in real-time domains. Firstly, the attribute of time should not be discarded or its effects minimized. By careful design on a micro and macro level, it is possible to utilise time to meet stringent real-time requirements. In some instances, time can be used to solve problems that would otherwise elicit inelegant solutions. Secondly, there is no doubt that systems must become increasingly intelligent in order to aid in the efficient and correct operation of modern process plants. It should be recognized that the type of intelligence and implementation techniques will vary depending on the application, since there is generally no known universal paradigm of intelligence. Rather than create large universal monolithic systems, it is more desirable to develop real-time intelligent systems that are small, efficient and manageable. This implies that the global system architecture must accommodate multi-paradigms of intelligence. Thirdly, the increasing complexity and size of today's modern engineering environment make system decomposition and distribution a necessity. A sound distribution philosophy is critical to ensure maximum system-wide integration and subsystem cooperation. System incompatibilities will cause knowledge exchange bottlenecks and anti-synergy effects which invariably limit the usefulness of knowledge systems and create 'islands of expertise'. The pragmatic approach to designing knowledge systems for tomorrow is to design for integration today.

REFERENCES

Allen, J.F. (1981). An Interval-Based Representation of Temporal Knowledge, *Proc. 7th International Joint Conference on Artificial Intelligence*, 1981, pp. 221-226.

Allen, J.F. and Koomen, J.A. (1983). Planning Using a Temporal World Model. *Proc. 8th International Joint Conference on Artificial Intelligence*, 1983, pp. 741-747.

Arlabosse, F. (1985). Reasoning with Time and about Time: Some Aspects of Temporal Logic, *Expert Systems and Optimisation in Process Control*. Technical Press. pp. 215-219.

Bennett, M.E. (1987). Real-time Continuous AI Systems, *IEE Proc.D Control Theory and Applications*, 134, part D, no. 4, pp. 272-277.

Chandrasekaran, B. (1986). Generic Tasks in Knowledge-Based Reasoning: *High Level Building Blocks for Expert System Design*, IEEE Expert, Fall 1986, pp. 23-30.

Dean, T.L. and McDermott, D.V. (1987). Temporal Data Base Management, *Artificial Intelligence*, 32, pp. 1-55.

Doyle, J. (1979). A Truth Maintenance System, *Artificial Intelligence*, vol. 12, No. 3, 1979, pp. 231-272.

Eliot, L.B. (1988). The Expert Systems Business, *IEEE Expert*, Fall 1988, pp. 5-6.

Gevarter, W.B. (1987). The Nature and Evaluation of Commercial Expert System Building Tools, *IEEE Computer*, May 1987, pp. 24-41.

Hayes-Roth, F., Waterman, D., Lenat, D.B., Eds. (1983). *Building Expert Systems*, Addison-Wesley Publishing Company, 1983.

Huhns, M.N. (1987), *Distributed Artificial Intelligence*, Pitman, London.

Kopetz, H., Lohnert, F., Merker, W., Pauthner, G. (1983). A Message Based DCCS, *IFAC Distributed Computer Control Systems*, 1983.

Leinweber, D., Gidwani, K. (1986). Real-time Expert System Development Techniques and Applications, *IEEE Western Conference on Knowledge-Based Engineering and Expert Systems*, 1986, pp. 69-73.

Leitch, R.R. (1987). Artificial Intelligence : the emergence of a formal basis for engineering, *IEE Proc.D Control Theory and Applications*, 134, part D, no. 4, p. 217.

Lun, V. and MacLeod, I.M. (1989). Distributed Knowledge Systems in Real-time Applications, *5th IFAC/IFIP Symposium on Software for Computer Control*, April 1988.

MacLeod, I.M. (1983). *A Study of Issues Relating to Real-time in Distributed Computer Control Systems*, Ph.D. Thesis, University of the Witwatersrand.

Milne, R. (1987). Artificial Intelligence for Online Diagonosis, *IEE Proc.D Control Theory and Applications*, 134, part D, no. 4, pp. 238-244.

Ramamoorthy, C.V. and Sheu, P.C. (1988). Object-Oriented Systems, *IEEE Expert*, Fall 1988.

Rich, E. (1983). *Artificial Intelligence*, McGraw-Hill International Edition.

Stankovic, J.A. (1988). Misconceptions About Real-time Computing, *IEEE Computer*, October 1988, pp. 10-19

Vere, S. (1985). Temporal Scope of Assertions and Window Cutoff, *Proc. 9th International Joint Conference on Artificial Intelligence*, 1985, pp. 1055-1059.

Wright, M.L., Green, M.W., Fiegl, G. and Cross, P.F. (1986). An Expert System for Real-Time Control, *IEEE Software*, March 1986, pp. 16-24.

Appendix A : Examples of micro-time statements

Definition statements :

state_variable(float, TEMP1)

Naming statements :

set_path(PDP1, MONITORING, TEMP_CONTROLLER)
set_system(PDP1)
set_group(MONITORING)
set_owner(TEMP_CONTROLLER)
  bucket (TEMP1, f)

Output statements :

with_validity_interval(CURRENT_TIME, CURRENT_TIME + 10)
  output (TEMP1);

with_validity(10)
  output (TEMP1);

Input statements :

```
input (TEMP2) and (TEMP3) filter (TEMP2  TEMP3)
   perform
               ALARM_CONDITION_1 = TRUE
or (TEMP5) and (TEMP6) filter (TEMP5  100) filter (TEMP6  90)
   perform
               ALARM_CONDITION_2 = TRUE
on_timeout(TIMER, DELAY)
```

General time statements :

wait(PROCESS_DELAY)

```
after(TIMER, STARTUP_TIME)
   perform
               with_validity(DURATION)
                        output (LOAD_CONTAINER)
```

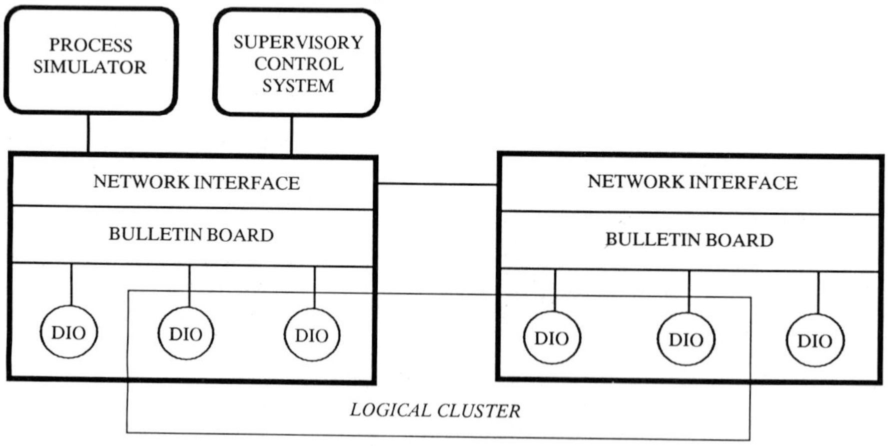

DIO : DISTRIBUTED INTELLIGENT OBJECT

NOTE THE LOGICAL CLUSTERING WHICH MAY OVERLAP PHYSICAL SYSTEMS.

FIGURE 1. ARCHITECTURE OF ADROIT

USING DISCRETE AI TECHNIQUES FOR DESIGNING A REAL-WORLD CONTROL SUPERVISOR

W. B. Smuts and I. M. MacLeod

Department of Electrical Engineering, University of the Witwatersrand, Republic of South Africa

Abstract. The mathematically based tools used by engineers to design control systems are not adequate for designing *supervisory* systems. The techniques developed in Artificial Intelligence (AI) research offer very promising tools for analysing and designing supervisory systems. However, in real-time, real-world applications, design considerations beyond those usually considered in AI research become important. While most AI techniques are based on *discrete* representations, the practical engineering applications of supervisory systems are in the *continuous* real world. The use of *discrete* AI techniques to implement a real-world control supervisor has been investigated and found to be feasible within certain guide-lines. An architecture for a control supervisor is proposed, followed by a discussion of the issues involved when using discrete AI techniques to implement the architecture.

Keywords. Supervisory control, real-time control, knowledge systems, artificial intelligence.

INTRODUCTION

A control supervisor can be described as *that* part of a control system, which (or who, in the case of a person) decides *when* to do *what*, in order to achieve certain goals. Usually the supervisor obtains information from the rest of the control system and gives high level commands to it, *without directly getting involved in the control loops.*

The pilot in control of a modern aircraft is a good example of a control supervisor. The autopilot keeps the airframe stable according to certain setpoints such as altitude, speed and heading. However, the autopilot alone cannot execute a mission. The *pilot* decides when to change the autopilot setpoints in order to reach the mission goals.

The mathematically based tools (time-domain methods such as state space analysis and frequency-domain methods such as Bode plots) used by engineers to design control systems are not adequate for designing *real-world* supervisory systems. In supervisory systems the emphasis shifts from *quantities* (calculating with numbers) to *qualities* (reasoning with symbols).

There are very powerful numerical techniques available to engineers for designing automatic controllers. All these techniques are based on the more fundamental numerical operators such as addition and multiplication. The logical techniques, on the other hand, are based on operators such as AND and OR. There are, however, very few (if any) logical methods currently used by engineers which compare in complexity and power to the high level numerical methods. This has been indicated in Table 1.

The authors believe that trying to analyse and design a control supervision system in terms of AND, OR and IF...THEN... ELSE... rules will prove to be as futile as trying to analyse and design an autopilot for an aircraft in terms of integration and differentiation operations.

The authors believe that the knowledge contained in the rules must *structured* and that a *strategy* has to be added to the way in which the rules are applied, before any success

Table 1 Levels of Abstraction in the numerical and logical methods commonly used by engineers.

Numerical Methods	Logical Methods
....	?
Z-Transform, Nichols Diagrams...	?
....	CASE Statements
Differentiation, Integration	IF...THEN...ELSE... rules
Multiplication, Division	Exclusive-OR, Coincidence
Addition, Subtraction	AND, OR

can be expected when implementing a comprehensive control supervisor. This view is supported by Sacerdoti (1977) when he states that:

> " ...the *structure* of knowledge about actions in a computer memory is as important as the *content* of that knowledge."

The techniques developed in Artificial Intelligence (AI) research offer very promising tools for analysing and designing supervisory systems. However, for real-time, real-world applications, design considerations beyond those usually considered in AI research, become important (Broadwell,1985).

Most of the techniques developed to date are based on *toy worlds* such as the blocks-world. The real world differs from these toy worlds in more aspects than just size.

The authors believe that one of the more important differences between the real world and the toy worlds is the fact that the real world properties are in most cases *continuous*, whereas the toy worlds are inherently *discrete*. It is also believed that the techniques based on discrete representations cannot be applied *blindly* to real-world situations. Either new techniques based on a continuous representation must be developed, or a valid and useful way must be defined in terms of which the continuous real world may be mapped into a discrete representation. In this paper an investigation of the second option is reported.

Many applications (mainly expert systems) have already been designed which *seem* to operate effectively in the real world. However, in most cases these are desk-top based *consulting* systems where a human operator forms a buffer between the system and the real world. The transformation of knowledge from the real world to the representation used in the system and vice versa, is done by the human operator. In a control supervision system, the idea is to *remove* the human from the system. Without the interpretation power of a human operator as part of the system, more careful consideration has to be given to the representation issue.

Similar work has been done by Moore (1984) and Visuri (1986). However, they concentrated more on *operator decision making aids* than on actually *replacing* the operator. Åström, Anton and Årzén (1986) and Trankle and Markosian (1985) tried to *enhance* the properties of an automatic controller, whereas the objective of the research described in this paper is to implement the control supervision functions, usually performed by man, as *part* of the system.

The issues involved in using *discrete* AI techniques to implement a real-world control supervisor are discussed within the framework of a proposed architecture. The first section provides a high-level discussion of the proposed architecture. The second section explains why it is claimed that a discrete world model can be used to implement a real-world control supervision system. Because *time* cannot be treated in the same way as the rest of the continuous properties of the world, it has been treated under a separate heading.

CONTROL SUPERVISION ARCHITECTURE

This section provides a discussion of the proposed control supervision architecture. For the purposes of this paper control supervision can formally be defined as follows:

> Control supervision is the process of using applicable *knowledge* and *facts* to decide (through a *reasoning process*) which *commands* to give to an *automatic controller* at specific moments in time, in order to guide the process (controlled by the automatic controller) to achieve certain *goals*.

The envisaged system and its environment can be represented as shown in Fig. 1.

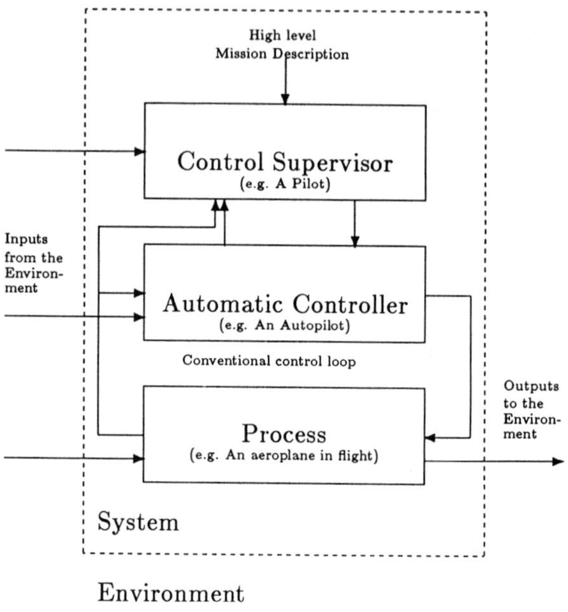

Fig. 1. Block Diagram of the System and its Environment.

The control supervisor performs a *logical* function, whereas the automatic controller performs a *numerical* function. These two processes are inherently different and call for two different design approaches.

The clear separation of the symbolic and numerical functions into different subsystems has already been advocated by Evers (1984). This approach also conforms to the principle of *Increasing Precision with Decreasing Intelligence*, described by Saridis and Valavanis (1988). According to Saradis this principle resembles Heisenberg's *principle of uncertainty*. It establishes a hierarchy in the distribution of intelligence of an intelligent control system and states that precision is not required where intelligence is high, and vice versa.

Since the beginning of AI research, there have been two schools of thought regarding the approach taken when modelling intelligent behaviour. The first tried to mimic the way in which humans solve problems and make plans. The second regarded the human approach as just *one* (and not necessarily the best) way in which to bring about intelligent behaviour and therefore attempted to derive the model for the solution from the problem itself, instead of simulating an agent able to perform the task. The approach used during this research was a combination of both. Although the work attempts to go beyond a mimicry of human abilities, the authors did not hesitate to use the human approach as a guideline.

By observing human control supervisors in action, the following activities have been identified as elements of a possible method of performing a control supervision task:

- Plan generation.
- Plan execution.
- Execution monitoring and exception handling.

Plan generation and execution has already received a lot of attention in AI research (Gevarter,1984; Sacerdoti, 1977; Sussman,1975). However, most of the planners form an *open loop* system. Plans are generated once and then executed without feedback of what actually happens during execution. The authors believe that more success can be expected if the loop is closed by adding *execution monitoring, exception handling and replanning* to the control supervision system. It is even believed that by closing the loop, better results can be expected from sub-optimum plans.

Execution monitoring and *exception handling* has not received the same amount of attention as plan generation. The exception handler can be defined as that part of the system which takes care of unexpected events such as breakages.

In the present model, exceptions are handled by:

- Generating new goals (called 'survival goals' in contrast to the predefined 'mission goals') and then replanning to incorporate the new goals in the plan.
- Changing the internal description of the abilities of the system and then replanning to generate a plan which will reflect these changes. (For example, in a 'means-end analysis' approach, the preconditions and results of operators can be changed to reflect exceptions which affect the abilities of the system. Some operators may even be disabled.)

A block diagram of the proposed architecture is shown in Fig. 2. (The environment is not explicitly indicated as in Fig. 1.) The mission description is provided by a human operator in the form of a list of mission goals. The *planner* generates a plan to reach the mission goals, while at the same time incorporating the survival goals. A description of the abilities of the system is used during the plan generation process. The *plan executor* executes the plan by giving commands to the automatic controller.

The *state* forms a description of the 'state of affairs' in the system and the process and is used by the *execution monitor and exception handler* to detect exceptions. Exceptions are handled by generating *survival goals* and by changing the description of the system abilities. A new plan is then generated which reflects the added survival goals and changed system abilities.

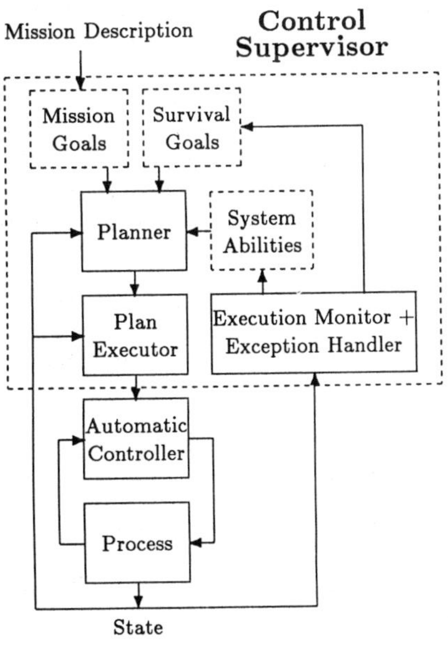

Fig. 2. Proposed Architecture for a Control Supervisor.

Within the framework of this architecture, the effects of using discrete AI techniques in the real world are investigated.

A DISCRETE WORLD MODEL

The issues involved in using a discrete model of the world and discrete AI techniques to generate plans, are discussed within the framework of the proposed control supervision architecture.

Planning can be seen as a simulation of the real world through the manipulation of symbols to investigate the expected outcome of actions without having to execute these actions. The effectiveness of the planning procedure depends to a large extent on how well the symbols represent the real world features. The mapping of these features into symbols can be seen as the construction of a *world model* and is generally known as the *Knowledge Representation Issue* in the AI literature. A *world model* is a simplified, abstract *representation* of a subset of the features of the real world.

Most planning systems developed to date are based on a *discrete knowledge representation* (Gevarter,1984; Sacerdoti, 1977; Sussman,1975). The techniques developed for planning in a discrete world, with a human operator in the planning and plan-execution loop to perform the transformation between the world model and the real world, cannot be applied *blindly* to planning in a real-world control supervision system.

Because the discrete planning techniques are fairly simple compared to what may be needed for planning in a continuous world, it is worthwhile looking for rules which can be used to map the continuous real world in a valid and useful way into a discrete representation.

Nyquist's Sampling Theorem states that a discrete (sampled) representation of a continuous variable contains all the information in that variable if the sampling frequency is chosen to be higher than twice the highest rate at which the variable changes (Papoulis,1980).

When using Nyquist's Sampling Theorem, it *seems* that the solution to the problem of applying discrete AI techniques to the real world is trivial. After the continuous real world features have been mapped into a discrete representation, by using a high enough sampling frequency, the discrete AI techniques can be applied directly.

However, when searching large quantities of knowledge, the *combinatorial explosion* (Raphael,1971) very soon makes the task totally unmanageable with current computing equipment. Sampling continuous variables at the Nyquist Sampling Frequency adds a few orders of magnitude to the combinatorial explosion.

It is conjectured that within certain guide-lines, discrete AI techniques can indeed be used to implement a control supervisor to operate in the real world. This claim is based on the assumption that in practical applications, missions are usually defined in such a way that the system is *expected* to do much less than what it actually *can* do.

The expression *highly discrete* is taken to refer to the mapping of continuous features to a discrete representation at a sampling frequency far below the Nyquist Sampling Frequency (Papoulis, 1980), and not necessarily at a constant rate. The values of variables in a highly discrete representation are usually used as *symbols* and not as *numbers*. These values are used for reasoning and not for doing calculations.

A good example of a highly discrete representation is the case where the map of a country is represented by the names of a few towns and the distances between them. This is in contrast to the more conventional way of using an x-y grid with a high enough resolution to reference locations on the map.

In such a geographical mission arena, the task of the control supervisor is limited to deciding which towns to visit and in which sequence, in order to reach the mission goals. Moving to the exact co-ordinates of a certain town and "fine-tuning" the position of the vehicle to be within δx and δy of the co-ordinates x and y, is a matter of *control* and not of *supervision*. This is a numerically based problem and not a logically based problem with which the control supervisor is concerned. This approach also conforms to the principle of *Increasing Precision with Decreasing Intelligence* which has already been mentioned.

For a *real-world* planning and plan execution system, with only a discrete number of goals to be reached in a discrete number of ways, it is postulated that a highly discrete world model can be used if:

- the system is given the ability to recover from any possible state in the real world back to a state that maps directly to the discrete world model;
- the system can *observe* the real state to a high enough accuracy to determine which recovery action to perform.

This can be compared to the case of a person crossing a river by stepping from stone to stone. Apart from being able to plan the route from stepping stone to stepping stone, the person needs the ability to get back onto the nearest stone, should he happen to fall into the water. Although he can reach *any point* in the river, he only has to consider *the stepping stones* as candidate states during generation of a plan to reach the other side of the river.

Time, however is a real-world property which needs special treatment.

REAL-TIME ISSUES

Time cannot be treated in the same way as other continuous properties such as distance and temperature. Time not only forms the independent variable of most of the functions describing the real world, but it also forms the property in terms of which the causality of actions and events is described. Part of the representation of time is thus embedded in the *planning strategy*.

Representing time as discrete *moments* (as in the Sampling Theorem), is not adequate when reasoning with actions and events, especially when concurrent and overlapping actions and events are possible. Actions and events are not instantaneous but occur over time *intervals*. In an application such as this (a real-world, real-time control supervisor), a real-time ability not only refers to a system that is "fast enough", but also to its ability to reason with temporal relationships. Work related to this subject has been done by Vere (1983) and Allen (1983).

A planning strategy based on the "means-end analysis" (Gevarter,1984) approach has been investigated. *Operators* are defined to describe actions, but instead of describing the preconditions for the application of an operator as a *state*, the preconditions are given in terms of other operators and events by using the seven basic temporal interval relationships defined by Allen (1981). These relationships are represented in Table 2.

TABLE 2 The Seven Basic Relationships between two Time Intervals X and Y.

Relationship	Pictorial representation
X before Y	XXXXXX YYYYYY
X equal Y	XXXXXX YYYYYY
X meets Y	XXXXXX YYYYYY
X overlaps Y	XXXXXX YYYYYY
X during Y	XXXXXX YYYYYYYYYY
X starts Y	XXXXXX YYYYYYYYYY
X finishes Y	XXXXXXXXXX YYYYYY

As an example, the preconditions for the application of Operator-A may be that Operator-A must be met by Operator-B, must be before Operator-C and may not be during Event-E. This differs from Allen's approach in that operators are linked directly in terms of other operators instead of linking them indirectly by the states caused by operators. It also solves the so-called "Frame Problem" (Raphael,1971) to some extent, because only the effect of operators on resources (and not a total state description) must be carried along with every candidate plan during plan generation. This approach makes it possible to model concurrent actions as well as actions by other agents acting in the same environment.

For those temporal relationships (such as *before* and *after*) of which the start and stop times are defined in terms of inequalities, *Linear Programming* techniques (Rothenberg,1979) have been used to find valid start and stop times for the actions.

CONCLUSION

Conventional numerical techniques cannot be used to design a comprehensive control supervision system. AI techniques offer valuable tools for designing such a system, but are based on *discrete* representations, whereas the real world consists of many *continuous* properties. This paper has shown that the discrete AI techniques can, within certain guidelines, be used to design a real-world control supervision system.

The concepts described in this paper have been implemented on a small scale in LISP and the results indicate that the above-mentioned guide-lines for using discrete AI techniques in the real world are indeed feasible and useful.

REFERENCES

Allen,J.F. (1981). An Interval-Based Representation of Temporal Knowledge. *Proc. 7th International Joint Conference on Artificial Intelligence*,pp.221–226.

Allen,J.F. (1983). Planning Using a Temporal World Model. *Proc. 8th International Joint Conference on Artificial Intelligence*, pp.741–747.

Åström,K.J.,Anton,J.J. and Årzen,K.-E. (1986). Expert Control. *Automatica*, Vol 22, Number 3.

Evers,D.C., Smith,D.M. and Staros,C.J. (1984). Interfacing an Intelligent Decision-Maker to a Real-Time Control System. *Spie*, Vol 485, pp.60–64.

Gevarter,W.B. (1984). In *Artificial Intelligence, Expert Systems Computer Vision and Natural Language Processing*. Noyes Publications, New Jersey.

Moore,R., Hawkinson,L., Knickerbocker,C. and Churchman,L. (1984) A Real-time Expert System for Process Control. *IEEE Conference on Artificial Intelligence*.

Papoulis,A. (1980). In *Circuits and Systems — A Modern Approach*. Holt-Saunders International Editions,New York.

Raphael,B.(1971). The Frame Problem in Problem-Solving Systems. In Findler,N.V. (Ed), *Artificial Intelligence and Heuristic Programming*, American Elsevier, New York.

Rothenberg,R.I. (1979). In *Linear Programming*. North-Holland,New York.

Sacerdoti,E.D. (1977). In *A Structure for Plans and Behaviour*. Elsevier, North-Holland, New York.

Saradis,G.N. and Valavanis,K.P.(1988). Analytical Design of Intelligent Machines. *Automatica*, Vol 24, Number 2.

Sussman,G.J. (1975). In *A Computer Model of Skill Acquisition*. Elsevier, North-Holland, New York.

Trankle,T. and Markosian,L. (1985). An Expert System for Control System Design. *IEEE Proceedings on Configuration Control*.

Vere,S.A. (1983). Planning in time: Windows and durations for activities and goals. *IEEE Transactions on Pattern Analysis and Machine Intelligence*, Vol 1, Number 3.

Visuri,P. (1986). Application of Intelligence to Digital Process Supervising Systems. *Software and Hardware Applications of Microcomputers, Proceedings of the ISMM International Symposium*.

HARDWARE AND SOFTWARE STRUCTURE OF A REAL-TIME EXPERT SYSTEM FOR CONTROL OF CHEMICAL PLANTS

T. Respondek and V. Krebs

Institute of Electrical Information Technology, Technical University of Clausthal, Leibnizstr. 28, D-3392 Clausthal-Zellerfeld, FRG

Abstract. This paper presents a hybrid software architecture for real-time expert systems (XPS), where knowledge based software components are embedded into the existing world of conventionally programmed process control systems for chemical plants. The paper shows, how an efficient low-cost real-time expert system can be designed using an available XPS shell running on a PC. The resulting XPS is provided for supporting the operator of the plant in starting up and closing down the process as well as for giving assistance in control and supervision/failure detection. The requirements and features of the XPS, which is applied to a prototype distillation column, are discussed and critically evaluated.

Keywords. AI based decision making techniques; monitoring and supervision; process and production control; process scheduling techniques; real-time expert systems

INTRODUCTION

It is well known that the design of control systems for complex processes, e.g. as they are found in chemical industry, is not an easy task. The implementation of the control laws first requires substantial modelling and identification activities, yielding a set of linearized differential or difference equations, which may be characterized as 'technical' or 'algorithmic' knowledge. However, these linear models are valid only in the range of the operating points and consequently the same holds for the regulators, which are either of PID type or represent some more sophisticated multivariable control laws. Difficulties arise when the process behaviour is highly nonlinear and thus cannot be described by linearized equations, e.g. as it happens for starting up or closing down procedures. In these operating modes the process is governed by a human operator who applies his 'heuristic' knowledge for the control strategy.

Advances in expert system (XPS) technology during the recent years allow the inclusion of the operator's heuristic knowledge in the knowledge bases of an XPS and to integrate this XPS into the process control system (Shibata and co-workers, 1987, Voss, 1988). A status report on real-time XPS is given in Bowen (1987). However, since most of today's XPS development tools are specified for offline use, it is not quite easy to apply them for online use. Therefore several features have to be met in order to obtain real-time performance.

An exemplary solution of this problem is presented for a system of automation designed for control of a distillation column. This prototype process is provided for a new method of synthesizing MTBE (Methyl-Tert-Buthylether), which is used as a leadfree antiknocking additive for fuel.

The hardware concept, as it is realized, consists of a series connection of three components, an interface computer and two Personal Computers (PC), one of them for process control and the other for the XPS shell to run on. In the sequel this hardware configuration as well as the hybrid software structure (i.e. algorithmic components for conventional process control complemented by a knowledge based XPS part) will be discussed and critically evaluated.

THE CONCEPT OF AUTOMATION WITH INTEGRATED REAL-TIME XPS

To develop an appropriate concept of knowledge based automation for a distillation column, it is useful to consider first of all the conventional control system without expert system technology.

While working in steady state, the process is controlled by five control loops for pressures, temperatures and flow rates. The controllers are implemented on a process control computer. Using this conventional system the control of the process is naturally in the operator's responsibility. Figure 1 explains the extensive range of tasks the operator has to attend to. While starting up the process, the control system works in open loop mode because of the completely nonlinear behaviour of the process, i.e. the process control computer provides output of data to the monitor only. So it is up to the operator to drive the process to the desired operating point by defining new control actions, by supervising the measurement data as well as the plant equipment etc. In case of a fault, the operator has to reason for the malfunction and then to eliminate it, while, at the same time, continuously watching the measurement data. Thus the operator works as a human expert controller, performing several jobs simultaneously.

The complexity of this prototype column already suggests the use of knowledge based technologies to support the operator.

Figure 2 shows a modified concept derived from the above mentioned requirements. The expert's knowledge is modelled in a separate XPS computer, but it has to be observed that the main authority remains with the operator who should be able to interfere and to take over the control at any time. Thus a hybrid software strucure is needed: it is significant to make further use of the conventionally programmed procedural software, which is well proven in controlling the process during steady state, but it is recommended to use knowledge based software for the heuristics and the strategies of the plant's operators for starting up and supervisory purposes.

Requirements for the XPS

As shown in Fig. 2 the XPS is connected to the process via the process control computer. With respect to this online operating mode, real-time performance is demanded, i.e. the factor 'time' has to be linked to the system concerning two different levels of requirements (Früchtenicht, Wittig, 1987):

- First a high speed of execution of the XPS is needed to cope with critical situations. In this sense the inference time of the XPS has to be short in relation to the changing speed of the process.
- Secondly the XPS should have the ability to handle with time dependent informations (temporal reasoning).

Moreover the XPS has to be qualified for continuous monitoring of the actual situation of the process which requires a special interrupt mechanism. It must be taken into account that a current XPS activity can be interrupted by the information contained in a new set of process data that signalizes the occurence of a more important event (e.g. a case of emergency) and therefore has to be dealt with first. This means that an event driven interrupt hierarchie is an important feature of the XPS.

The XPS development tool

Considering the possibilities for building an XPS, it is obvious that there are several ways of finding a proper solution (Krebs, 1988).

One way is the development of the software by the XPS-designer. However, this means to devote a huge amount of time-consuming programming activity to the pursuit of an exactly fitting solution to the problem. On the other hand, there is the possibility of buying fully programmed XPS development tools, which are available at several levels of quality in terms of their ability of knowledge representation and reasoning as well as the hardware they run on. With regard to cost limitations in transferring expert system technology into real industrial applications, the following boundary conditions are met in the proposed and applied concept:

- Use of a Personal Computer instead of an AI machine
- Use of an XPS shell instead of a knowledge representation language
- Use of DOS instead of a multitasking operating system (the latter is preferable but - as usual - the XPS shell runs under DOS).

As a consequence of the application of a low-cost shell, there are only restricted possibilities for knowledge representation but on the other hand all the good (and bad) characteristics of the given inference engine. It should be mentioned that the boundary conditions in this pilot project concerning cost and required hardware (and availability) excluded tools like G2 and MUSE, which are especially designed for real-time purposes.

After evaluating a large number of tools for possible real-time use within a certain price level, it was decided to buy a system called SAVOIR, which is produced by ISI (Intelligent Systems International), U.K. This shell is a very flexible Pascal based production system with rules and demons for knowledge representation and forward and backward chaining for inference, available for PC's as well as for mainframes.

However, to match the features of the shell with the above mentioned requirements for real-time XPS, extensive modifications of the SAVOIR tool were neccessary. For example the original I/O routines SAVOIR provides, had to be replaced by a special I/O system, because when running the original routines, all the inference engine's activities are stopped until the user prompts a keyboard <RETURN> command. This feature would be opposite to the required continuous monitoring of the process state.

THE REALIZATION OF THE KNOWLEDGE BASED SYSTEM OF AUTOMATION

Figure 3 shows the hardware as well as the software structure of the system as it is in use for release of the human operator and thus brings a higher degree of automation to the process.

As mentioned above, most of today's XPS development tools are not specially designed for real-time applications, hence they are not able to process a great number of algorithmic data.

Therefore an interface is needed between the different knowledge levels of the process control computer on the one side, and the XPS on the other side, i.e. a mapping between algorithmic and knowledge based computing has to be provided.

This task of transformation is taken over by two software modules.
First there is the real-time interface which has to guarantee the exact coordination of data transfer between the two computers for preventing timing problems and in addition works as a data buffer.
Secondly we have a data preprocessing module, which is performing the essential task of linking the different knowledge levels of the process control computer and the XPS computer.
To diagnose the current situation, the XPS requires both, information about the actual data and information about the time history of the process. To enable an effective temporal reasoning, it is not neccessary to consider the complete history, but rather to shape the memory of the past by using either rectangular or exponential moving windows for data weighting as shown in Fig. 4. These moving windows, extended over a certain period of time from the present to the past, analyze a set of data, sufficient for computing the mean, the variance, and the gradients of the important measured process data. Now the purpose of this module becomes clear: the data preprocessing module provides time variable data for the XPS derived from the process control signals. However, instead of simple numeric values the information for the XPS is transformed, e.g. to the following type:

"temperature(t+dt)>temperature(t), speed_of_increasing := high " etc.

Combining the results from all important variables of the chemical process with the knowledge base, the XPS is able to infer the actual state of the plant and to give a diagnosis, consequently followed by a proposal for the next action.

The user interface gives assistance in convenient communication of the operator with all components of the process. To allow a comprehensive overview, it is neccessary to use several windows on the monitor, to show all important measured values, to give information about the control loops (i.e. control loops open or closed, automatic or manual control, values of set points and control elements etc.). Another window is needed to show the activities of the XPS, i.e. to give a diagnosis of the process behaviour as well as suggestions for the next steps to come.

At last there is a supervising program, which drives the whole system by coordination of all software components being implemented in the XPS computer. To avoid runtime problems the supervising program is part of the knowledge base.

The knowledge base itself contains a set of rules representing the expert's knowledge and strategies of running the process. These rules are expressed in a special programming language provided by the XPS shell. An example is shown below:

```
DISPLAY 'Increase cooling rate onto 50%'
 ASSOONAS (Heating = 40)
      AND (Profile_of_temperature ==
            'stable')
      AND (Flow_rate < 10)
```

The meaning of this rule is as follows: There has to be a display on the monitor instructing the operator that the cooling rate has to be increased onto 50%, as soon as some pre-conditions concerning the heating, a profile of temperature, and a flow rate become true. In this special case most of the preconditions depend on the results of the data preprocessing, e.g. the value of profile_of_temperature is deduced by measurement of single temperatures along the column. Thus there is indeed a dynamic determination of values representing the actual state of the process.

Figure 5 shows the operating cycle of the XPS computer. According to the nonprocedural character of the software this figure can only demonstrate the principle of the XPS activities.

On the left side of this figure the main cycle is depicted. Before the actual start of the process, extensive preparations have to be executed. During this situation the XPS is used as a system for diagnosis. By using the knowledge base 'initial preparations' and by communication with the operator, it is ensured that all the actions required for a safe start-up of the process are fully accomplished, e.g. the correct positions of valves, pump capacities etc.

After these preparations the supervisory program assigns the control of the starting procedure to the knowledge base 'starting-up'. This knowledge base is embedded in a complex flow of information, because the XPS needs input data not only from the process but also from the operator as well as communication with the dynamic data base for inferring the rules. Each kind of action, including output to the monitor and to the real-time interface, is performed rulebased. The network of connections on the right side of Fig. 5 characterizes the nonprocedural operating mode of the rulebased system. The inference engine of the XPS guarantees a correct performance of all functions by cyclic applying forward and backward chaining to the rules.

CONCLUSIONS

This example of a real-time XPS for support of the operator of a chemical plant shows, how knowledge based software can be embedded into the hierarchical structure of process control systems. The problems resulting from the dynamic changes of the process, call for a hybrid software structure, to combine the advantages of both, the conventional process control, and the XPS control.

Field tests with this knowledge based process control system demonstrated that execution time of the XPS (about 2 sec.) is no major problem using today's hardware technology (32 bit PC); however, it has been found more complex to include the 'time' in the knowledge base, especially if the development tool does not meet all features for this purpose.

First experiences with this system show that the resulting hybrid system architecture is an efficient and low-cost possibility to design real-time XPS for monitoring and control purposes.

REFERENCES

Bowen, B.A. (1987). Real-Time Expert Systems: A Status Report. AGARD LS No.155.

Früchtenicht, H.W., Wittig, T. (1987). Ein Ansatz für Echtzeit-Expertensysteme. Automatisierungstechnische Praxis, 29,78-82.

Krebs, V. (1988). Wissensmodellierung bei Diagnose-Expertensystemen. Messen, Steuern, Regeln, 31, 444-446.

Shibata, M. and co-workers (1987). Application of Expert Systems for Blast Furnace Operation Control. 10. IFAC-World Congress, Preprints Vol.6, 282-287.

Voss, H. (1988). Architectural Issues for Expert Systems in Real-Time Control. IFAC-Workshop on Artificial Intelligence in Real-Time Control, Preprints, 1-5.

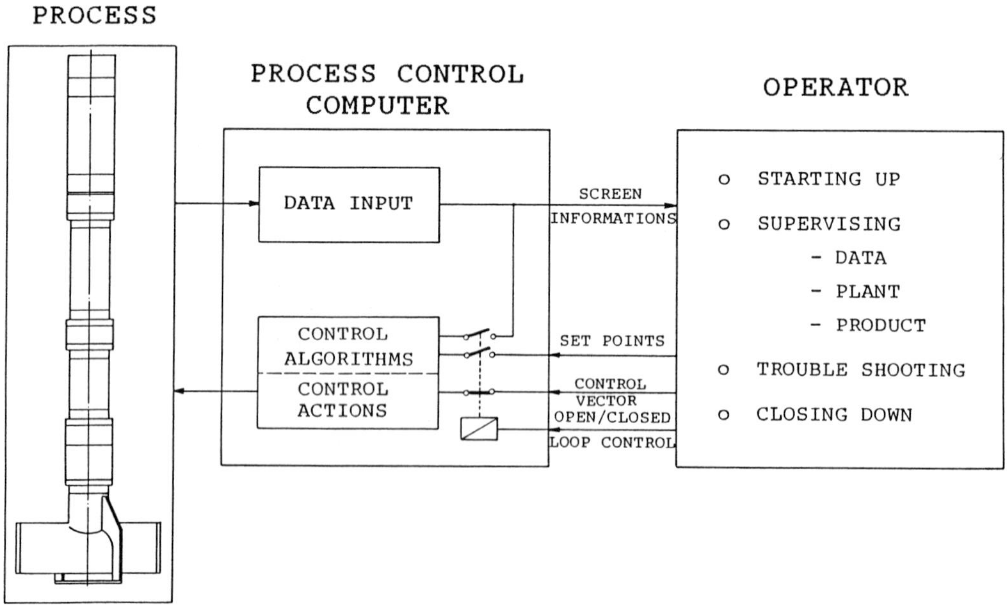

Fig. 1. Conventional system for process control

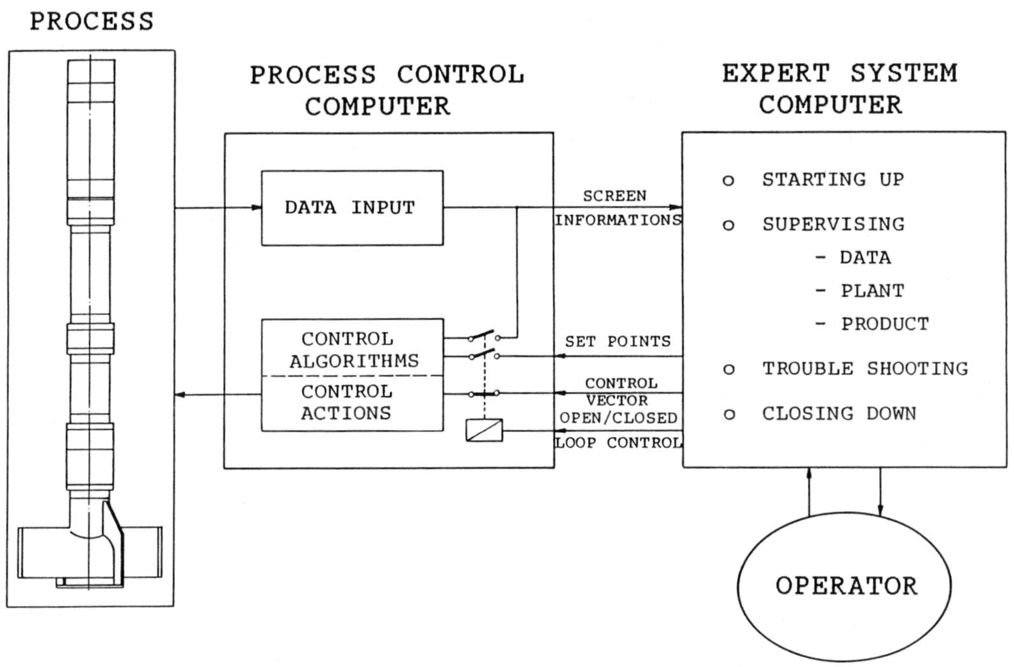

Fig. 2. Process control system supported by XPS technology

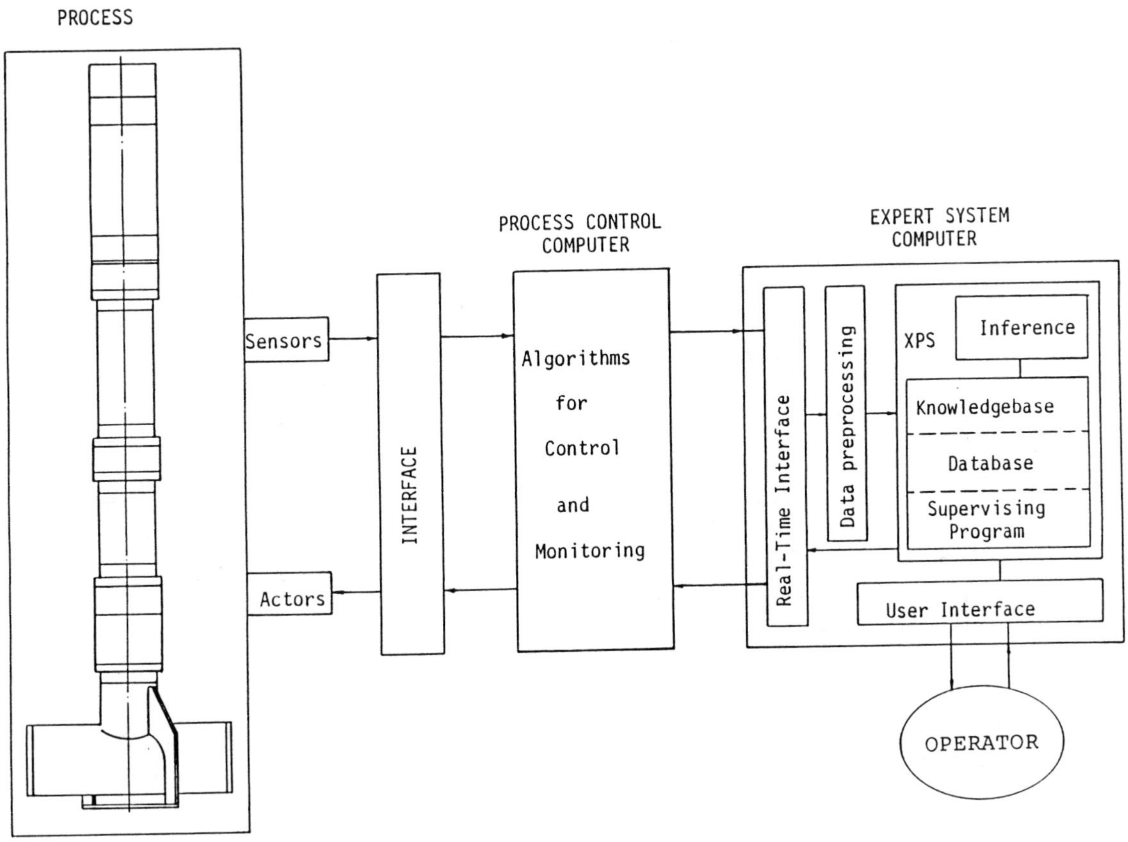

Fig. 3. Hardware and software structure of the realized knowledge based system of automation

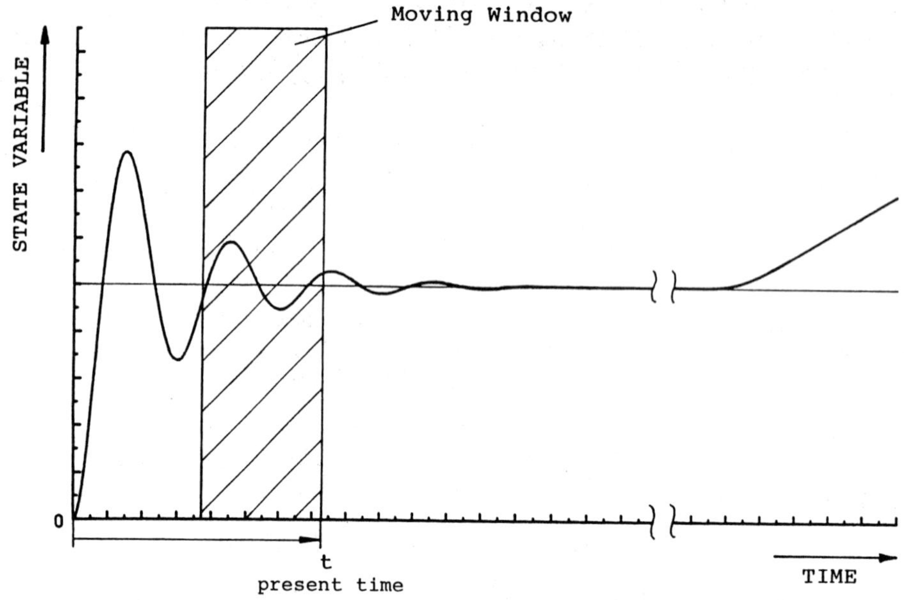

Fig. 4. Example for data preprocessing using a moving window

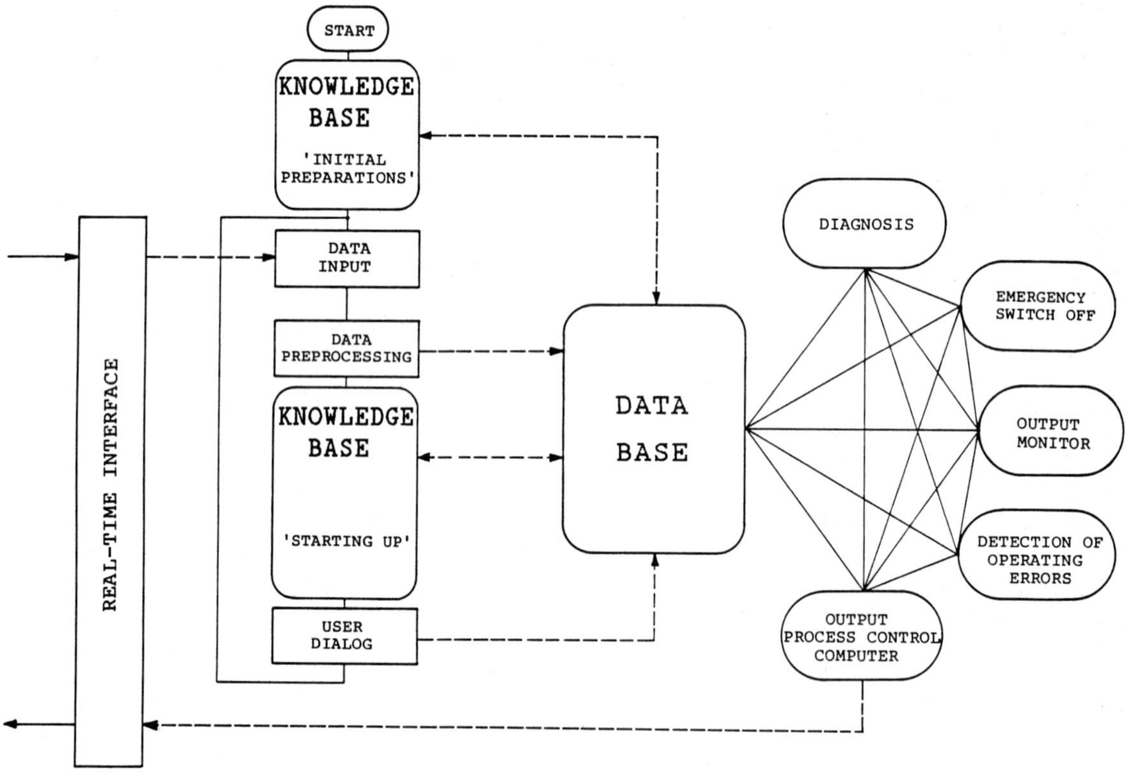

Fig. 5. Software structure of the real-time XPS

MODELLING AND CONTROL FOR NONLINEAR TIME-DELAY SYSTEM VIA PATTERN RECOGNITION APPROACH[1]

Lan Zhou*, Nan Ye and Yong-zai Lu****

**Mold High Technology Institute, Zhejiang University, Hangzhou 310027, PRC*
***Research Institute of Industrial Process Control, Zhejiang University, Hangzhou 310027, PRC*

ABSTRACT This paper addresses a development of the pattern recognition based system modelling and the relevant state feedback control for nonlinear time–delay systems. The study involving in this paper is mainly to propose an algorithm of statistical fuzzy pattern classification and the learning based on the stochastic approximation.

As a case study, the application of the proposed strategy and algorithm to the fluidized catalytic cracking unit in large production scale refinery shows the satisfactory results, merits and the potential applications in other industrial processes.

KEYWORDS System modelling, Pattern recognition, Pattern classification, Learning, Nonlinear system, State feedback

INTRODUCTION

With the rapid progress of modern control theory and techniques, the mathematical description based system modelling and the relevant control strategies / algorithms have been successfully applied to some industrial processes. However, there are still some difficulties in dealing with the modelling and advanced control for complex systems widely existing in industry, due to the system complexity, uncertainty and lack of the priori–knowledge concerning model structure and time–varying characteristics as well. As a result, it has been becoming an attractive research area to seek the novel approaches to establishing system models and related control strategies with less prior–knowledge of the system under study. Fortunately, the rapid development of artificial intelligence techniques has made it possible to describe the system characteristics using nontraditional ways, such as expert system, fuzzy set theory and pattern recognition etc. (Saridis, 1979).

Depending on the analysis of the system information and principle, a group of the features describing the system behaviors could be extracted through using the system input / output / state data sequences, and further be used to set up pattern description model. This provides a new way to avoid the difficulty of determine the system model structure which is usually required in traditional identification approaches. So far, many reports in pattern recognition based adaptive control (Bristol, 1977), fault diagnosis (Se–Young, 1986) and state estimation (Ye, 1988) etc. have been published.

[1] This study was supported by China National Natural Science Foundation and China Petrol–Chemical General Cooperation

This paper presents a new algorithm for pattern recognition based dynamic system modelling with a statistical fuzzy pattern classifier (SFPC) as proposed. The research results demonstrate that the proposed algorithm is superior to the existing work and is valid to solve the problem of noncontinuous output of general pattern classifier under consideration.

STATISTICAL FUZZY PATTERN CLASSIFIER FOR SYSTEM MODELLING

Problem Statement

Supposing a system model under consideration which is not available is governed by the following nonlinear dynamic equation:

$$y(k+1) = F(y(k), u(k)) \tag{1}$$

where $u(k) \in U$ is the input vector, r–dimension
$y(k) \in Y$ is the output vector, n–dimension
$F(\cdot)$ is the nonlinear operator

The problem statement of pattern recognition based system modelling is first to establish a standard (or so–called initial) pattern by means of the off–line input / output data sequences $\{u_k, y_k, k=0, k_f\}$, and then the real–time output can be determined by using the established pattern associated with the real–time input data without knowing the model structure as shown in equation (1).

Classical pattern recognition methods have been developed mainly for the analysis of cognitive processes for that a precise measure of dissimilarity between the classes is given. As a matter of fact, the general outputs of dynamic system are varying continuous to some extent, so in order to get the qusi–continuous outputs via pattern classifier, the only way is to increase the output classes. This will cause the complexity of the pattern recognition based model and the largely increased in computer storage which will cause difficulties for on–line industry computer system. To solve this problem, an algorithm of statistical fuzzy pattern classifier is presented in the following section since the concepts of homogeneity and of separation can not be made precise.

Membership Function

There are many possibilities for choosing membership function. The one we proposed here is heuristically determined based on the geometrical properties of the data set. Consider the output y can be divided into N subobject sets, i.e. N classes, denoted as $w_1, w_2, \ldots w_N$. Where each class $\{ w_i, i=1, N \}$ may be represented by C_i, i=1, N kernels. The membership function μ_{ik}, i=1, N; k=1, C_i of an event X is estimated by its effective distance to the kth kernel $\bar{D}_{ij}$, as an efficient measure of the membership function of classification, is defined as shown in Fig. 1.

$$\bar{D}_{ik} = g(D_{ik} / r_{ik}) \quad i=1, N; k=1, Ci \tag{2}$$

where D_{ik} is the distance (e.g. Euclidean distance, Mahalanobis distance etc.) between X and X_{ik}, which is defined by:

$$D_{ik} = d(X, X_{ik}) \tag{3}$$

r_{ik} is the efficient range of the kth kernel;
$g(\bullet)$ is the nonlinear operator;

Then the fuzzy membership function μ_{ik} is given by:

$$\mu_{ik} = f(\bar{D}_{ik}) \quad i=1, N; \quad k=1, Ci \tag{4}$$

let $m = \sum_{i=1}^{N} Ci$, m represents the total number of the kernels.

For simplicity and without confusing, denotes ik as i and i=1, m.

As is well known, the range of μ_i is set to [0,1] generally, so some conditions must be added in order to make the range of $\mu_i \in [0,1]$. In fact, μ_i is not only a function of $\bar{D}_i$, but also of $\bar{D}_j$ $(i \neq j)$. Two conditions are added to the definition:

Condition 1) The membership function μ_i is inversely proportional to the efficient distance $\bar{D}_i$, that is:

$$\frac{\mu_i}{\bar{D}_j} = \frac{\mu_j}{\bar{D}_i} \quad 1 \leqslant i,j \leqslant m \tag{5}$$

In the physical meaning, it implies that the closer the pattern is to a class kernel, the higher is its membership function.

Condition 2) The usual normalization condition

$$\sum_{i=1}^{m} \mu_i = 1 \tag{6}$$

It is easy to infer the μ_i expression from these two conditions.

$$\mu_j = \frac{\bar{D}_i}{\bar{D}_j} \mu_i \tag{7}$$

So, using (6) and (7)

$$\mu_1 + \mu_2 + \cdots + \mu_i + \cdots + \mu_m = 1 \tag{8}$$

$$\frac{\bar{D}_i}{\bar{D}_1} \mu_i + \frac{\bar{D}_i}{\bar{D}_2} \mu_i + \cdots + \mu_i + \cdots + \frac{\bar{D}_i}{\bar{D}_m} \mu_i = 1 \tag{9}$$

$$\mu_i = \frac{\bar{D}_1 \bar{D}_2 \cdots \bar{D}_{i-1} \bar{D}_{i+1} \cdots \bar{D}_m}{(\bar{D}_2 \bar{D}_3 \cdots \bar{D}_m) + (\bar{D}_1 \bar{D}_3 \cdots \bar{D}_m) + \cdots + (\bar{D}_1 \bar{D}_2 \cdots \bar{D}_{m-1})} \tag{10}$$

In the case of m = 2, (10) can be written as

$$\mu_1 = \frac{\bar{D}_2}{\bar{D}_1 + \bar{D}_2} \tag{11}$$

$$\mu_2 = \frac{\bar{D}_1}{\bar{D}_1 + \bar{D}_2} \tag{12}$$

Equations (11)—(12) can be used as approximate expressions for μ_i in real computations where m > 2. They are a set of rough estimates of (10) by considering only the two shortest effective distances $\bar{D}_i$ among the m possible ones. It is a limitation of the precision of membership estimate in the sense that one assumes that all other values of μ_i are zero in order to satisfy constraint (6). Here the value 2 must be thought of as a possible limitation of number of distances to be considered: usually one can limit computation of μ_i to the q nearest sets and get a rough estimate of μ_i, This will make the algorithm simpler and faster, and the value has to be chosen by the user.

It should point out that the membership function is related to concrete geometric positions of classes in the distribution of the given sets. In other words, the expressions μ_i and μ_j contain both $\bar{D}_i$ *and* $\bar{D}_j$. In addition, μ_i is not dependent on the order number of X in the data set, so the classification of patterns is stable.

Multi – Centre Pattern Description

In pattern description, the main problem is how to describing the real pattern space simply and efficiently. A kind of multi–hyperbox pattern description method has been introduced to dynamic system (Ye, 1988). It is efficient, but is rather complex in most situation. This paper we discuss a kind of multi–centre pattern description method developing from the Optimal Upturn Performance Index Classifier (OUPIC) (Tao Gu, 1982) to describe the input space of the dynamic system.

As it has been supposed in the former section, the output y can be divided into N classes $w_1, w_2, \cdots, w_N$, there are N steps to get the description of the N classes $\{ w_i, i=1, N \}$.

For w_k, $k=1, N$

(i) Get the event set X_k that belongs to w_k from the data set, and the initial centre is produced by using the following method:

a. Calculating the mean vector and intraset distance of the observed events in the event set

$$XM = \frac{1}{N_s} \sum_{i=1}^{N_s} X_{ki} \tag{13}$$

$$XD = \frac{1}{N_s} \sum_{i=1}^{N_s} \| X_{ki} - XM \| \tag{14}$$

where XM is the mean vector of X_k
XD is the mean intraset distance
N_s is the number of events in X_k
X_{ki} is the ith pattern feature vector

b. Find the first initial centre, it is the event which is nearest to the total mean vector.

Suppose the distance between X_{ki} and XM is defined by:

$$DM_i = \| X_{ki} - XM \| \tag{15}$$

then the first initial centre C_1 is defined by:

$$\text{if } DM_1 = \min\{ DM_{ki} \}, \text{ then } C_1 = X_{kl},\ i=1, N_s \tag{16}$$

c. The other initial centres are defined by:

$$\text{if } \| X_{kj} - C_f \| > \alpha \cdot XD, \text{ then } C_e = X_{kj} \tag{17}$$

where α is variable element, the initial value is α_0.
$j \in \{1, 2, \cdots, N_s\}$
$e = 2, 3, \cdots, N_c$
N_c is the number of initial centres.
$f = 1, 2, \cdots, e-1$

(ii) The total observed events are classified to the centre of the nearest distance.

Consider $DF_{i,e} = X_{ki}^t \cdot C_e - C_e^t \cdot C_e / 2$ (18)

$i=1, N_s$, $e=1, N_c$

if $DF_{i,e} > DF_{j,e}$, $j \neq i$
then $X_{ki} \in$ the cluster defined by C_e.

(iii) Calculating each centre of the clusters separately and renewing the cluster centres under fixed N_c

Consider C_e^N is the centre of cluster e and the observed events of cluster e are $X_{k,e}$, then

$$C_e^N = \frac{1}{N_e} \sum_{i=1}^{N_e} X_{kej}, e = 1, N_c \tag{19}$$

where N_e is the observed events number of cluster e.

if $C_e^N \neq C_e$, then the C_e^N will be considered as the new cluster centres to repeat step (ii),(iii).

(iv) Calculating the performance index M, and:

$$M = \frac{1}{N_c(N_c - 1)} \sum_{i=1}^{N_c} \left(\frac{N_i}{D_i^2 + D_i} \sum_{\substack{j=i \\ j \neq i}}^{N_c} D_{i,j} \right) \tag{20}$$

where $D_{i,j} = \| C_i^N - C_j^N \|$, $i=1, N_c-1$, $j=i+1$, N_c is the intreset distance between cluster i and j.

$$D_j = \frac{1}{N_j} \sum_{e=1}^{N_j} \| X_{ke} - C_j^N \| \quad j=1, N_c \tag{21}$$

is the mean intraset distance.

(v) Successive decreasing α to change N_c, repeat (i)—(iv), and denotes:

$$M_{max} = \max\{ M^N, M^{N-1} \}$$

where N represents the iterative number.

(vi) When the minimum value of α and / or the maximum value of N_c are reached, it is the time to end the iterative process. The cluster results (N_c, C_e^N, D_e, $e=1,N_c$), corresponding to the maximum M, are the description of $\{w_k\}$.

The descriptions of w_k, $k=1$, N can be obtained by repeating the step (i)—(vi) separately.

SFPC for Dynamic System Modelling

(i) SFPC algorithm

From the definition of fuzzy membership function and pattern description processes, a kind of statistical fuzzy pattern classifier is proposed in this section.

Consider the output set can be divided into N subobjects $w_1, w_2, \cdots, w_N$, and the description of every w_i, $i=1$, N can be gotten using the method that has been proposed. The results denote as C_i, N_{ci}, C_{ei}, D_{ei}, $e=1,N_{ci}$, $i=1,N$, and furthermore the corresponding output of every C_i is defined as the mean output of the observed events that belong to w_i, denotes as: y(e,i).

Suppose the event to be classed is X, calculating the distance $\overline{D(e,i)}$ between X and C_i to obtain the membership function μ(e,i). The corresponding output will be:

$$y_k = \sum_{\substack{e=1,N_{ci} \\ i=1,N}} \mu(e,i) y(e,i) \tag{22}$$

Equation (22) is the fuzzy classifier algorithm.

(ii) Learning of the initial pattern description

In order to cope with the incompleteness of initial gathered data and the time–varying of system in terms of the fresh sampling data, learning for the initial pattern is necessary. On the other hand, when discussing the pattern description and classification methods, the performance index of the dynamic model and the relationship between the N subobjects have not be considered. Here a learning algorithm based on stochastic approximation is developed to deal with these problems.

The performance index of the dynamic model is selected as the following general form:

$$J=\frac{1}{K_f}\sum_{i=1}^{K_f}(y(i)-\hat{y}(i))^2 \tag{23}$$

where K_f is the number of data in the data sets.
y(i) is the real output of the dynamic system
$\hat{y}(i)$ is the output estimated by the pattern description–classification model

Combining the model performance index, the index in stochastic approximation could be:

$$\text{Min}J=\frac{1}{2K_f}\sum_{s=1}^{K_f}(y(s)-\hat{y}(s))^2 \tag{24}$$

Then the iterative algorithm of stochastic approximation is:

$$C_{ei}^{K+1}=C_{ei}^{K}+\alpha_K(y(s)-\hat{y}(s))\frac{\bar{D}_2}{\bar{D}_1(\bar{D}_1+\bar{D}_2)^2}(y(e_1,i)-y(e_2,j))(X_i-C_{ei})$$

$$C_{ej}^{K+1}=C_{ej}^{K}-\alpha_K(y(s)-\hat{y}(s))\frac{\bar{D}_1}{\bar{D}_2(\bar{D}_1+\bar{D}_2)^2}(y(e_1,i)-y(e_2,j))(X_i-C_{ej}) \tag{25}$$

Moreover α_K satisfies:

$$\lim_{K\to\infty}\alpha_K=0,\quad \sum_{K=1}^{\infty}(\alpha_K)^2<\infty,\quad \sum_{K=1}^{\infty}=\infty \tag{26}$$

NUMERICAL EXAMPLE

Considering a nonlinear system:

$$y(k+1)=y(k)-.0459(u(k)-y(k))-.035(u(k))^{\frac{1}{12}} \tag{27}$$

$$u(k+1)=u(k)+.093(y(k)-u(k))-.078(1-e^{(-\frac{1}{0.148}+\frac{0.01486}{y(k)})}) \tag{28}$$

Supposing u(k) is the input variable that satisfies equation (28), y(k) is the output variable and could only be analyzed off–line, and there are d time–delay between $y(k)_{measure}$ and $y(k)_{output}$.

The objective domain y ∈ (5., 8.5) and is divided into ten subobjects in the simulation. A comparison for y(k) estimated results between using the SFPC algorithm proposed in this paper (a) (c) (e) and using the general minimal distance classifier (b) (d) is shown in Fig. 2. The estimation results under different d are also shown in the Figure. The y represents the data from the real system model.

INDUSTRIAL APPLICATION EXAMPLE — THE REAL TIME ESTIMATION AND FEEDBACK CONTROL OF THE GASOLINE VAPOUR— PRESSURE IN FCCU

As is well known, vapour–pressure is one of the major qualitative criteria of gasoline in fluidized catalytic cracking unit (FCCU) in refinery. But because of the nonlinear property of the process, it is very difficult to estimate the vapour–pressure accurately on–line with mathematical model. In other aspect, the vapour–pressure usually can not be measured on–line, only the off–line analysis data can be obtained. So now the vapour–pressure is not controlled by computer in many refineries.

The application of pattern recognition based system modelling techniques makes it possible to estimate the vapour–pressure on–line, so as to realize real–time control on gasoline vapour–pressure.

Input / Output Relation

Through analysis, three input variables are selected, i.e. stabilizing tower temperature x_1, stabilizing tower pressure x_2 and the heat change of stabilizing tower divided by input gasoline weight flow x_3.

The relation between input and output (the vapour–pressure) y is as follows

$$y(t)=f(x_1(t),x_2(t),x_3(t-d)) \tag{29}$$

where f(•) is unknown nonlinear function
d is time delay

Sample Data Processing

Pattern recognition based modelling technique is dependent on input / output data. A large amount of analysis data { $y(t_k)$, $k=1,K_f$} and corresponding measurable data { $x_1(t_k)$, $x_2(t_k)$, $x_3(t_k-d)$, $k=1,K_f$} can be accumulated from the industrial process. But the sampled input / output data may be with stochastic error which will have great influence on the accuracy of the model established with pattern recognition approach. For increasing the accuracy of the model, the input / output data need to be preprocessed.

Because the input data can be measured continually, some existing filtering method can be used. In order to reduce the error of off–line sampled output data, a data filtering approach connected with feature space is proposed here. The variation areas of input or feature variables { $x_1(t)$, $x_2(t)$, $x_3(t-d)$ } constitute the feature space. We first divide the feature variables into a number of small sections so that the feature space is also divided into a number of subspaces (Fig. 3). In a subspace, there may be several sampled input data with different output value. Suppose there are a number of data groups in the jth subspace as follows

$$\begin{cases} x_1^j(t_1),\ x_2^j(t_1),\ x_3^j(t_1-d) & y^j(t_1) \\ x_1^j(t_2),\ x_2^j(t_2),\ x_3^j(t_2-d) & y^j(t_2) \\ \vdots & \\ x_1^j(t_{K_f}),\ x_2^j(t_{K_f}),\ x_3^j(t_{K_f}-d) & y^j(t_{K_f}) \end{cases}$$

For all input / output data belonging to the jth subspace, we use average weighting recursive filtering approach. We have

$$\left.\begin{aligned} y^j &= \sum_{i=1}^{K_f} v_i y^j(t_i) \\ x_1^j &= \sum_{i=1}^{K_f} v_i x_1^j(t_i) \\ x_2^j &= \sum_{i=1}^{K_f} v_i x_2^j(t_i) \\ x_3^j &= \sum_{i=1}^{K_f} v_i x_3^j(t_i) \end{aligned}\right\} \tag{30}$$

Where v_i, $i=1,K_f$ are weighting parameters, and

$$\sum_{i=1}^{K_f} v_i = 1$$

After data preprocessing, all the data vectors $\{ (x_1^j, x_2^j, x_3^j)', j=1, K_f\}$ can be taken as sample patterns because their pattern classes can be determined according to their corresponding output value $\{ y^j, j=1, K_f\}$.

Establish Class Representation

From the sample patterns given above, the multi–center representation of pattern class can be established with the algorithms proposed in the former section.

Estimation Results

Depending on the multi–center representation of all pattern classes and the statistical fuzzy pattern classification algorithms, the vapour–pressure of gasoline can be estimated on–line (Fig. 4). Fig. 5 shows the estimation results in a real production scale FCCU.

Real Time Control

With the on–line estimation of gasoline vapour–pressure, the real time control of the qualitative criterion can be implemented in the way of cascade control (Fig. 6). The stabilizing tower temperature x_1 is considered as control variable to regulate the vapour–pressure y, furthermore, the temperature x_1 is controlled with a feedback control loop. The setpoint of y is an area (50, 55), which will meet the needs of real industrial process. From Fig. 7 we can see that the qualitative criterion of gasoline is improved with real–time control.

CONCLUSION

The main merit of pattern recognition based system modelling technique is to avoid the difficulties of determining the system structure. It can be seen from the above discussing that all the modelling procedures are based on the system data sequences. The proposed SFPC pattern description and classification method is appropriate for dynamic system modelling and useful for increase the model accuracy.

The industrial application example shows the applicability of pattern recognition based modelling method for the most complicated industrial processes is difficulty to be modelled by the general modelling technique. To most industry process, pattern recognition based modelling method is quite simple and satisfied.

REFERENCE

Tao Gu (1982). An Optimal Upturn Performance Index Classifier—OUPIC. *Scientia Sinica (Series A), vol.25, 565–570.*

Nan Ye, and Yong–zai Lu (1988). An Application of Pattern Recognition to System Modelling. *Proceedings of 8th IFAC Symposium on Identification and System Parameter Estimation, Beijing.*

Saridis, G. N. (1979) Application of Pattern Recognition Method to Controls. *IEEE Trans. Automat. Contr., AC–26 ,638–645*

Se–Young, OH. (1986) A Pattern Recognition and Associative Memory Approach to Power System Security Assessment. *IEEE Trans. Syst. Man and Cybern., SMC–16, 62–72.*

Julius, T. Tou and Rafael, C. G. (1974). Pattern Recognition Principles. Addision–Wesley.

Bristol, E. H. (1977). Pattern Recognition as An Alternative to Parameter Identification in Adaptive Control. *Automatica, vol.13, 197–202.*

Abraham Kandel, (1982). Fuzzy Techniques in Pattern Recognition. Wiley–Interscience Publication.

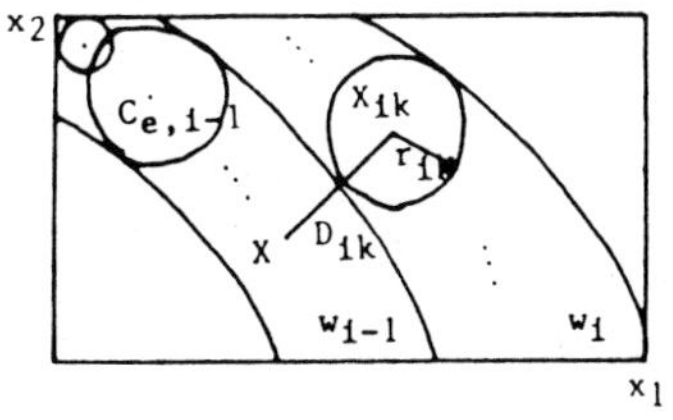

Fig.1. Illustrative definition of the fuzzy membership

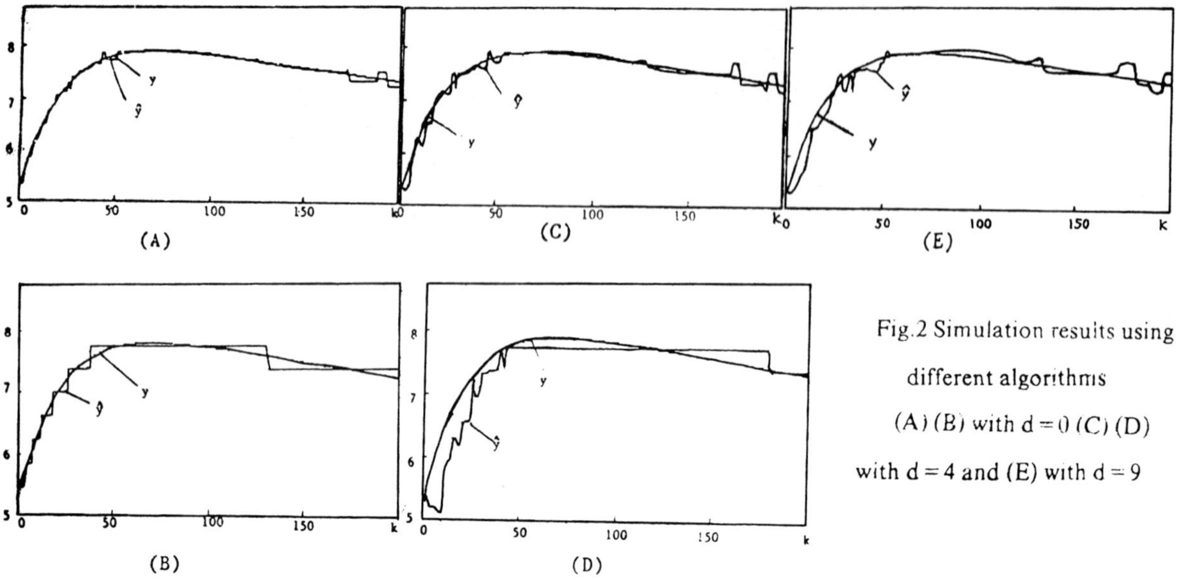

Fig.2 Simulation results using different algorithms (A) (B) with d = 0 (C) (D) with d = 4 and (E) with d = 9

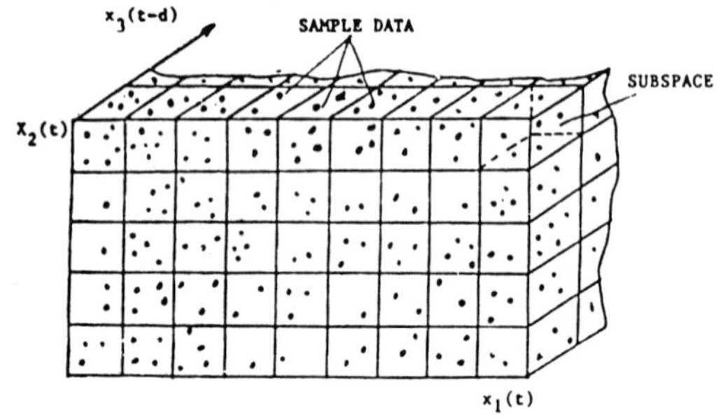

Fig.3 Division of feature space

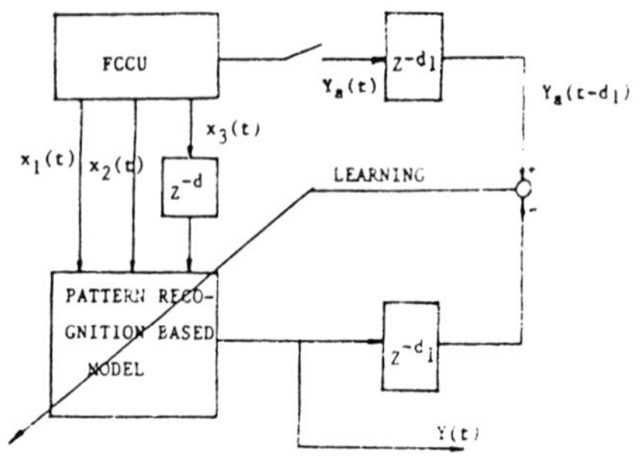

Fig.4 Diagram of real time estimation

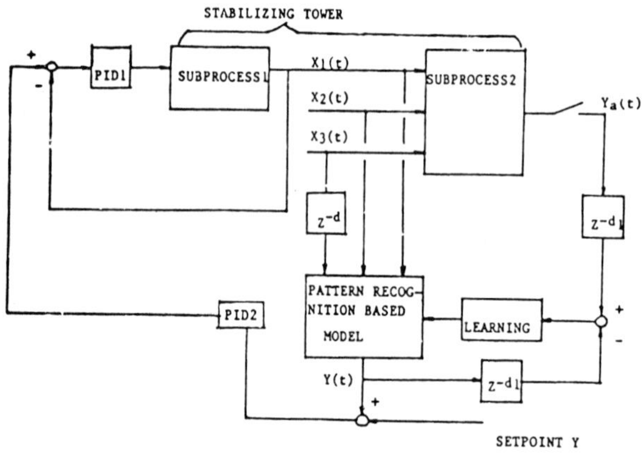

Fig.6 Diagram of real time control

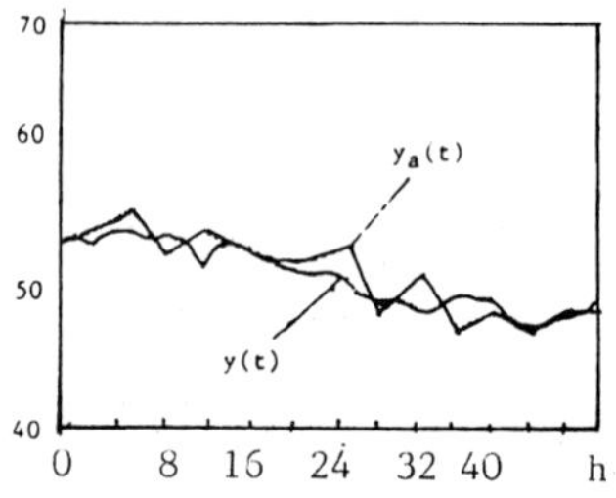

Fig.5 Estimation results

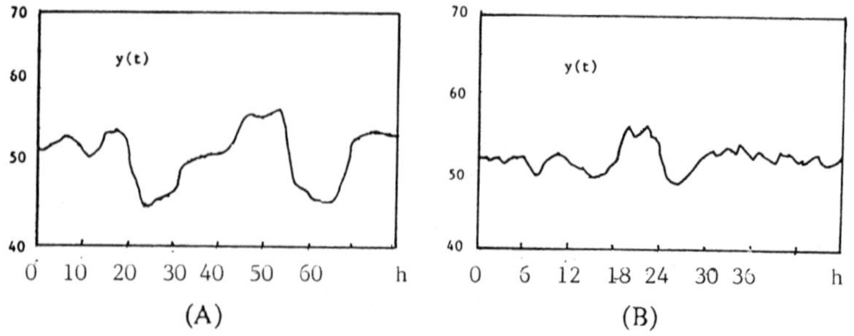

Fig.7 The variation of y without (A) and with (B) control

A CLUSTERING METHOD OF KNOWLEDGE ACQUISITION IN A REAL-TIME CONTROL SYSTEM

Yu-Ji Huang

*Department of Computer Science and Engineering,
Northeast University of Technology, Shenyang, PRC*

Abstract. The goal of knowledge clustering is that acquired knowledge is divided into several classes according to some principles and the knowledge in an identical class should have some general features on the concepts of classifying attributes so as to overcome some disadvantages produced by the centralized store of knowledge and to raise the working efficiency of a knowledge base. This paper describes a goal-oriented conceptual clustering method in the course of acquiring knowledge in a real-time production command system. This method makes use of background knowledge, concept attributes of knowledge, and clustering goals in a clustering knowledge base to infer clustering attributes of knowledge. The paper also discusses the components of a clustering algorithm model base and a clustering process.

keywords. Knowledge clustering; artificial intelligence; knowledge base; classification;attribute.

INTRODUCTION

Knowledge clustering is mainly used in a knowledge acquisition system of large scale knowledge bases. according to some principles, knowledge acquired will be divided into several classes and individually stored in relevant knowledge bases so as to reduce query time and raise the using efficiency of knowledge.

This paper outlines a knowledge clustering method in a real-time production command system. Based on frame representation of knowledge, we make use of background knowledge, conceptual attributes of knowledge, clustering goals to get clustering attributes of knowledge. Therefore, this method could be regarded as a goal-oriented conceptual clustering method. The clustering algorithm model base offers some algorithms used in the clustering process which is a recursive procedure. The final clustering result is K classes of acquired knowledge.

A REAL-TIME PROBLEM

RPC System

Consider an instance, A Real-Time Production Command System (briefly, RPC). As shown in Fig. 1.

A production process of an enterprise could be affected by many factors. Generally speaking, there are two information sources in production. One is the external source including sales calculation, materials & supplies, and energy resources etc. The other is the internal source including production capability, staff quality etc. The information above is an important basis with which managers and decision makers command and control a production process. At the same time, the RPC system collects a large quantity of feedback information and constantly adjusts the production process so that the enterprise can get the best economic benefits. Another important component of the RPC system is a knowledge base and its management system. The functions of the KBMS include offering decision basis, knowledge and measures; making quantitative or qualitative analysis to the problems in production.

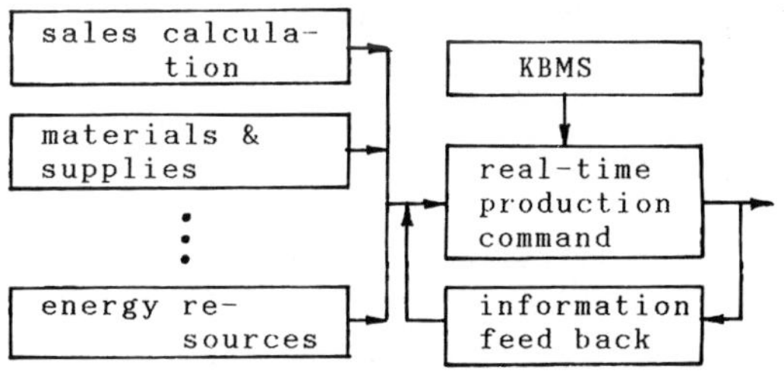

Fig. 1. RPC system

Knowledge Representation in RPC

In this system, knowledge representation and store functions are expanded in a relation database to construct EDS (Expanding Database System) (Han, Shi , 1988; Schmids, 1986). The system offers users (users and knowledge engineers) knowledge definition language (KDL) and knowledge manipulation language (KML).

Knowledge representation is closely concerned with knowledge acquisition. The konwledge in the KBMS of RPC is presented in the form of frames combining with rules (a kind of hybrid knowledge representations) (Qiu 1988; Shen, 1988). Here, take frames as the dominant factors and embed rules into attribute slots of frames. The structure of a frame is shown in Fig. 2.

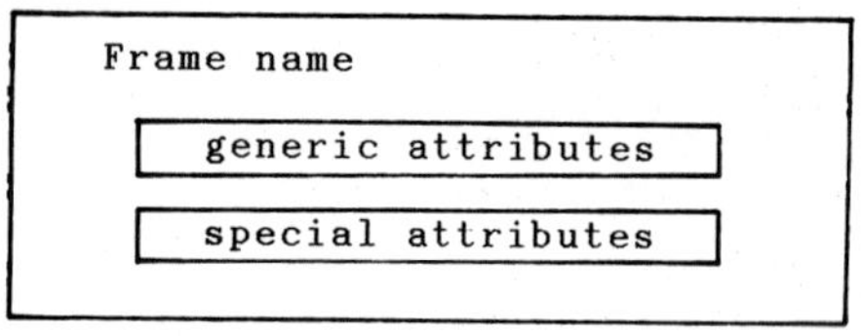

Fig. 2. Structure of a frame

Generic attributes of a frame describe context relations, associations, and some general features which its instance frames possess. Special attributes of a frame describe its own special features. the values of a attribute may be other frame names, a computational expression, a rule set, procedures, or specific values etc. This knowledge representation form has many advantages. An important one of them is that attributes of a frame can provide a knowledge clustering process with an efficient basis.

KNOWLEDGE CLUSTERING METHOD

Knowledge Acquisition & Classification

There are two ways to acquire knowledge.

(1) Using a man-machine interface, experts and knowledge engineers provide a system with their knowledge including experience, laws, hypotheses, and theory obtained in practice, i.e knowledge acquisition.

(2) Using inductive,deductive,and analogical methods etc., a system can obtain knowledge from objective circumstances, i.e machine learning (Li, Cai, 1988).

Because a real-time production command process is very complex the quantity of knowledge accumulated in the system constantly increases. If knowledge acquired is centred and stored together the system will be given much trouble. For this reason, knowledge classification becomes an important part of the KBMS during knowledge acquisition and store. This can reduce or avoid unefficient knowledge query and be in favor of knowledge maintenance. Of course, abstraction, classification, and construction of knowledge is still the difficult problems that AI scientists face (Douglas, 1987; Simmonds, 1987). Next Section presents a knowledge classification method.

A Knowledge Clustering Method

Clustering technique can be usually divided as following :

(1) clustering analysis
(2) environment clustering
(3) conceptual clustering
(4) goal clustering.

Ma Z.F. (1988) gave theoretical clustering. In AI fields, clustering technique is mainly used in aspect of machine learning. Knowledge clustering illustrated in Fig. 3 is a goal-oriented conceptual clustering method.

The first step is to determine classifying attributes of knowledge to be classified. Classifying attributes of knowledge is different from knowledge attributes in a frame. Classifying attributes are the attributes directly concerned with the clustering goal and considered in the clustering process. Knowledge attributes in a frame could be called as initial attributes. Classifying attributes are obtained in part from initial attributes and in part from results of inference relying on some initial attributes and background knowledge.

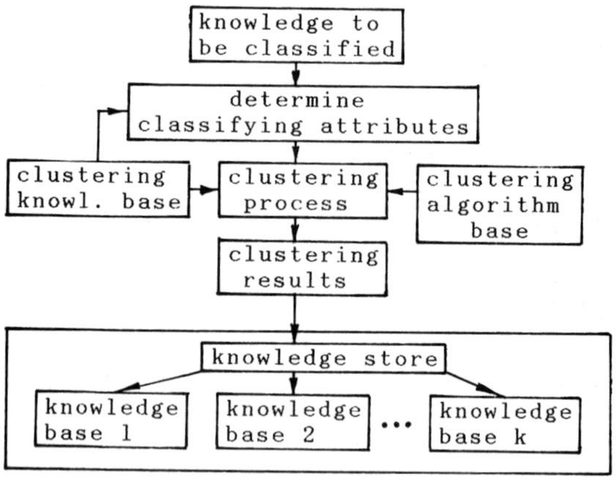

Fig. 3. A knowledge clustering method

The clustering knowledge base consists of three parts :

(1) background knowledge (Stepp, 1986)
 (a) value fields, types, and some special values of classifying attributes.
 (b) rules
  <1> logical rule such as :

  [made(gear A)],[qlf(gear A)] ==> [store(gear A)]

  "if gear A has been made and been qualified then store it into a storehouse."

  <2> computational rule such as:

  [weight(axle B)] = [vol(axle B)]*[s-grav(axle B)]

  Using the rules, classifying attributes can be derived from low-level concepts and attributes provided initially.

(2) clustering goal network
It is used for guiding the search for relevant inference rules and classifying attributes. In simple circumstances, it may be a tree.

(3) clustering criterion
The clustering criterion could be determined according to specific circumstances such as : to maximize the number of attributes that take different values in different classes ; maximize the number of attributes that singly discriminate among all classes.

The clustering knowledge base plays an important role for determining clustering attributes of knowledge. The clustering attributes are described by a series of vectors of clustering attribute values. Each vector stands for a object (knowledge).

Clustering Process (Michalski, 1983)

The first step of the clustering process is to choose initial seeds from clustering attribute vectors. Then, the clustering algorithms in the algorithm model base are called to form a clustering result of acquired knowledge. After that, the termination conditions are tested to see whether the clustering termination criterion is satisfied. If not, new seeds are chosen from the result above and the clustering process restarts again. This is a recursive procedure. Finally, we will get a clustering result and the evaluation to the result. The knowledge in all classes will be stored in individual knowledge files.

These clustering algorithms, provided by the clustering algorithm model base, include cover set computation algorithm, complex queue algorithm, complex combination computation algorithm, and choice seed algorithm etc. The clustering process is illustrated as following :

```
PROCEDURE : Clustering
  choose initial seeds e_i∈E, i=1,2,...k
  DO WHILE  terminal conditions are not
            satisfied
     IF first iteration = "n"
        choose new seeds e_i i=1,2,...k
        from K complexes in set V;
     ENDIF
     BEGIN
        determine a cover for each seed
        against the other seeds;
        constuct combinations of complexes
        from covers;
        select an optimal disjoint cover
        of E depending on clustering
        criterions;
        form a clustering result:
           V = {complex_i} i=1,2,...k;
     END
  ENDDO
  IF some classes can be merged
     execute mergence operation
  ENDIF
RETURN
```

The vectors of classifying attribute values (as input information of the clustering process) construct a finite set E. Suppose, the number of classes is K. In order to speed convergency of a clustering process, K objects which have the maximal differences among classifying attribute values are selected as initial seeds. A cover of each seed e against the other seeds is presented $RG(e_i|E_0,m)$ i=1,2,... k where E_0 is the set of remaining seeds and m is a boundary value of the number of complexes in a cover. Each cover consists of some complexes which are restraints to a classifying attribute. The goal of setting a boundary value is to reduce search space. The clustering process dynamically generates a search tree. The complex queue algorithm is used to queue to complexes in every cover. Then, a search tree is queried on the deep-first strategy. After calculating combinations of complexes, determine disjoint covers of E and depending upon clustering criterions, calculate the value of clustering quality of each complex combination and select the optimal one as the final clustering result:

$$V = \{complex_i \mid i=1,2,...k\}$$

This result is used as initial conditions for next clustering process.

In each iteration, except the first one, new seeds need to be chosen from complexes in set V using the choice seed algorithm. When terminal conditions are satisfied the clustering process terminates and K classes are obtained. Some classes will be merged together if possible.

CONCLUSION

This paper describes a goal-oriented conceptual clustering method of knowledge acquisition in a real-time system. In this paper, authors have discussed approaches to determine classifying attributes using background knowledge, inference rules and clustering goal network in a clustering knowledge base and outlined a clustering algorithm model base. In this method, attributes of knowledge presented in the form of a frame, context relations, and clustering goals are considered so as to be able to explain clearly classifying results. This is an attempt to classify and store a large scale knowledge in computers.

REFERENCES

Douglas, D.D. (1987). Knowledge representation for Expert Systems: A Survey and Evaluation of Techniques. AI: Rerent Development. Feb., 15-27.
Han, J.C., and Shi, Z.Z. (1988). On Knowledge Base System. Computer Science, 6, 51-55.
Li, Y.C., and Cai, Q.S. (1988). The Rapid Development of Machine Learning. Computer Science, 1, 30-34.
Ma, Z.F. (1988). Clustering Technique and Theoretical Clustering, Computer Sci., 4, 47-52.
Michalski,R.S. (1983). The Theory and Methodology of Inductive Learning, In R.S. Michalski and others (Ed.), Mahine Learning: An AI Approach, Tioga. 83-134.
Michalski, R.S. (1983). Learning from Observation: Conceptual Clustering, In R.S. Michalski and others (Ed.), Mahine Learning: An AI Approach, Tioga. 331-363.
Qiu, D.H. (1988). Knowledge Representation and Reasoning: On Hybrid Knowledge Representation. Computer Science, 5, 15-19.
Schmids, J.W. (1986). Knowledge Management System--The Conceptual Level. IFIP.
Shen,Y.D. (1988). PFKR: A PROLOG Frame Based Knowledge Representation System. Computer Journal, Vol. 10, 609-621.
Simmonds, W.H. (1987). Representation of Real-Time Use. 1st IFAC Workshop on IRTC, 63-67.
Stepp,R.E., and Michalski, R.S. (1986). Conceptual Clustering of Structured Objects: A Goal-Oriented Approach. AI, 28, 43-69.

TOWARDS INTELLIGENT PID CONTROL

K. J. Åström*, C. C. Hang and P. Persson***

**Department of Automatic Control, Lund Institute of Technology, Box 118, S-221 00 Lund, Sweden*
***Department of Electrical Engineering, National University of Singapore, 10 Kent Ridge Crescent, Singapore 0511*

Abstract. Auto-tuners for PID controllers have now been commercially available for a few years. These controllers are automating the task normally performed by an instrument engineer. The auto-tuners include some technique for extracting process dynamics from experiments and some control design method. They may even be able to select to use PI or PID control. For a higher degree of automation it is desirable to also automate tasks normally performed by process engineers. To do so it is necessary to provide the controllers with reasoning capability. This seems technically feasible with the increased computing power that is now available in single loop controllers. This paper describes a PID controller with such reasoning capabilities.

1. Introduction

In the design of an intelligent or knowledge based feedback controller (Åström et al 1986, Årzén 1987, 1988), it would be desirable to incorporate the expert knowledge of design engineers so that it can make decisions on the choice of control algorithm and provide diagnostics on the effectiveness of the control system. A system with such facilities would make the task of the operator and the instrument engineer more interesting. It would also make it possible for the instrument engineer to improve the reasoning of the system. For real-time implementation it would also be desirable to have as much deep knowledge as possible, in place of large number of possibly conflicting rules. It would also be desirable that the controller to a limited degree could explain its own reasoning, e.g. why derivative action was used. It should also be able to tell if PID is appropriate in the particular case and possibly also suggest alternative control schemes.

In this paper we attempt to develop formal tools to assess what can be achieved by PID control of a class of systems with the Ziegler-Nichols tuning formula and to characterize a class of systems where PID control is appropriate. Based on empirical results and approximate analytical study, we introduce two numbers, namely the normalized dead time θ and the normalized process gain $\mathcal{K}$, to characterize the open loop process dynamics and two numbers, the peak load error λ and the normalized rise time τ, to characterize the closed loop response. Simple methods of measuring these parameters are proposed. It is shown that θ and $\mathcal{K}$ are related and either of them can be used to predict the achievable performance of PID controllers tuned by the Ziegler-Nichols formula. Using these relations the intelligent controller can thus interact with the operator and advise on choice of control algorithm.

We have established useful relations, which can be used to assess whether the PID controller is properly tuned. The simplicity of the relations allows the development of a first generation of intelligent controllers using current technology. Significant insight into the properties and heuristic aspects of PID control is gained. Such knowledge can be formally discussed and further refined. It is believed that the approach can be extended to other classes of systems and this is a topic of current research.

The paper is organized as follows. The restricted class of processes that we are concerned with is introduced in Section 2. Some useful dimensionless numbers are introduced in Section 3. In Sections 4 and 5 some relations between the features are derived by approximate analysis and empirical refinement based on simulation. The results are used in Section 6 to discuss the performance that may be achieved with PID control based on Ziegler-Nichols tuning. Some characteristics are given in Section 7.

2. Process Characteristics

It is assumed that the process dynamics is linear and stable. The characteristics will be further restricted both in the time and the frequency domain. Feedback with simple controllers only is considered.

Time Domain Characterization

It will be assumed that the step response is monotone or essentially monotone, i.e. monotone except for a small initial part. Such systems can be characterized by the parameters K_p, L, and T, where K_p is the *static process gain*, L is the *apparent dead time* and the T is the *apparent time constant.* The parameters T and L are obtained by graphical construction, where the tangent is drawn in the inflection point of the step response. The transfer function

$$G(s) = K_p \frac{e^{-sL}}{1+sT} \tag{1}$$

is a crude analytic approximation of the the transfer function of the class of processes that we are considering. Notice however that the transfer functions considered are not restricted to this class.

The class of systems considered is the same as that used in the classical works on Ziegler-Nichols tuning. There are important classes of systems that are excluded, e.g., systems having integrators and systems with resonant poles. Systems having integrators may have monotone step responses but they are not stable. Systems with resonant poles do not have essentially monotone step response.

Frequency Domain Characterization

A different frequency domain characterization of process dynamics will also be introduced. It is assumed that the Nyquist curve is monotone or essentially monotone, i.e. both the phase and the amplitude are monotone functions of the frequency. The first intersection with the negative real axis defines the *ultimate frequency*, ω_u, and the *ultimate gain*, K_u. Lack of monotonicity can be accepted at frequencies, where the phase shift is larger than 180°.

3. Features

Dimension-free parameters, like Reynold's numbers, have found much use in many branches of engineering. They have however not been much used in automatic control. In this section it is attempted to introduce some numbers that are useful in assessing control system performance.

Normalized Dead-time

The normalized dead-time is defined as the ratio of the apparent dead-time and the apparent time constant, or formally

$$\theta = \frac{L}{T} \tag{2}$$

This number is thus easily obtained from a record of the step response. It has been known from practical experience that the normalized dead-time may be used as a measure of the difficulty of controlling a process. Processes with a small θ are easy to control and processes with a large θ are difficult to control. The parameter θ was actually called the *controllability ratio* by Deshpande and Ash (1981). Fertik (1975) introduced the name *process controllability* for the quantity $\theta/(1+\theta)$. To avoid possible confusion with the standard terminology of modern control theory we will use the word *normalized dead time.*

Normalized Process Gain

The process gain K_p is not dimension-free. It can however be made dimension free by multiplication with a suitable controller gain. The ultimate gain K_u, i.e., the controller gain that makes the process unstable under proportional feedback control, is a suitable normalization factor. The normalized process gain, $\mathcal{K}$, can be defined as

$$\mathcal{K} = K_p K_u \tag{3}$$

This number is easily obtained from the Nyquist curve. It also has a physical interpretation as the largest process loop gain that can be achieved under proportional control. The number is useful to assess the control performance. Roughly speaking, a large value indicates that the process is easy to control while a small value indicates that the process is difficult to control.

The normalized process gain is directly obtained from a Nyquist curve of the process. It can also be obtained from an experiment with relay feedback, see Åström and Hägglund (1984).

Since the processes we consider are stable they have a static error under proportional feedback. The static error obtained for a unit step command

$$e_s = \frac{1}{1+K_pK_c} > \frac{1}{1+\mathcal{K}} \tag{4}$$

where K_c is the proportional gain used. The inequality follows because $K_pK_c < \mathcal{K}$. The number $\mathcal{K}$ can thus be used to estimate the static error achievable under proportional control and also to determine if integral action is required to satisfy the specifications on static error.

Peak Load Disturbance Error

The response to step load disturbances is an important factor when evaluating control systems. The effect of a load disturbance depends on where the disturbance acts on the system. In this section it will be assumed that the disturbance acts on the process input. With a controller without integral action a unit step disturbance in the load gives the static error

$$e_l = \frac{K_p}{1+K_uK_c} > \frac{K_p}{1+\mathcal{K}} \tag{5}$$

The quantity e_l/K_p is dimension-free.

When a controller with integral action is used the static error due to a step load disturbance is zero. A meaningful measure is then the maximum error due to a load disturbance. To obtain a dimension-free quantity it is also divided by the process gain. The following variable is thus obtained

$$\lambda = \frac{1}{l_0 K_p} \max e(t) \tag{6}$$

where l_0 is the amplitude of the step disturbance.

Normalized Closed Loop Rise Time

The closed loop rise time is a measure of the response speed of the closed loop system. Again, to obtain a dimension-free parameter it will be normalized by the apparent dead time L of the open loop system. The parameter is thus

$$\tau = \frac{t_r}{L} \tag{7}$$

D	T_u	os	us	θ	$\mathcal{K}$	τ	$\mathcal{K}\lambda$
0.1	1.4	75	26	0.15	21	0.80	1.26
0.2	2.0	60	14	0.19	10.5	0.95	1.57
0.4	2.8	50	5	0.26	5.7	1.0	1.53
0.6	3.6	35	2	0.34	4.0	0.94	1.48
1.0	4.8	26	3	0.49	2.7	1.02	1.40
1.5	6.0	19	9	0.69	2.0	0.93	1.35
2.0	7.2	14	14	0.89	1.7	0.85	1.26
2.5	8.3	12	17	1.09	1.5	0.82	1.28
3.0	9.4	20	20	1.26	1.4	0.79	1.25

Table 1. Experimental results for a system with the $G(s) = e^{-sD}/(s+1)^2$.

n	T_u	os	us	θ	$\mathcal{K}$	τ	$\mathcal{K}\lambda$
3	3.7	50	13	0.22	8.0	1.07	1.52
4	6.0	40	10	0.32	4.0	1.16	1.40
6	10.6	26	11	0.49	2.4	1.14	1.30
8	14.6	17	14	0.64	1.88	1.08	1.18
10	18.8	12	17	0.76	1.60	0.96	1.18
15	29.0	0	24	1.05	1.36	0.9	1.16
20	39.0	5	30	1.28	1.25	0.8	1.14

Table 2. Experimental results for a system with the $G(s) = 1/(s+1)^n$.

α	T_u	os	us	θ	$\mathcal{K}$	τ	$\mathcal{K}\lambda$
0	3.7	50	13	0.22	8	1.15	1.52
0.1	3.8	50	15	0.23	6.2	1.09	1.49
0.25	4.3	48	11	0.28	4.5	1.09	1.44
0.5	5.0	38	3.8	0.38	3.2	1.16	1.41
1.0	6.0	21	3.8	0.58	2.0	0.98	1.34
1.5	6.5	9.6	7.7	0.76	1.45	0.89	1.30
2.0	7.0	-1.9	16	0.98	1.15	0.84	1.24

Table 3. Experimental results for a system with the $G(s) = (1-\alpha s)/(s+1)^3$.

4. Empirics

The Ziegler-Nichols closed-loop tuning procedure was applied to a large number of different processes. It was attempted to correlate the observed properties of the open and closed loop systems to the features introduced in Section 3. In this section we will present the empirical results. Processes with the transfer functions

$$G_1(s) = \frac{e^{-sD}}{(1+s)^2} \tag{8}$$

$$G_2(s) = \frac{1}{(1+s)^n}, \quad 3 < n < 20 \tag{9}$$

$$G_3(s) = \frac{1-\alpha s}{(1+s)^3}, \quad 0 < \alpha < 2.5 \tag{10}$$

will be investigated. These models cover a wide range of dynamic characteristics such as pure dead-time and nonminimum phase response. The main features of the models are summarized in Åström et al (1988).

The normalized apparent dead-time was measured from the step responses. The ultimate gain was determined by simulation. Parameters of PID regulators were determined by a straight forward application of the Ziegler-Nichols closed-loop method without fine tuning, i.e. with values of proportional gain K_c, integral time T_i and derivative time T_d set as $0.6K_u$, $0.5T_u$, and $0.125T_u$ respectively. The closed loop performance is judged based on the closed loop step and load responses.

The results obtained are summarized in Tables 1–3. The tables give a parameter that characterizes the process, the ultimate period T_u, the overshoot os, the undershoot us of the closed loop step response, the apparent normalized dead-time $\theta = L/T$, the normalized loop gain $\mathcal{K}$, the normalized closed loop rise time $\tau = t_r/L$, and the normalized peak load error $\mathcal{K}\lambda$.

The results for the first process are summarized in Table 1. The closed loop behavior was judged to be satisfactory for $0.15 < \theta < 0.6$. The overshoot for θ in the low range is too high. This is however easily reduced by using the setpoint weighting factor modification, see Åström and Hägglund (1988). For large values of θ there is a pronounced undershoot in the step response. The results for the second process are summarized in Table 2. The closed loop behavior was judged to be satisfactory for $0.22 < \theta < 0.64$. The overshoot for θ in the low range is too high. This is however easily reduced by using the setpoint weighting factor modification. For large values of θ there is a pronounced undershoot in the step response. Similar results are obtained for the third process as summarized in Table 3.

5. Relations

We have thus introduced two normalized numbers, namely the normalized dead-time θ and the normalized process gain $\mathcal{K}$, to characterize the open loop dynamics and two numbers, the peak load error λ and the normalized closed loop rise time τ to characterize the closed loop response. Some relations between these numbers will now be established. In doing so we will also develop an intuitive feel for the meaning of the numbers.

Normalized Dead-time and Process Gain

As can be seen from Tables 1–3 there appears to be a relation between normalized process gain $\mathcal{K}$ and normalized dead time θ. For specific systems it is possible to find the relations exactly, see Åström et al (1988). For first order systems with dead time we have:

$$\theta = \frac{\omega_u L}{\omega_u T} = \frac{\pi - \arctan\sqrt{\mathcal{K}^2 - 1}}{\sqrt{\mathcal{K}^2 - 1}} \qquad (11)$$

See Åström et al (1988). This relation is shown graphically in Figure 1.

It is possible to find exact expressions for the relations between $\mathcal{K}$ and θ for the processes given by equations (8), (9) and (10). They can also be obtained experimentally as discussed in Section 4. The relations are shown in Figure 1. The graphs indicate that for processes with higher order dynamics the product $\mathcal{K}\theta$ is approximately constant. This is important because it means that the normalized process gain $\mathcal{K}$ can be used instead of the normalized dead time θ to assess achievable performance.

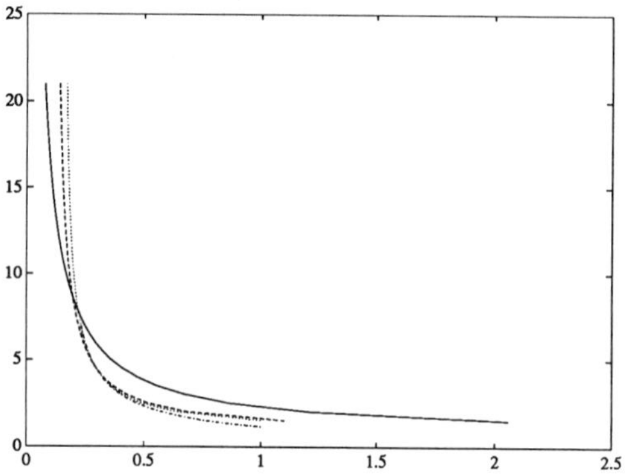

Figure 1. The normalized process gain $\mathcal{K}$ as a function of apparent normalized dead time θ for systems (1), (8), (9), and (10).

Peak Load Error and Normalized Dead-time

Consider the closed loop system obtained with the process and the controller. Assume that the disturbance enters at the plant input with PID control and Ziegler-Nichols tuning. The transfer function from the load disturbance to the output is

$$G_d(s) = \frac{1}{G_c(s)} \frac{G_p(s)G_c(s)}{1 + G_p(s)G_c(s)} \qquad (12)$$

A PID controller with Ziegler/Nichols tuning has the transfer function

$$G_c(s) = \frac{K_c(s+\alpha)^2}{2\alpha s}$$

where

$$\alpha = \frac{1}{2T_d} = \frac{4}{T_u}$$

This choice gives good rejection of load disturbances as discussed by Hang (1989). With Ziegler-Nichols tuning the closed loop system has a bandwidth $\omega \approx 7.4/T_u$. The transfer function (12) can then be approximated by

$$G_d(s) \approx \frac{1}{G_r(s)} = \frac{2\alpha s}{K_r(s+\alpha)^2}$$

The corresponding unit step response is

$$H(t) = \frac{2\alpha t}{K_r} e^{-\alpha t}$$

It has a maximum

$$\frac{2}{eK_r} = \frac{0.74}{K_r} = \frac{1.23}{K_u} \qquad (13)$$

at

$$t = 2T_d$$

We thus find that the parameter $\mathcal{K}\lambda$ can be expected to be constant. This is also supported by the experimental results given in Tables 1–3 which gives

$$\mathcal{K}\lambda \approx 1.3 \qquad (14)$$

The knowledge of λ can be used by an intelligent controller to check if a PID controller with Ziegler-Nichols tuning can be used to satisfy the given specifications to peak load error. From the analysis we also find that the peak error occurs $T_u/4$ time units after the step disturbance is applied.

Closed Loop Rise Time

The experimental results given in Tables 1–3 show that the normalized rise time is approximately constant. Hence

$$\tau \approx 1 \qquad (15)$$

In physical terms this implies that $t_r \approx L$, compare with equation (7). This means that the Ziegler-Nichols method gives a closed loop system with a rise time approximately equal to the apparent dead-time of the open loop system.

6. Ziegler-Nichols Tuning

The results obtained will now be used to evaluate PID controllers with Ziegler-Nichols tuning. We can first observe that the Ziegler-Nichols tuning procedure is very simple. It is based on a simple characterization of the process dynamics, either parameters a and L from the step response or the critical point on the Nyquist curve parameterized in K_u and ω_u. We have also obtained two relations $\tau \approx 1$ and $\mathcal{K}\lambda \approx 1.3$ which characterizes the closed loop performance. The condition $\tau \approx 1$ implies that Ziegler-Nichols tuning tries to make the closed loop rise time equal to the apparent dead-time.

When can Ziegler-Nichols Tuning be used?

The results obtained show that Ziegler-Nichols tuning will give good results under certain conditions and that these conditions can be characterized by one parameter, θ, or $\mathcal{K} = K_u K_p$.

The results are summarized in Table 4. Four cases are introduced in the table. They are classified as follows:

Case 1, $\theta < 0.15$ or $\mathcal{K} > 20$: Ziegler-Nichols tuning may not give the best results in this case. The reason is that it is possible to use comparatively high loop gains. There are many possible choices of controllers. A P or PD controller may be adequate if the requirements on static errors are not too stringent. A proportional controller could be chosen if a static error around 10% is tolerable. (This estimate is based on the assumption that the controller gain is half of the ultimate gain). If smaller static errors are required it is necessary to use integral action. In some cases performance can be increased significantly by using derivative action or even more complicated control laws. Temperature control where the dynamics is dominated by one large time constant is a typical case. We have observed that the derivative time $T_d = T_i/4$ obtained by the Ziegler-Nichols rule is too large in this case. It gives a long tail in the step response; a better value is $T_d = T_i/8$. □

Case 2, $0.15 < \theta < 0.6$ ***or*** $2 < \mathcal{K} < 20$***:*** This is the prime application area for PID controllers with Ziegler-Nichols tuning. It works well in this case. Derivative action is often very helpful. □

Case 3, $0.6 < \theta < 1$ ***or*** $1.5 < \mathcal{K} < 2$***:*** When θ approaches 1 Ziegler-Nichols tuning becomes less useful. This is easy to understand if we recall that the tuning procedure tries to make closed loop rise time equal to the apparent dead time. It is difficult to achieve tight control with Ziegler-Nichols tuned PID controllers. Other tuning methods and other controller structures like Smith predictors, pole placement, or feedforward could be considered. □

Case 4, $\theta > 1$ ***or*** $\mathcal{K} < 1.5$***:*** PID control based on Ziegler-Nichols tuning is not recommended when θ is larger than 1. The reason why PID controllers work so poorly for $\theta > 0.6$ is partly due to inherent limitations of PID controllers and partly due to the Ziegler-Nichols tuning procedure. Modifications of the Ziegler-Nichols rule were proposed by Cohen-Coon (1953). By choosing other tuning methods it is however possible to tune PID controllers to work satisfactorily even for $\theta = 10$, see Åström (1988). □

A parallel effort by Hang and Åström (1988) has gone further than merely using θ to predict the effectiveness of the Ziegler-Nichols tuning formula. The following modification to eliminate manual fine tuning has been recommended. When $\theta < 0.6$ the main drawback of the Ziegler-Nichols formula is excessive overshoot. This can be overcome by setpoint weighting where the weighting factor is a simple function of θ. When $\theta > 0.6$ the integral time computed by the Ziegler-Nichols formula needs to be modified by a factor which again can be expressed as a simple function of θ. These modifications are essential to obtain high quality PID control without manual fine tuning.

Table 4 indicates that a broad classification of Ziegler-Nichols tuned PID controllers can be made based on the normalized dead-time. This observation is useful if we try to build control systems with decision aids where the instrument engineer or the operator is advised also on controller selection.

Implications for Smart Controllers

There are several simple auto-tuners that are based on the Ziegler-Nichols tuning procedure. A drawback with them is that they are unable to reason about the achievable performance. The result of this paper indicates that there is a simple modification. By determining one of the parameters θ or $\mathcal{K}$ it is thus a simple matter to provide facilities so that a simple auto-tuner can select the controller form P, PI, or PID and also give indications if a more sophisticated control law would be useful. For an auto-tuner based on the transient method this can be achieved by determining not only a and L but also K_p and including a logic based on Table 4. For relay based auto-tuners it is necessary to complement the determination of ω_u and K_u with determination of K_p. This can easily be made from measurement of average values of inputs and outputs in steady state operation. It is also possible to modify the relay tuning so that the static gain is also determined. The accuracy of the tuning formula over a wide range of θ-values can be markedly improved by the use of the correlation formula of Hang and Åström (1988) as discussed above.

On-line Assessment of Control Performance

The results of this paper can also be used to evaluate performance of feedback loops under closed loop operation. Consider, e.g., the relation (15) for the normalized rise time. The rise time can be measured when the set point is changed. If the controller is properly tuned then the closed loop rise time should be equal to the apparent dead time. If the actual rise time is significantly different, say 50% larger, it indicates that the loop is poorly tuned. This type of assessment is particularly useful

θ	Tight Control is Not Required	Tight Control is Required		
		High Measurement Noise	Low Saturation Limit	Low Measurement Noise and High Saturation Limit
Class I < 0.15	P	PI	PI or PID	P or PI
Class II 0.15 ∼ 0.6	PI	PI	PI or PID	PID
Class III 0.6 ∼ 1	I or PI	I + A	PI + A	PI or PID + A + C
Class IV > 1	I	I + B + C	PI + B + C	PI + B + D

Table 4. A: Feedforward compensation recommended, B: Feedforward compensation essential, C: Dead-time compensation recommended, D: Dead-time compensation essential.

when the damping is adequate but it is not certain whether the control is too sluggish. Note that the Foxboro's EXACT adaptive controller, based on pattern recognition, Bristol (1977), cannot make this kind of judgement. Similarly the relation (13) can be used by introducing a perturbation at the controller output. If the maximum error deviates from that predicted by (13) we can suspect that the loop is poorly tuned.

7. Conclusions

In this paper it has been attempted to analyze simple feedback loops with PID controllers that are tuned using the Ziegler-Nichols closed loop method. It has been shown that there are some quantities that are useful to assess achievable performance and to select suitable controllers. These quantities are the *normalized process gain* ($\mathcal{K}$), the *normalized dead-time* (θ), the *normalized closed loop rise time* (τ), and the *peak load error* (λ). Simple methods to determine these parameters have also been suggested.

It has been shown that $\mathcal{K}$ and θ are related and that they can be used to assess the control problem. A small θ indicates that tight control is possible with P or PI control but also that significant improvements is sometimes possible with more sophisticated control laws. Processes with θ in the range from 0.15 to 0.6 can be controlled well by PID controllers with Ziegler-Nichols tuning. The results show clearly that Ziegler-Nichols tuning gives poor results when the normalized dead-time θ is larger than 0.6. There are also relations like $\tau \approx 1$ and $\mathcal{K}\lambda \approx 1.3$, that may be used to assess the closed loop response time and the load rejection properties. The results indicate that it would be useful to determine at least one of the parameters $\mathcal{K}$ or θ in connection with controller tuning because these parameters are so important for assessment of achievable performance.

Acknowledgements

This work has been supported by the Swedish Board for Technical Development (STU) under contract DUP 85-3084P.

8. References

ÅRZÉN, K. E. (1987): "Realization of expert system based feedback control," PhD dissertation, CODEN: LUTFD2/TFRT-1029, Department of Automatic Control, Lund Institute of Technology, Lund, Sweden.

ÅRZÉN, K. E. (1989): "An architecture for expert system based feedback control," to appear in Automatica.

ÅSTRÖM, K. J. (1988): "Dominant Pole Placement Design of PI Controllers," CODEN: LUTFD2/TFRT-7381, Department of Automatic Control, Lund Institute of Technology, Lund, Sweden.

ÅSTRÖM, K. J. (1989): "Assessment of achievable performance of simple feedback loops," *1988 IEEE Decision and Control Conference*, Austin, Texas, Also available as Report TFRT-7411, Dept of Automatic Control, Lund Institute of Technology, Lund, Sweden..

ÅSTRÖM, K. J. and T. HÄGGLUND (1984): "Automatic tuning of simple regulators with specifications on phase and amplitude margins," *Automatica*, **20**, 645–651.

ÅSTRÖM, K. J. and T. HÄGGLUND (1988): *Automatic Tuning of PID Controllers*, ISA, Research Triangle Park, NC, USA.

ÅSTRÖM, K. J., J. J. ANTON, and K.-E. ÅRZÉN (1986): "Expert Control," *Automatica*, **22**, no 3, 277–286.

ÅSTRÖM, K. J., C. C. HANG and P. PERSSON (1988): "Heuristics for assessment of PID control with Ziegler-Nichols tuning," Report CODEN: LUTFD2/TFRT-7404, Department of Automatic Control, Lund Institute of Technology, Lund, Sweden.

BRISTOL, E. H. (1977): "Pattern Recognition: An Alternative to Parameter Identification in Adaptive Control," *Automatica*, **13**, 197–202.

COHEN, G. H. and G. A. COON (1953): "Theoretical Consideration of Retarded Control," *Transactions of the ASME*, **75**, 827–834.

DESHPANDE, P. B. and R. H. ASH (1981): *Computer Process Control*, ISA, Research Triangle Park, NC, USA.

FERTIK, H. A. (1975): "Tuning Controllers for Noisy Processes," *ISA Transactions*, **14**.

GOFF, K. W. (1966): "Dynamics in Direct Digital Control, Part I," *ISA Journal*, **13**.

GOFF, K. W. (1966): "Dynamics in Direct Digital Control, Part II," *ISA Journal*, **13**, 44–54.

HANG, C. C. (1989): "Controller zeros," *IEEE Control systems Magazine, to appear.*

HANG, C. C. and K. J. ÅSTRÖM (1988): "Refinements of the Ziegler-Nichols Tuning Formula for PID Auto-tuners," *Proc. ISA Annual Conf. Houston, USA.*

KRAUS, T. W. and T. J. MYRON (1984): "Self-tuning PID controller uses pattern recognition approach," *Control Engineering*, June, 106–111.

ZIEGLER, J. G. and N. B. NICHOLS (1942): "Optimum Settings for Automatic Controllers," *Transactions of the ASME*, **64**, 759–768.

AN EXTENDED FEEDBACK STRUCTURE OF INTELLIGENT COMPUTER-AIDED CONTROL SYSTEMS DESIGN BASED ON OBJECT-ORIENTED LANGUAGE

O. Ono

Department of Electrical Engineering, School of Science and Technology, Meiji University, 1-1-1 Higashimita, Tama-ku, Kawasaki, Kanagawa, Japan

Abstract. *In this paper we consider about the structure of an intelligent computer-aided control systems design (CACSD) based on object-oriented language. We also indicate a frame in which the controlled system is a receiver and the control design is a message. From this view we construct the extended feedback structure of a design process. The graphics produced by object-oriented language is important for designing control systems, because it is concerning with the characteristics of a control system but also presenting the structure of a control. We point out that the graphics or the symbols are treated as input and output patterns produced from the design process. It is displayed as a complex potential which is an extended form of the Bode diagram. The complex function expresses a control structure as the transformation of a transfer function. Finally We explain a graphic data-base for intelligent control systems design and a human fuzziness which is transferred into the computer through graphics or symbols.*

Keywords. *Intelligent computer-aided design; Feedback structure; Object-oriented language; Application of computer graphics.*

1. Introduction

For several years applications of object-oriented language have been appeared in the control theory sphere[1),2)]. The reason is that the modern control theory really needs iteration of matrix operations, algebraic operations which have many physical parameters. As well known, the other hand, the classical control theory treats several kinds of graphics such as Bode diagrams, Nyquist charts. These graphics are still important as well as numerical and symbolic operations when we design a control system by using a computer. Then we consider an intelligent graphics data-base for computer-aided control systems design. Especially, in this paper we use a small computer and also LISP machine with a symbolic manipulation language and object-oriented language like Smalltalk-80, and Common LISP with Flavor. These languages are well known and affect the future computer-aided systems. Using these we regard inputs and outputs data as graphics on two or three dimension space.

Furthermore we produce a principle of feedback in the process of a human thinking. As well known this concept has been important since the classical control theory was founded. However, it is difficult to present this process as a mathematical model, so we need a new frame about the process. In this paper we handle graphics on two dimension computer display and treat a control system as a transfer operation of graphics. Lastly, we introduce a data-base for designing a control system and indicate an intelligent CACSD system.

2. Control design

In designing control system using computer (CACSD) it is frequently happened to take the following three steps,

a. analysis,
b. synthesis,
c. design.

In particular Rosenbrock[3] states that design is the creative act of constructing a control system. At present there are several synthesis methods for a control system, for example, pole placement, state feedback control with observer, LQG control, and H-infinitive optimal control. However, the comparison of control results is a part of humanity. There are many CACSD packages produced till now, the evaluation is still remained for human thinking.

We should reconsider the feedback structure which coincides with designing a control system. It is usually used in signal flow diagram which shows a structure of control system, but also is indicating the human thinking process. When we require the specification after searching output display produced from computer simulation, the graphics or symbolic patterns are effective for communicating with a digital computer. In this paper we propose the design process based on graphic patterns produced by symbolic manipulation language and construct the system by means of object-oriented programing. We can install artificial intelligence into the computer-aided control design based on graphics.

Fig. 1. CACSD with feedback structure

In the above computer-aided control system design, graphics representation is a communication method with a computer in which the feedback structure is indispensable through the design process. This design operation is fitted to object-oriented language apparently. The design process proposed here is shown abstractly in Fig. 1..

3. Graphics based on object-oriented language

Recently some object-oriented languages appear in designing control systems and are useful for model building from physical subsystems. Now a day we can install object-oriented language into a small computer and curry it out easily. Using the object-oriented programing the graphics are realized by a simple message and offer effectiveness for man-machine interface. For example, the modelling of mechanical systems, electrical systems, and chemical systems need usually characteristics of physical subsystems, and then they need object-oriented representation.

We also consider graphics in control engineering which naturally appear in study of engineering problem. The diagrams are important part in the control theory and we can set a controller in the system arising from them. There are Nyquist-diagrams, Bode-diagrams, Nichols-charts, pole-zero placements, and so on. These graphics are presented by object-oriented language and indicate not only control structure but also system characteristics. They are corresponding with complex plains, for example, Bode-diagram is presenting gain and phase of complex number. That is, the control system design is simply said to be a transformation of the complex function. The function and transformation are not only characterizing a control system but also corresponding with design or synthesis. The operation is curried out by using object-oriented language.

First, we consider complex functions like transfer functions or matrix transfer functions. These function maps from complex plain to nxm dimension complex space.

$$G(.) : C \dashrightarrow C^{nxm}.$$

When we treat single-input single-output (SISO) system, C^{nxm} is to be usual complex plane. In the case of state space model which is system {A,B,C,D}, the following equations are produced,

$$G(x+jy)=RG(x,y)+jIG(x,y), \quad (1)$$
$$RG=CFB, \quad IG=CHB,$$

$$F=-(A-xI)(y^2I-(A-xI)^2)^{-1}$$
$$H=-y(y^2I+(A-xI)^2)^{-1}$$

It is important to search two inverse sets which are mapping to zero or infinity. If G is rational, these sets are separate points, however, it is not always the case. Then we must consider to present G-function by some way. We present a color graphical display as one of the presentations. Hitherto we recognize characteristics of system from simple response carves or pole-zero placement on complex plane, but as the same way we can also recognize systems by using of color graphical display after enriching our experiences. We can understand the system from its color graphical display. For example, singular points are immediately indicated and if there are some kinds of singulars we can distinguish them by the surround circumastances[4),5)].

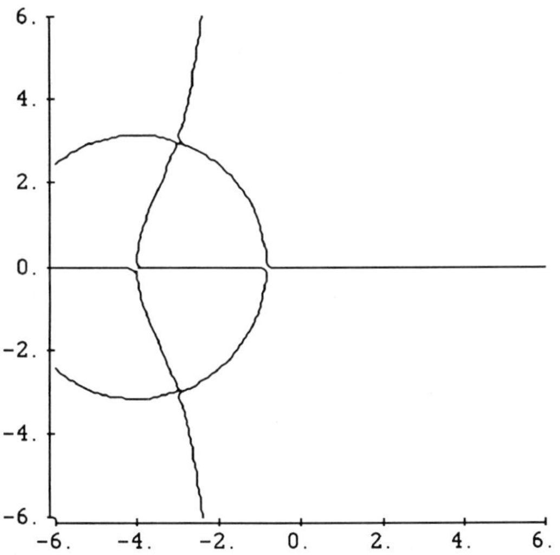

Fig. 2. Color pattern of control system (2D)

In the case of a representation using Markov parameter we also display the graphic pattern approximately. It is presented as following,

$$G(s)=g_0+g_1s^{-1}+g_2s^{-2}+\ldots+g_ms^{-m}/(1-ps^{-1}) \quad (2)$$

This function is parameterized by means of angular coordinate,

$$G(r,\theta) = RG(r,\theta) + jIG(r,\theta) \quad (3)$$

$$RG(r,\theta) = \sum_{i=0}^{m-1} g_i r^{-i}\cos(i\theta) - q^{-1}((1 - pr^{-1}\cos\theta)$$
$$g_m r^{-m}\cos(m\theta) - g_m r^{-m}\sin\theta\sin(m\theta))$$

$$IG(r,\theta) = \sum_{i=0}^{m-1} g_i r^{-i}\sin(-i\theta) - q^{-1}((1 - pr^{-1}\cos\theta)$$
$$g_m r^{-m}\sin(-m\theta) - g_m r^{-m}\sin\theta\cos(m\theta))$$

$$q = (1 - pr^{-1}\cos\theta)^2 + (pr^{-1}\sin\theta)^2$$

In object-oriented language this operation is fitted to graph-massage and G is one of variables which has several parameters. These parameters are expressed as state space matrices {A, B, C, D} or system matrix {T, U, -V, W}. Anyhow the variable G has some kind of parameters which are called attributes in symbolic manipulation language. A variable G is equivalent to graphics like from Fig. 3 to Fig. 6..

G ===><Graphics>.

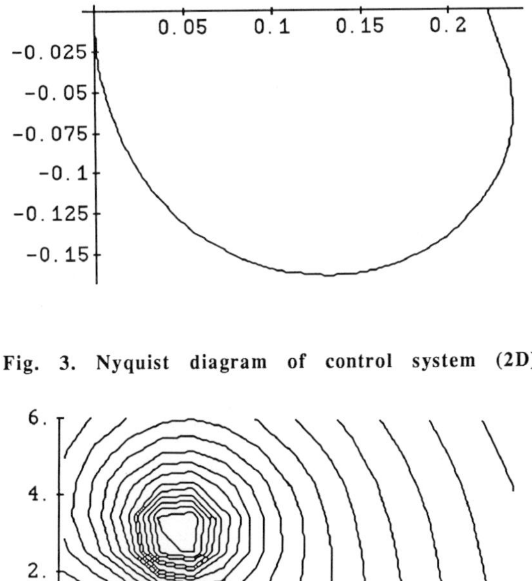

Fig. 3. Nyquist diagram of control system (2D)

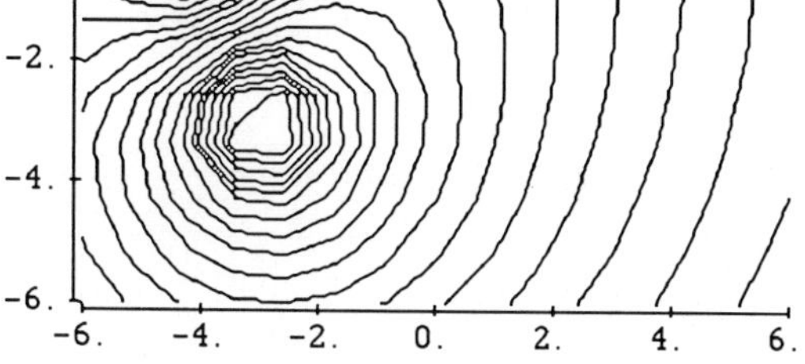

Fig. 4. Potential of control system (2D)

The velocity potential of the above control system is represented as the following graphic pattern. The pole and zero are shown distinctly on the complex plane.

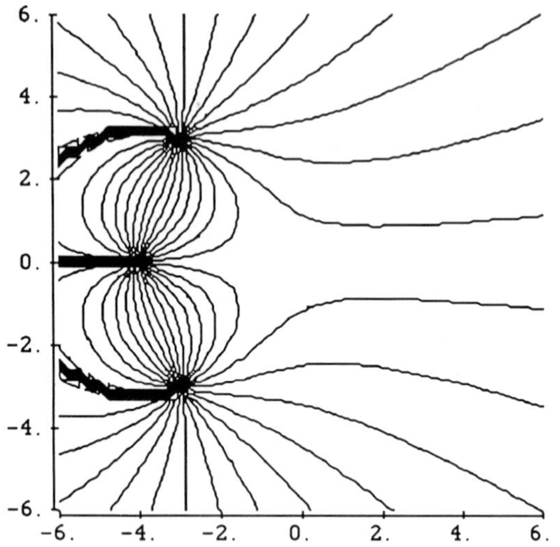

Fig. 5. flow function of control system (2D)

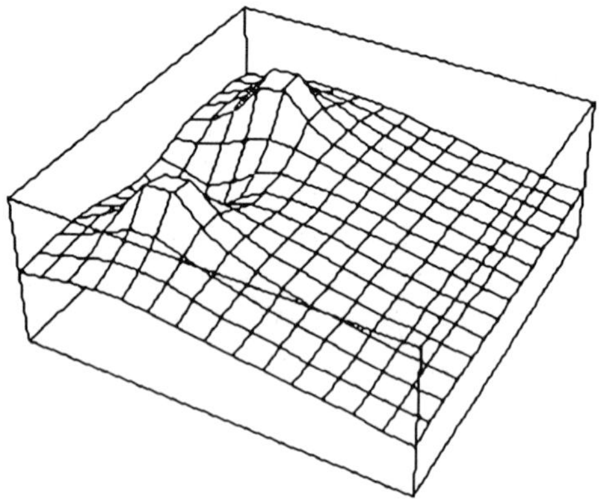

Fig. 6. Graphics of control system (3D)

Above examples are presented from the following transfer function,

$$G(s)=\frac{s+4}{s^2+6s+18} .$$

Next we consider transformations of complex functions. When we construct control system with some controller, a transfer function is mapped to another transfer one.

$$T : [G] \dashrightarrow [G], \qquad (4)$$

where [G] shows a set of complex functions or matrix complex functions. We assume the transformation T has some parameters and it appears as design operation. For example, they are pole placement, LQG control, state feedback with observer, and so on. These designs are parameters of design massage. And also we can send a graphic massage into the designed object. Therefore we can redisplay characteristics of control system and indicate results of controller effect. In this paper we also consider a graphic presentation of a transformation, that is, we can display control design as graphics. For example we can show a gain feedback control system. It is a linear transformation (Möbius transformation) and can be presented as the following matrix in projection coordinate system,

$$T:\begin{bmatrix} k & 0 \\ k & 1 \end{bmatrix}. \qquad (5)$$

We can construct a graphic message and a transformation message using object-oriented language. If we can assume infinitive feedback which means infinitive iteration feedback loops, we put the idea of complex dynamical system into the control theory.

4. Intelligent CACSD

In automatic control engineering the concept of feedback has been a key term and it has still important meaning not only on signal level but also on intelligent level. We have to emphasize that the term "feedback" should be used in artificial intelligence[6]. It is important idea and was already indicated in the early classical automation theory. We can show this idea abstractly in the following Fig. 7.. The concept of feedback will lead to intelligent computer-aided engineering. It is usually used in signal flow diagram which shows a structure of control system, but also is indicating the human thinking process. We should reconsider the feedback structure which coincides with designing a control system when we require the specification after searching output display produced from computer simulation.

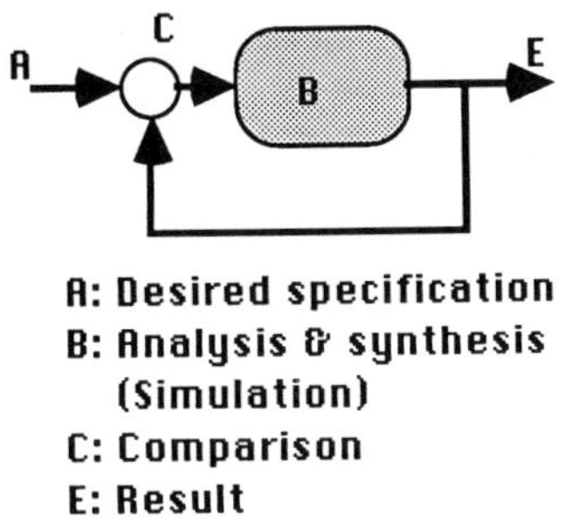

Fig. 7. An extended feedback structure of CACSD

Now we have many computer-aided control systems design packages which are already published, however, they need human power at the comparison point even using these CACSD packages[7]. Then we must construct the feedback structure like Fig. 7. into a computer-aided design system. This leads to artificial intelligence in control engineering field and it will have several input-output facilities such as speech signal or graphics. The idea about feedback is too simple to dare to produce but it is important basic notion on computer-aided method. From the above figure it is easily pointed out that the arrows are corresponding with message routes, therefore this feedback structure is suited to object-oriented programming. The true meaning of feedback can be carried out by using of an advanced computer such as a LISP machine.

In software engineering the object-oriented programing is not so particular, but in control engineering there is no usage of this type practically. If we use a frame of Smalltalk-80 such as

<receiver> <message>,

a basic operation in proposed CACSD system is simply written as the following,

<control system><design>.

The result object is usually the output to a designer through display, but in this paper it stored into the data-base in shape of some pattern.

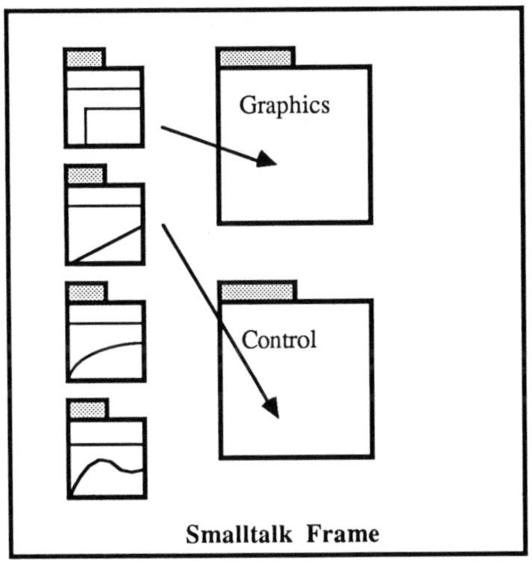

Fig. 8. Intelligent CACSD

The computer make comparison using these data-base and select several design fitting to required specification. This loop is previously mentioned to be feedback structure and we should reconsider this frame of feedback through a new point of view. Super computers working in these field are sufficiently effective and two kinds of interfacing media such as phonetics and graphics are important. They are input and output interface in an intelligent CACSD system. Up to now no one propose like above consideration because it is hard to work on even advanced computer.

5. Graphics data-base

In this paper we treat the desired specification for control system as a graphic pattern and also results of design as graphics. The comparison can be carried out in computer if we use graphic input-output patterns for designing control system. These graphics can be easily data-based in computer memory, therefore it will lead to intelligence for control design. Recently human fuzziness is pointed out to be important for artificial intelligence. If we deal with freehand graphical input pattern, a concept of fuzziness is installed into a computer system. This system is shown in Fig. 9. abstractly.

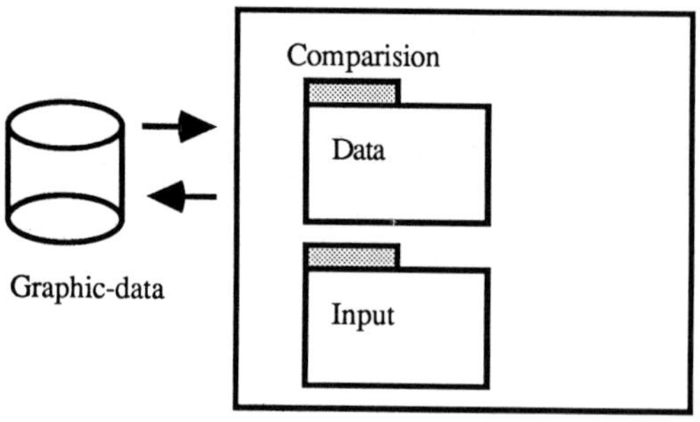

Fig. 9. Graphics data-base

6. Conclusion

In computer-aided control systems design we use a object-oriented language as displaying graphics and indicate that it is well fitted to design operation. If we will have a new analysis or synthesis method, it can be installed into the system easily. The new frame proposed in this paper is summarized as following,

(a) graphic pattern is useful for not only displaying characteristics of control systems but also showing design structures,
(b) we point out that the principle of feedback structure based on graphic patterns is effective in an intelligent CACSD system,
(c) we can construct the graphical patterns data-base for selecting synthesis methods,
(d) and we indicate that operations in an intelligent CACSD system are well suited to object-oriented programing.

References

(1) Astrom, K. J.:"Computer Aided Tools for Control System Design," Computer -Aided Control Systems Engineering, 3/40 North-Holland, Heidelberg (1985)
(2) Denham, M. J. and A. J. Laub ed.:"Advanced Computing Concepts and Techniques in Control Engineering", Springer-Verlag (1988)
(3) Rosenbrock, H. H.:"Computer-Aided Control System Design", Academic Press, London (1974)
(4) Ono, O.:"A Characteristics Analysis of Control System by Using Computer Graphics", Trans. IEE Japan, Vol.108-C, No.1, 1/5 (1988)
(5) Ono, O.:"A Characteristic Analysis of Control Systems by Symbolic Manipulation Language", Journal of Hokkaido University Computer & Control Research, Vol.1 No.3 15/19 (1988)
(6) Ono, O.:"On an Extended Feedback Structure for Control Systems Design Based on Input-Output Pattern", SICE 21th Hokkaido Branch Conf. (1988)
(7) Pang, G. K. and A. G. MacFarlane:"An Expert Systems Approach to Computer-Aided Design of Multivariable Systems", Springer-Verlag, Heidelberg(1987)

AN EXPERT SYSTEM SHELL FOR ANALYSIS OF REAL TIME SIGNALS

Tong Wei-Guang* and Zhao Lin-Liang**

**Department of Automatic Control, Shenyang Architectural and Civil Engineering Institute, Shenyang, 110015, PRC*
***Department of Computer Science, Northeast University of Technology, Shenyang, 110006, PRC*

Abstract. The interpreting and analysis of real time sampled signals is important for improvement of quality of products. This article developed an expert system shell ASESS for interpreting and analyzing the real time signals based on the analysis-synthesis (A-S) inference technology which frequently used by human expert in considering complex problems. The A-S technology is introduced. In order to meet the need of speed of real time control, in ASESS two measures are taken: 1. Knowledge classification and meta-rules are applied. 2. The system is developed with the combination of three languages: Assembler, Fortran and Prolog. Considering the vagueness in inference of human experts, the fuzzy inference technology are applied. The knowledge base of ASESS can be separated from inference engine and can be edited easily, so the system ASESS can be used effectively in different cases by adding appropriate knowledge in that field.

Keywords. Expert systems; analysis-synthesis; meta-rules; real time diagnosis.

INTRODUCTION

In modern process plants the improvement in the quality of products through better application of the technology of diagnosis and analysis of products can potentially provide economic benefits of significance. In production processes, a large quantity of signals sampled from real time processing need to be detected and analyzed quickly and accurately. The classical detecting technology using computer is of high speed, but can not analyze the signals in detail and draw inference accurately from sampled signals. On the other hand, human expert in his area may have years of experience in observing sampled signals and quality of products, he is aware of process equipment failures and the patterns of behavior induced, he also know how to operate and correct the failures to improve the performance, so he can analyze and interpret the real time sampled signals and gain the satisfied results. However, human expert suffer from an inherent lack of low level numerical computation capacity and a poor memory and their reaction to stimulation is rather slow. So, in the application to real time process, human experts may not infer quickly enough to meet the need of inference speed. The combination of computer and expertise can compensate for the weakness and attain high level performance.

For these reasons, expert systems should be used to synergistically combine the classical detecting technology and human expertise. In (Waterman, 1986), There listed about 181 expert systems in different fields. Also, expert systems are applied to real time control field increasingly. Voss (1988) discussed an expert process control system architecture (EPCS). In human expertise about diagnosis and analysis, there is vagueness between the failures and its character. To represent the ambiguous the Fuzzy Set Theory (Zadah, 1965) is applied. In this article, applying an analysis-synthesis inference technology, we developed an expert system shell (ASESS) for interpreting and analyzing real time sampled signals. This system can be used to various cases by addition of appropriate expert knowledge.

In the case of real time control, the important problem for expert system to be used is the speed of inference. To quicken the process of interpreting and analyzing, in ASESS two measures are taken: 1. The system is developed with three languages: Assembler, Fortran and Prolog. Assembler is a language suitable for real time processing, and the Fortran is faster in calculating than other language. So the sampling of signals and mathematic calculating can be done quickly. 2. Knowledge classification and meta-rules are applied. So in logical processing, only the relevant rules in knowledge base are searched and the inference process is shortened.

BUILDING THE SYSTEM

Expertise About A-S

In analyzing and interpreting the real time sampled signal for diagnosing faults and analyzing the quality of production, most of human experts use an analysis-synthesis (A-S) inference technology, that is, first, they analyze the signals from different angles and different sides according to the real environment, and then they synthesize the results of analysis and obtain the conclusion. In the analysis-synthesis inference technology, a set of performance characteristic values of the sampled signals are extracted by calculating the signals using relevant methods. for example, a group of sampled electricity signal can be characterized by their frequency, amplitude, average value, and variance. For every character of signals, there is a standard value. the deviation of a characteristic value from its standard value indicates that there may exist different failures of operations or equipment. By analysis to these deviations and synthesis of the possible failures the main failure can be found and corrected, so that the quality and quantity of the products can be improved.

Knowledge Representation

Generally, a deviation of a characteristic value may be caused by several failures of operations or equipment to different extents, while a failure of operation or equipment may be identified by different deviations of characteristic values in varying degrees. The expertise about analysis of signals is represented with rules as following:

```
IF      The deviation of the 1st
          characteristic value is D1, and
        The deviation of the 2nd
          characteristic value is D2, and
          ...
THEN    The reason of deviation is F
          with possibility C
```

where $0 < C \leqslant 1$. In the case of a failure being inferred from two rules with two possibilities C1 and C2 respectively, the consequential possibility C of the failure F is calculated as follows:

$$C = C1 + C2*(1 - C1)$$

For a failure being inferred from N rules with N possibilities respectively, N>2, then the consequential possibility C of the failure F with possibilities Ci, i=1, 2, ..., N, can be obtained by using the above equation N-1 times. Finally, we can get the set of all failures with their own possibilities:

$$\{F_1(C_1),\ F_2(C_2),\ \ldots,F_M(C_M)\}$$

Sort this set of failures according to their possibilities, we can obtain a new series of failures

$$\{F'_1(C'_1),\ F'_2(C'_2),\ \ldots,F'_M(C'_M)\}$$

where $C'_1 \geqslant C'_2 \geqslant \ldots \geqslant C'_M$. Obviously, the F'_1 is the main failure of the process. According to this consequence, we can regulate and correct the failure of operations or equipment.

Knowledge Acquisition

As an expert system shell, its knowledge base must be able to be separated from its inference engine. In Turbo-Prolog, all statements are divided two categories: facts and rules. The rules can not be managed by program. Fortunately, however, the facts in Turbo-Prolog can be managed by using dynamic data base and be accessed by using initiative predicates. So, in outside of main program, the knowledge can be represented with facts instead rules. For example, the rule

```
A if B and C.
```

can be represented with the fact

```
rule([B,C], A).
```

using this measure, the expertise can be represented in a rule file and can be accessed by main program. Such a rule file can be managed easily.

Structure of Knowledge Base

In order to represent the knowledge appropriately, and, more importantly, infer the conclusion quickly, the frame structure are used to represent the analysis-synthesis knowledge. In logical programming, the searching and backtracking consume a large part of processing time, so the measure to shorten the time of searching and backtracking must be taken. In ASESS, all rules are classified in to some categories according to the character of signals, and each category of rules is stored in a slot of the rule frame (RUFRAME). The structure of the rule frame is shown in Fig. 1.

Rule Frame

Slot name	Slot value
Sname1	:
:	:
Snamei	rule(antecedent , consequence) rule(antecedent , consequence) : rule(antecedent , consequence)
:	:

Fig. 1. The structure of rule frame

In the inference process, for a deviation of a characteristic value, only the rules in one slot are searched, so the inference is quickened. The slot is motivated by the meta-rule as following:

IF The deviation is about category *i*,
THEN Use the rules in slot Sname*i*.

Inference Engine

The system uses a forward reasoning strategy. By calculating the sampled signals, the characteristic values are extracted and put into slots of an extracted value frame (EVFRAME), the standard characteristic values and their tolerances are stored in the slots of a standard value frame (SVFRAME). Comparing each slot value of EVFRAME with that of SVFRAME, if these two values do not match, that is, the difference between the extracted value and the standard value is larger than the tolerance, the rules in a corresponding slot of RUFRAME are motivated by use meta-rules, so the conclusions are inferred.

SYSTEM STRUCTURE

Prolog is a declarative logical programming language and easy to execute logical inference, but its calculation speed is relative low and it can not response the interrupt request. However, the Fortran language can calculate data with high speed, and the Assembler language is of short responding time and suitable for industrial processing. So in the system the main program is developed with Turbo-Prolog, the extraction of characteristic value of sampled signals is completed by a subprogram written with Fortran, and the sampling subprogram is developed with Assembler language. The interface of Prolog with other two subprograms is provided by a Prolog initiative predicate "system( )" which can be used to call other executed files. The structure of the system is shown in Fig. 2.

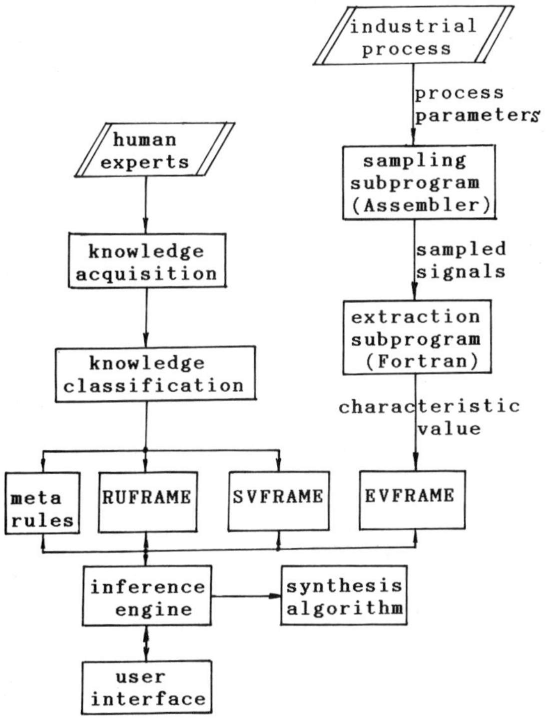

Fig. 2. System structure

CONCLUSION

Analysis-synthesis inference technology is a method frequently used by human experts in consider complex problems. The ASESS, in which A-S is applied, can obtain the results of diagnosing and analyzing the real time signals in the level approximate to the human experts. Comparing with experts, the ASESS has the advantage of high inference speed. According to the results of diagnosis, the operating and equipment failures can be corrected so the quality of products and efficiency of production can be improved.

The method to speed up the inference in ASESS is to apply the rule classification and use meta-rules to select appropriate rules. The ASESS is of high reliability and simplicity, and can meet the need of real time diagnosis. By adding appropriate knowledge in different fields, the ASESS can be built into various expert systems. Based on ASESS, an expert system RES, which is used to analyze the quality of electric motor, is built and has gained satisfied results.

Further research on ASESS is to speed up inference, for example, parallel processing can be applied.

REFERENCES

Charniak, E. and D. McDermott. (1985). Introduction to Artificial Intelligence. Addison-Wesley Publishing Company.

Rich, Elaine. (1983). Artificial intelligence. McGraw-Hill Book Company.

Voss, H. (1988). Architectural issues for expert systems in real time control. 1st IFAC Workshop on AIRTC.

Waterman, Donald A. (1986). A guide to expert systems. Addison-Wesley Publishing Company

Zadeh, L.A. (1965). Fuzzy set. Information and Control, 8.

AN EXPERT SELF-LEARNING FUZZY CONTROLLER

Yu-Lan Zhou* and Zhengyue Qiu**

**Equipment Institute, Chengdu Steel Pipe Co., Chengdu, PRC*
***Department of Automatic Control, Northeast University of Technology, Shenyang, PRC*

Abstract. This paper is about an Expert Self-Learning Fuzzy Controller (ESLFC) in which the control policy can improve automatically by use of Fuzzy sets,expert system and pattern recognization techniques of Artificail Intellegence (AI). It can apply to real-time control of complex systems with nonlinearity,time-variant and uncertainty. Based on the combustion process control of an industrial boiler, a number of simulation experiments are carried out to prove its feasibility.

Key Words. Fuzzy systems; self-organizing systems; multi-level structure; process parameter estimation; computer simulation; thermal plant.

INTRODUCTION

For the purpose of controlling complex plants with nonlinearity,time-variant and uncertainty, ideal control systems are expected to have intelligent functions such as simultaneous utilization of memory,learning or multilevel decision-making in response to "fuzzy" or qualitative commands. With the development of Fuzzy sets theory, a new generation of control, Fuzzy control,is developed in 1970s on the basis of simulating the control behaviors of human beings. But up to now the commonly used Fuzzy Logic Controllers(FLC) still suffer from some inherent limitations. Their control rules are merely descriptive that is,just a copy of the experience of the operators. And the rules once formulated can not adapt itself to operation condition changes.

In this paper,we propose an Expert Self-Learning Fuzzy Controller (ESLFC) by introducing the technology of expert system and pattern recognization of artifical intelligence into simple fuzzy logic control systems. The structure of ESLFC is hierachical,which consists of three levels,that is,main control level, expert self-learning level, and parameter self-tuning level. In this system, Fuzzy sets are used to model uncertainty. Its self-learning function can successively improve the control performance on line. Unlike the usual adaptive control, this system does not strictively depend on system models. Based on the combustion process control of an industrail boiler, a number of simulation experiments are carried out and good results are obtained,which show the good control properties and adaptivity of the system.

THE PRINCIPLES OF ESLFC

A Simple Fuzzy Logic Controller and Its Problems

A fuzzy logic control system is composed of Fuzzy control rules, inference and decision-making. In general,the Fuzzy control rules may be put into the following form:

$$\text{if } \underset{\sim}{A}_i \text{ then if } \underset{\sim}{B}_i \text{ then } \underset{\sim}{C}_i\ ,\quad i=1,2,\ldots N \tag{1}$$

where $\underset{\sim}{A}_i$ and $\underset{\sim}{B}_i$ denote the linquistic values of the state variables,and $\underset{\sim}{C}_i$ denotes the linquistic values of the control variable.

The rules may be treated as Fuzzy implications:

$$\{\text{if } \underset{\sim}{A}_i \text{ then if } \underset{\sim}{B}_i \text{ then } \underset{\sim}{C}_i\} \equiv \{\underset{\sim}{A}_i \Rightarrow \underset{\sim}{B}_i \Rightarrow \underset{\sim}{C}_i\} \tag{2}$$

where "$\Rightarrow$" stands for the operator of the implication. A set of the rules given by equations (1)-(2) creates the "memory" of the controller which is essentially rewritten in the following form of the fuzzy relations (matrix) R:

$$\{\underset{\sim}{A}_i \Rightarrow \underset{\sim}{B}_i \Rightarrow \underset{\sim}{C}_i\} = \underset{\sim}{A}_i \times \underset{\sim}{B}_i \times \underset{\sim}{C}_i = \underset{\sim}{R}_i \tag{3}$$

$$\underset{\sim}{R} = \bigcup_{i=1}^{N} \underset{\sim}{R}_i \tag{4}$$

operator "x" is defined as:

$$u_{\underset{\sim}{R}_i}(x,y,z) = u_{\underset{\sim}{A}_i}(x) \wedge u_{\underset{\sim}{B}_i}(y) \wedge u_{\underset{\sim}{C}_i}(z) = \text{Min}\{u_{\underset{\sim}{A}_i}(x),\ u_{\underset{\sim}{B}_i}(y),\ u_{\underset{\sim}{C}_i}(z)\}$$

$$x \in X,\quad y \in Y,\quad z \in Z \tag{5}$$

with u.(.) being the membership function of correponding Fuzzy sets.

"U" denotes Max operator

$$u_{\underset{\sim}{R}}(x,y,z) = \underset{i}{\text{Max}}\ u_{\underset{\sim}{R}_i}(x,y,z),\quad i=1,2,\ldots N \tag{6}$$

For a certain group of fuzzy sets of the process state $\underset{\sim}{A}'$ and $\underset{\sim}{B}'$,the value of output varaible is calculated by means of the composite rule of inference:

$$\underset{\sim}{C}' = \underset{\sim}{A}' \circ (\underset{\sim}{B}' \circ \underset{\sim}{R}) = (\underset{\sim}{A}' \times \underset{\sim}{B}') \circ R \tag{7}$$

Its membership function is

$$u_{\underset{\sim}{C}'}(z)=\underset{x\in X}{\mathrm{Max}}\,\underset{y\in Y}{\mathrm{Min}}[\mathrm{Min}(u_{\underset{\sim}{A}'}(x),u_{\underset{\sim}{B}'}(y),u_{\underset{\sim}{R}}(x,y,z))] \quad (8)$$

$\underset{\sim}{C}'$ is still a fuzzy set. In order to derive a deterministic control action,one output value is chosen from $\underset{\sim}{C}'$ according to the grades of the memberships and particular application problems. For example

$$\mathrm{Uopt}(n)=\frac{\sum_{k=1}^{K} u_{\underset{\sim}{C}'}(z_k)z_k}{\sum_{k=1}^{K} u_{\underset{\sim}{C}'}(z_k)} \quad (9)$$

or,in the case of unimodel membership function of $\underset{\sim}{C}'$

$$u_{\underset{\sim}{C}'}(\mathrm{Uopt}(n))=\underset{z\in Z}{\mathrm{Max}}\ u_{\underset{\sim}{C}'}(z) \quad (10)$$

For a Fuzzy logic controller,in which the inputs are system error e and its rate q,and the output is Uopt, the input-output relation of the controller can be considered as a mapping:

$$\mathcal{F}: [\underset{\sim}{e}(n),\underset{\sim}{q}(n)] \longrightarrow \mathrm{Uopt}(n)$$

$$\mathrm{Uopt}(n)=\mathcal{F}[\underset{\sim}{e}(n),\underset{\sim}{q}(n)] \quad (11)$$

In fact,the control rules of existing FLCs have the form

if <process-state> then <control-action>

Where <...> denotes some fuzzy proposition about the underlying variables. By conventional control theory, an FLC constructed in this way is no more than a non-linear gain controller which mapps the process states directly into control actions. In order to control complex plants,we propose the ESLFC which makes use of the technology of self-learning control, expert system and pattern recognization in the field of artifical intelligence.

Expert System

Expert system is an intelliegent programic system with an amount of expert knowledge which is used to solve practical problems in a particular field. As in the FLC case,the underlying premise of the expert system paradigm is that in certain domains there is problem solving expertise that can not be expressed mathemalically but can be captured by means of approprecIate representation techniques. However,expert systems are not restricted to a single format of this 'knowledge base'. There have been much research on what constitutes knowledge ,how it is organized and how it is used. Here we introduce the rule-based expert syetem techniques in FLC system to enrich the structure and content of the knowledge that is availabe to the FLC,while retaning its flexibility. This system contains more complex knowledge about process control, and it uses this knowledge in more flexible ways. It will allow more complex hierachies of rules, such as

If <process-state> Then
<intermediate variable-1>
...
...
If <intermediate-variable-K> Then
<control-action>

where the intermediate variable resperents some implied non-measurable state that can affect the control actions. At the next level of comlexity,It will permit knowledge to be included. Thus we could have meta-rules that are used to decide which low-level rules to apply, i,e

if <process-state-1> then
<apply-rule-set-A1>
if <process-state-2> then
<apply-rule-set-A2>
...
...
if <process-state-k> then
<apply-rule-set-An>

The Structure of ESLFC

In order to make the system fit for a large range of plants,we imbed the FLC with self-learning function via expert system technology. This ESLFC system (shown in Fig.1) consists of three levels, that is, main control level (MC), expert self-learning level (ESL) and parameter self-tuning level (PST).

In Fig.1, X_1,X_2,X_3 stand for identification of characters, RB_1,RB_2 and RB_3 the rule bases, I_1 ,I_2 and I_3 inference and decision-making engines in the three levels respectively.

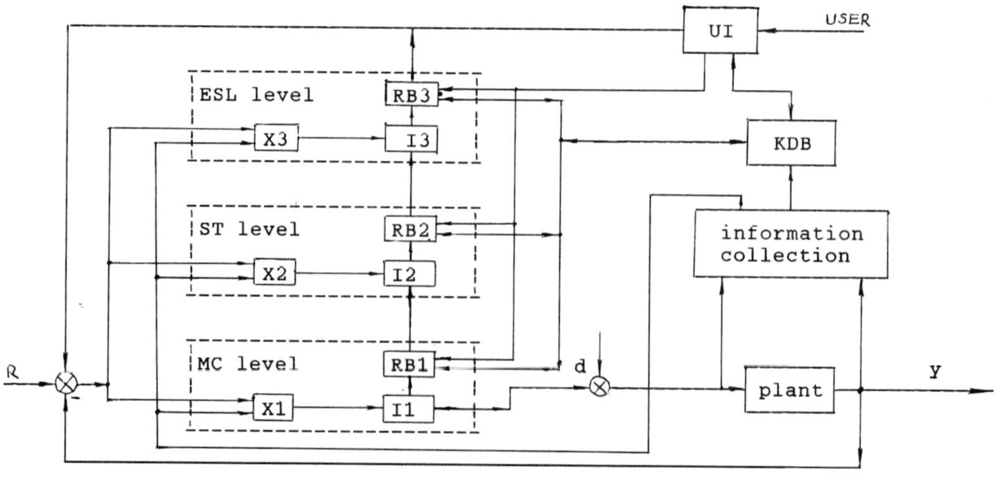

Fig. 1 block diagram of ESLFC system

KDB is the common knowledge data base, which stores facts, evidences, hypotheses and goals. Facts include static data, such as measurement ranges, operating points and various thresholds. Evidence includes dynamic data obtained from sensors or experiment results. Because observations of the plant are usually noise-containminated or incomplete, the experience of skilled operators can be used to provide hypotheses which may offset the lack of direct information. One important aspect of hypotheses is used in state estimation.

Goals are another important entry of the KBD. There are static goals, such as performance index, and dynamic goals which are generated on line by the system itself.

In the sequel, we will deal with the three levels in detial seperately.

The control rules in MC level. The control rules in MC level contains control strategies which are divided in four modes. One out of the four modes is selected according to the state of characteritstic error (e) and its rate of change (q). Define characteristic set as

$$\Phi_1=\{e, q, \underset{\sim}{e}, \underset{\sim}{q}\} \qquad (12)$$

where "e" and "q" stand for error and its rate of change, respectively. "$\underset{\sim}{e}$" and "$\underset{\sim}{q}$" stand for fuzzy set of "e" and "q", respectively.

The control rules are expressed as

r1: if $|e(n)|>\delta$ then $Uopt(n)=s\times Um$
r2: if $\eta<|e(n)|<\delta$ then
    $Uopt(n)=r_2\times Uopt(n-1)$
r3: if $|e(n)|\bar{\in}\langle Zo\rangle$ & $|q(n)|\bar{\in}\langle Zo\rangle$ then
    $Uopt(n)=\mathscr{F}[e(n),q(n)]$ & $k=\beta$
r4: if $|e(n)|\in\langle Zo\rangle$ & $|q(n)|\in\langle Zo\rangle$ then
    $Uopt(n)=e(n)$ & $k=\alpha$
r5: if $|e(n)|>\eta$ then $u(n)=Uopt(n)$
r6: if $[u(n-1)+k\times Uopt(n)]>UM$ then
    $u(n)=UM$
r7: if $[u(n-1)+k\times Uopt(n)]<UL$ then
    $u(n)=UL$
r8: if $[u(n-1)+k\times Uopt(n)]\in[UL,UM]$ then
    $u(n)=u(n-1)+k\times Uopt(n)$
r9: if M=1 then $e(n)= R-y(n)$
r10: if M=2 then $e(n)= R-\hat{y}(n)$

where
$Uopt(n)$—the medimum output of controller
$u(n)$—the output of the controller
UM—the maxmum of the admissible output
UL—the minmum of the admissible output
Um—the minmum of the output of controller
s—$s=SGN(e(n))$
r_2—reducing factor
δ, η—two experince values
$\langle Zo\rangle$—zero level of fuzzy set
$q(n)$—$q(n)=e(n)-e(n-1)/T$
k—integral gain
$y(n)$—output of the plant
$\hat{y}(n)$—predicted output of the fuzzy control model of the plant
M—flag of system model type

Rules 1-4 represent the four modes: two open-loop control modes and two closed-loop control modes. Rules 1-2 are used with Rule 5 to give out the output of the controller directly. Rules 3-4 are used with Rules 6-8, which have the function of integration, to give out the output of the controller. Rule 9 and Rule 10 are used to calculate the system error e when the plant is judged to be without or with delay respectively.

Expert self-learning level. The pattern recognization technique developed in the Expert Self Learning (ESL) level enables the system to deal with a variety of plants. When the character of the plant-controlled is unknown, the initial parameters of the controller is set based on the previous knowledge and let the system run. In the system learning process, ESL level extracts the closed-loop transient reponse characterictis set:

$$\Phi_3=\{e, q, \dot{y}, T_\tau, T_\delta, Em, J1, J2\} \qquad (13)$$

where
e—error   q—$q=de/dt$
$\dot{y}$—rate of output change
T_τ—delay-time
T_δ—the keeping time during $|e|>\delta$
Em--the maximum of overshoot
J1--$J1=\sum t\cdot e(t)$, J1--$J2=\sum e(t)$

According to the characteristic set, ESL level establish the following classification rules:

r1: if $u(t)=0$ & $y(t)=0$ then
    M=2 & P=0 & $T_\tau=t$ else M=1.
r2: if $|T_\delta-T_\tau|>D1$ then P=1.
r3: if $\eta<|e|<\delta$ & $e.q<0$ & $\dot{y}(t)\in[Y1,Y2]$
    then P=2
r4: if $Em\in(Em_1, Em_2)$ & $J1>Q_1max$ then P=3
r5: if $|Em|>Emax$ & $J2>Q_2max$ then P=0

where D1, Y_1, Y_2, Em, Em, Emax, Q_1max and Q_2max are experience values, which are stored in the KDB. P is the flag of the parameter to be adjusted, M is the flag of the system model type. M=1 indicates the model without delay, M=2 indicates the model with delay.

Parameter Self-Tuning (PST) Level. PST level tunes on-line some parameters in MC level under the instruction of ESL level. The characteristic set is

$$\Phi_2=\{P, M, \dot{y}, e, q, J, T_\delta\} \qquad (14)$$

where P, M, e, q and $\dot{y}$ are the same as in ESL level, and
T_δ—keeping time during $|e|>\delta$
J—$J=e.q$

When $J=e(n)q(n)>0$, the error changes towards set-point, then control action should be reduced. When $J=e(n)q(n)<0$, the control action should be increased. The rules are as follows

1. P=0:
Estimate the control parameters and experience values.

2. P=1 : $Um=r R/k=r_1\times Um$.
$r_1(n)=r_1(n-1)+\Delta r_1(n)$,
    if $[r_1(n-1)+\Delta r_1(n)]\in[R11,R12]$
$r_1(n)=r_1(n-1)$, esle

where $\Delta r_1(n)$ is adjusted on-line according to T_δ in the following way

if T_δ=B then $\Delta r_1(n)=a$
if T_δ=M then $\Delta r_1(n)=0$
if T_δ=S or O then $\Delta r_1(n)=-a$

3. P=2:
$r_2(n)=r_2(n-1)+\Delta r_2(n)$,
    if $[r_2(n-1)+\Delta r_2(n)]\in[R11,R12]$
$r_2(n)=r_2(n-1)$, else

where $\Delta r_2(n)$ is adjusted on-line according to $\dot{y}$, i.e.

if $|\dot{y}|<Y1$ then $\Delta r_2(n)=b$
if $|\dot{y}|>Y2$ then $\Delta r_2(n)=-b$
if $|\dot{y}|\in[Y1,Y2]$ then $\Delta r_2(n)=0$

4. P=3:
$\beta(n)=\beta(n-1)+\Delta\beta(n)$, if [$\beta(n-1)+\beta(n)$] $\in$ [B1,B2]
$\beta(n)=\beta(n-1)$, else

where $\Delta\beta(n)$ is adjusted on-line according to J and e, i.e.

if J>0 & $|e(n)|$=B then $\Delta\beta(n)=0$
if J>0 & $|e(n)|$=S then $\Delta\beta(n)=-c$
if J<0 & $|e(n)|$=B then $\Delta\beta(n)=c$
if J<0 & $|e(n)|$=S then $\Delta\beta(n)=0$

where B,M,S and O stand for fuzzy sets. R11,R12,R21,R22,Y1,Y2 B1 and B2 experience values. a,b and c are parameters

SIMULATION EXPERIMENTS

The combustion process control of a boiler is very important and difficult. This system is a multivarible plant with several input variables,such as,air-input and chain speed,and three output varibles: pressure P, O_2 % in soot and negative pressure in the chamber of the furnace S_L. The usual control method used is PID regulator,which is not satisfactory to get good control performance. And so do the other control systems established on the basis of linear control theory,which requires strict mathematical models.

Based on the combustion process control of an industrial boiler, a number of simulation experiements are carried out to prove the feasibility of ESLFC.

Experiment 1. vapour pressure control. The main concern is to get good tracking property to user's demand and disturbance-resistance. Fig 2 is a quatitative mathematic model of the dynamic process vapour pressure of SHL20-13 boiler.

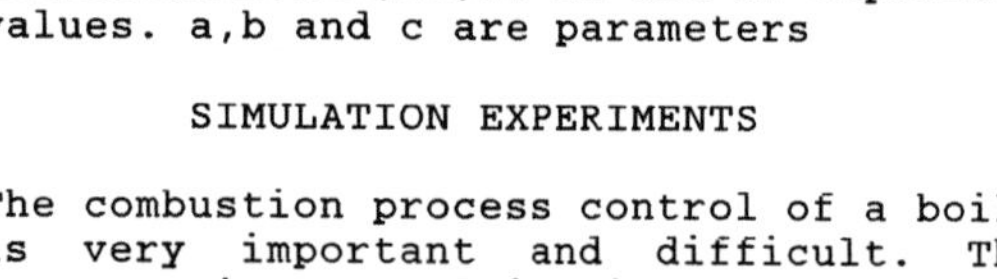

Fig. 2
λ_D—load disturbance
u_B—coal disturbance
P—vapour pressure
v—ratio of air to coal
$G(s)=(0.3/(1+180s)).\exp(-60s)$
$G_{F_1}(s)=1/(1+180s)$
$G_{F_2}(s)=G(s)$

Assume the performance index is ITAE

$$J=\sum t\ |e(t)|. \quad (15)$$

Based on the process model given in Fig.2, the following simulation experiments are carried out.

Experiment 1.1: On the learning ability of the ESLFC. Fig.3 shows the control results. Curve-1 is the result of first running of ESFLC with initial parameters $r_1(0)=6, r_2(0)=0.9$, δ%=50%, η% =30% and $\beta(0)=0.15$. Curve-2 is the control result of the second running after the learning and adjustment in the first running.

Experiment 1.2: On the disturbance-resistance property. Fig.4 shows the pressure regulation precess to $U_B=4$. Curve-1 is the control result of by ESFLC system and the performance ITAE $J_1=17.8$ and transient process time $t_{s_1}=300s$. Curve-2 is the control result by PI control system and $J_2=37.73$, $T_{s_2}=540s$.

Experiment 1.3: Fig.5 shows the pressure regulation process to $\lambda_D=3$ by ESLFC and PI systems. Curve-1 is the result by ESLFC and J1=26.18,T_{s1}=200s. Curve-2 is the result by PI, regulator and J2=36.58,T_{s2}=340s.

From the above results,we can see the performence of ESLFC system is superiour to PI system.

Experiment 2. Now consider the control problem of O_2% in the boiler.In a SHL 20-13 boiler,an approximate control model of O_2% can be taken as

$$G(s)=K/[(T_1S+1)(T_2S+1)] \quad (16)$$

Experiment 2.1: Fig. 6 shows the control result when the parameters in G(s) take the usual values,that is,K=0.742,T_1=3 and T_2=1.

Experiment 2.2: This experiment is to show the adaptivity of ESLFC to plant parameter changes,in comparison with PI regulator.

We still take the performance index ITAE with J1 and J2 denoting the values of the systems by ESFLC and PI respectively. At first let the plant parameters in G(s) be K=0.742,T_1 =3 and T_2 =1. Under this condition,we set the control parameters of ESFLC anf PI to be the best. Then the adaptivity property of ESFLC anf PI can be shown in experiments with plant parameters changed.

Fig.7 shows the control results of ESLFC and PI when K=0.742,T_1=3 and T_2=1.

Figs.8-12 show the results of ESLFC and PI when the plant parameters change to various values as shown in the figures.

From these experiments it is obvious that the system controled by ESFLC works much better than the system controlled by PI regulator.

CONCLUSION

The Expert Self-Learning Fuzzy Control (ESLFC) system proposed in this paper aims at the control problem of complex systems, for which mathematical models are hard to set up. By expert system technology,the ESLFC system is constructed in multi-level hierachial form. There are three levels: main control level(MC),Expert self-learning level(ESL) and parameter Self-tuning level(PST). The self-learning and adjustment function enables the system to improve its control performance on-line. Unlike adaptive control,this self-tuning dose not strictly depend on mathematical model.

Finally a number of simulation experiments are carried out to test the control properties of ESLFC in comparison with PI regulator. The plant models are based on the combustion process of an industrial boiler. The simulation results prove the good tracking and robust properties of the ESLFC.

REFERENCE

King,P.J. and Mamdani,E.H. (1977), The application of Fuzzy control systems to industrial processes. Automatica, 13, 235-242.

Procyk,T.J. and Mamdani,E.H. (1979), A linguistic self-organizing process controller. Automatica, 15, 15-30.

Astrom,K.J.,Anton,J.J. and Arzen,K.E. (1986), Expert control, Automatica, 22, 277-286.

Shirlay,R.S. (1987), Some lessons learning using expert systems for process control. American Control Conference, Vol.2, 1342-1346.

Saridis,G.N. (1977),Self-organizing con- Dekker Inc.

Fu,K.S. (1972) Learning techniques in system design:a brief review. Proc. of the IFAC 5th World Congress Part 3, 3701-3714.

Davis,R. (1982) Expert systems.Where are we and where do we go from here?. Artif. Intell. 3-22.

Mendel,J.M. (1973) Reinforcement learning models and their applications to control problems. JACC of the American Automatic Control Council.

Mcfaddena,R.W. (1984) Multiparameter trim: it pays in combustion control. Intech.,31(5)

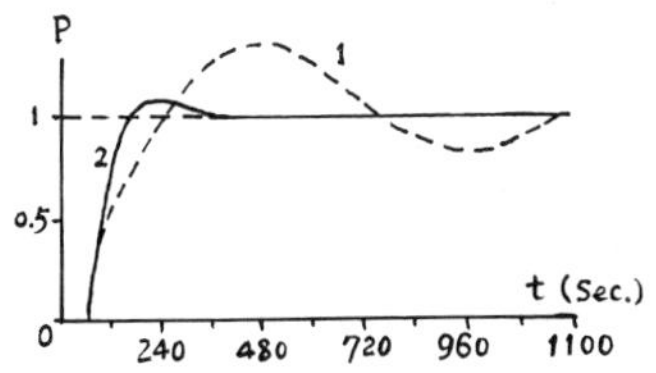

Fig.3 Pressure control results of ESLFC
1-- 1st running, 2-- 2nd running

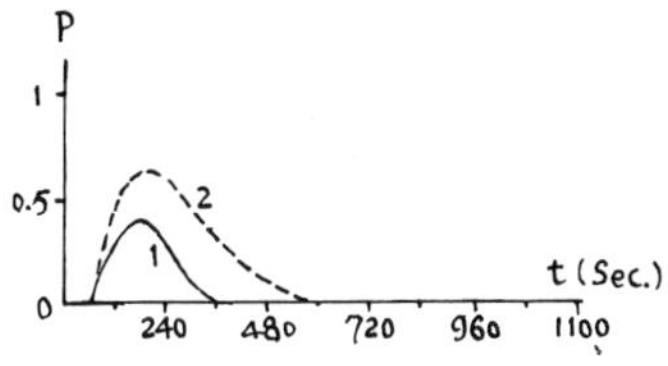

Fig.4 Pressure control results (U =4)
1-- ESLFC, 2-- PI

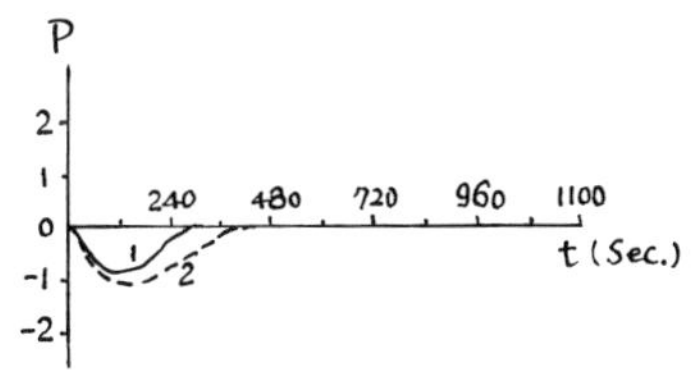

Fig.5 Pressure control results (=3)
1-- ESLFC , 2-- PI

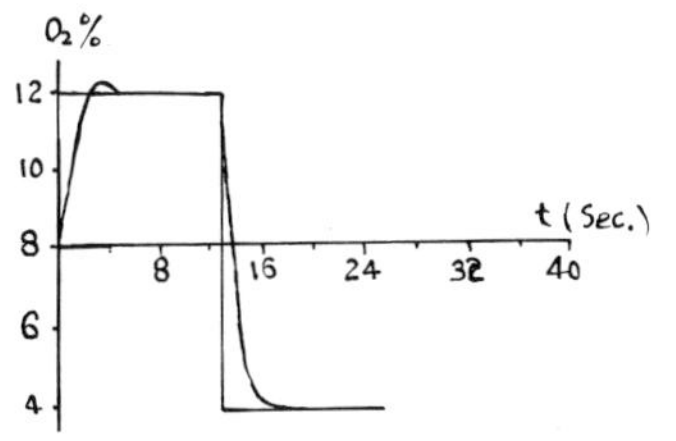

Fig.6 Oxygen O_2% control result by ESLFC

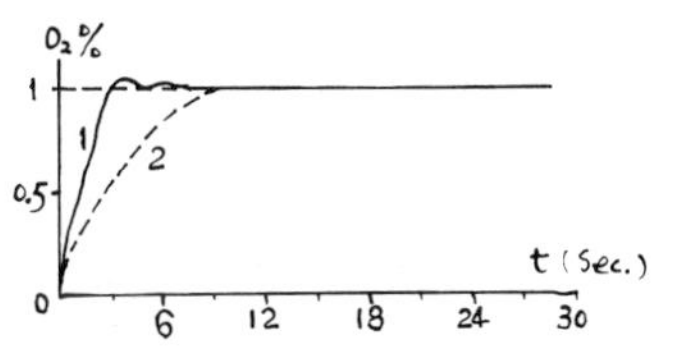

Fig.7 Results of experiment 2.2
K=0.742, T1=3, T2=2,

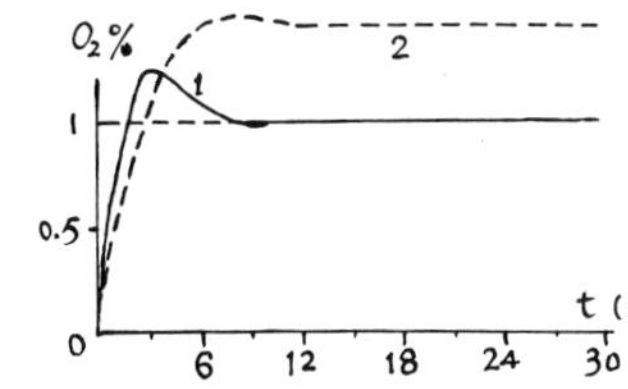

Fig.8 Results of experiment 2.2
K=1.5, change about 100%

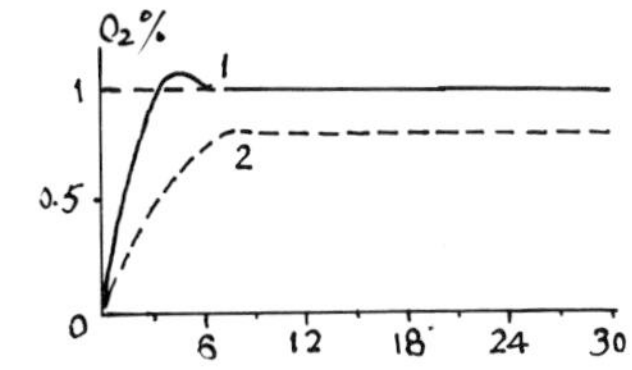

Fig.9 Results of experiment 2.2
K=0.6, change about 19%

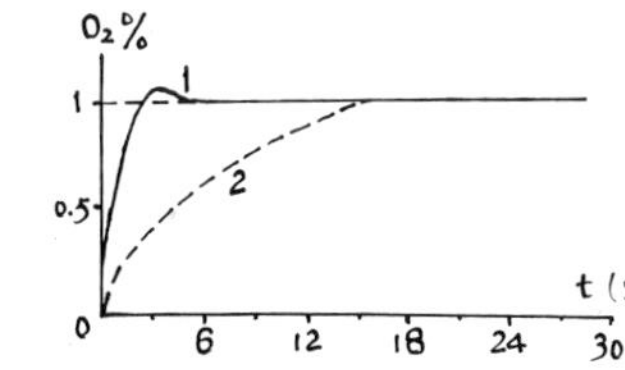

Fig.10 Results of experiment 2.2
T1=5, change about 66%

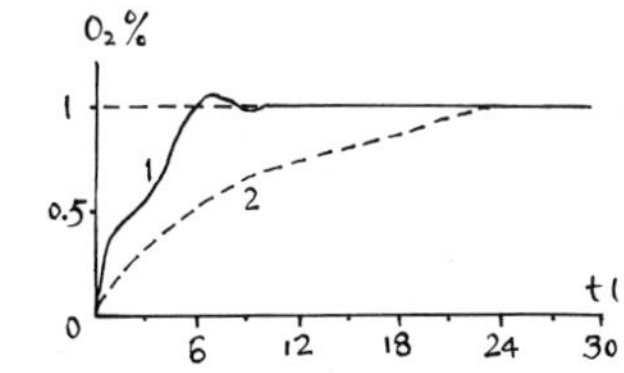

Fig.11 Results of experiment 2.2
T1=8, change about 160%

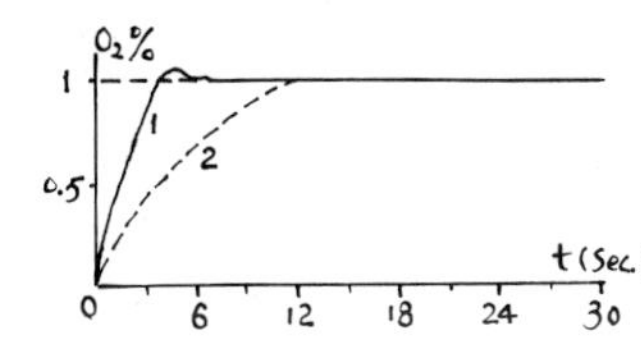

Fig.12 Results of experiment 2.2
T2=1.5, change about 50%

ASYNCHRONOUS METHODS FOR EXPERT SYSTEMS IN REAL-TIME APPLICATIONS

Th. Beck and R. J. Lauber

Institute of Control Engineering and Industrial Automation of the University of Stuttgart, Pfaffenwaldring 47, D-7000 Stuttgart 80, FRG

Abstract:

Asynchronous behaviour turns out to be one of the key factors for the use of expert systems in real-time application. The paper dicusses methods to treat asynchronous events as well as parallel inferences in expert systems. We will show that the combination of knowledge based techniques with the concepts of real-time programming languages and real-time operating systems seems to be a promising way to obtain real-time capability of expert systems. Furtheron, we suggest a method for the realization of these concepts with respect to the integration of the expert system into a conventional real-time software system.

Keywords:

Expert systems, knowledgebased systems, integration of expert systems, compilation of expert systems.

Introduction

During the last years the development of knowledge based techniques has been one of the basic topics in AI research. There are a lot of papers discussing the advantages and the use of expert systems in certain applications (diagnosis, configuration etc.). Often indicators are given that an expert system might be appropriate for problem solving in a real-time domain.

However, the use of knowledge based techniques in real-time application is still a challenge because there are mostly no concepts provided in the expert system shell supporting this kind of application. We think that an amount of research is still needed until a real-time expert system will work in a satisfactory way.

The term 'real-time' can be defined by the requirements for timeliness and simultaneousness. This definition includes the most common usage 'fast' of the term 'real-time', but points out that there are further important requirements to meet.

With respect to the real-time capability of expert systems, it must be possible for expert systems to react to asynchronous events. In most cases events such as dangerous failure in a technical process can not be planned ahead but it is necessary to react to them immediately. It is also helpful if expert systems can do more than one inference (sometimes mutually dependent inferences) at a time. The supervision of two dependent parts of a technical process hits this class of problems. At last, the time needed for the solution by the inference engine has to meet the required time constraints.

In general we can list some problems occuring by the use of expert systems in real-time applications:

- There is only a fixed amount of time for infering the solution. The expert system should provide the best possible response within a given deadline. Therefore, it is one goal in real-time expert system research to develop new strategies of knowledge processing.
- The inference of a real-time expert systems could be interrupted by asynchronous events to process new important incoming data. The events can vary in importance.
- To serve two or more events with same priority the expert system must be capable of doing some inferences in parallel.
- Tempus fugit. The time never stands still. There are problems such as time representation and the problem to reason about time. New data may be in contradiction to some stored data. It must be possible to handle a non monotonic knowledge base.

There are other problems concerning the environment of the expert system:

- An interface to the technical process has to be provided. The physical continuous values of sensors have to be translated to the symbolic level the expert system is working on.
- The expert system should be integrated in a conventional problem solution.
- There are always limited resources in a real-time system.

The paper especially discusses some methods to treat asynchronous events and parallel inferences in a real-time expert system. Furtheron, we suggest a method for the realization of these concepts with respect to the integration of the expert system into a conventional real-time software system.

A view on conventional real-time software systems

The structure of a conventional real-time software system is highly modular. A real-time software system is built up by a set of tasks running in parallel, exchanging data, suspending or activating each other. Each of the tasks is designed to solve a part of a complex problem. The tasks are running under control of a real-time operating system. It provides means for the resource management such as IO control and memory management. On the other side it is also responsable for the scheduling of tasks. Furtheron, event handling is provided by a real-time operating system.

The tasks in conventional real-time software systems are realized by non-real-time languages (C, PASCAL) and assembly languages inserts, or languages with real-time programming ability (PEARL).

With the help of real-time programming languages the facilities of real-time operating systems could be used easily by the programmer. For instance, it is easy to express that a task should be activated cyclicly or that a certain task should be suspended from running. In PEARL, for example, the cyclic activation of a task named 'diagnosis' looks as follows:

```
every 3 sec activate diagnosis;
```

Even interrupts are easy to use in such languages. Let 'alarm' be an interrupt specified in a PEARL programm and let 'fault_diagnostics' be a task in a real-time software system. The statement

```
when alarm activate fault_diagnosis;
```

expresses that the task 'fault_diagnosis' would be executed as soon as the event 'alarm' occurs.

Expert systems as tasks in a real-time software system

Bringing the concepts of knowledge based systems (knowledge representation, knowledge processing etc.) together with the concepts of real-time programming languages and real-time operating systems seems to be a promising way to obtain real-time capability of expert systems.

The idea is to run an expert system as a task under control of a real-time operating system.

By this point of view an expert system becomes a part of a complex real-time system; it is fully embedded into a software system. From the viewpoint of a real-time operating system there is no difference in handling an 'expert system task' or a 'conventional task'.

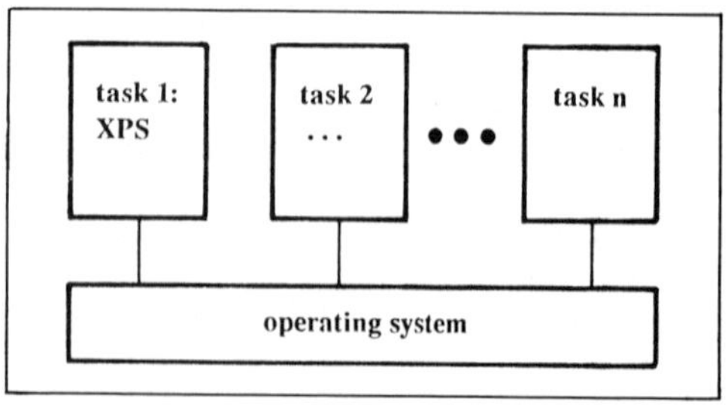

Figure 1: Expert system under control of a real-time operating system

By this way we can use the asynchronous methods of the real-time operating system for expert systems as well, if it is possible to run expert systems as tasks in a real-time software system.

Asynchronous events

Reacting to events turns out to be a basic requirement for real-time expert systems. We are able to make out several types of events differing only in the place of occurency but not in the way the expert system should react to them.

External events

They occur outside the expert system, for example in a technical process. In most cases sensor data is send to the process computer system triggering processor interrupts. The interrupt triggers the activation of an interrupt service routine which could be even an expert system task.

Internal events

They occur inside the expert system and are often called demons in literature. They are similar to signals known from operating systems but they are mostly not handled in parallel as they should be. For example:

- a value of the knowledge base is needed
- a value of the knowledge base is determined
- a certain state of the knowledge base is reached
- or a simple internal clock event.

All these events are asynchronous and two or more can occur at the same time each of them requesting its own action. The expert system must be capable of processing the input data in parallel with different priority.

By our treatment of expert systems as tasks in larger real-time software systems we can use the facilities of the operating system even for expert system to handle the mentioned events.

The interrupt handling and task scheduling is managed by the operating system. Out of this reason there is no management overhead in the expert system itself.

Transforming expert systems

Taking notice of expert system shells (KEE, ART, Babylon, KNOSSOS ...) it seems to be impossible to run an expert system realized on the base of these shells as a task in a real-time system. The expert system requests a great amount of resources which are always limited in real-time software systems running on micro computers.

In the following we will discuss our idea to transform an expert system to the level of conventional programming languages to solve the mentioned problems.

We developed a compiler with the ability to transform an expert system to an equivalent program realized in a conventional programming language (C, PASCAL). Equivalent in the sense that the generated program shows the same external behaviour as the original expert system. Figure 2 shows the principal proceeding of the transformation.

The compiler accepts the knowledge base of an expert system realized on base of a knowledge representation language which was derived from PATHOS as an input. Frames, rules and relations are the basic elements of this language as described by Permantier and Lauber [1987].

The output of the compiler is a conventional program which in its external behaviour, is equivalent to the original expert system. For our researches we selected C to be the language of the generated program because it is available for a wide range of computer systems.

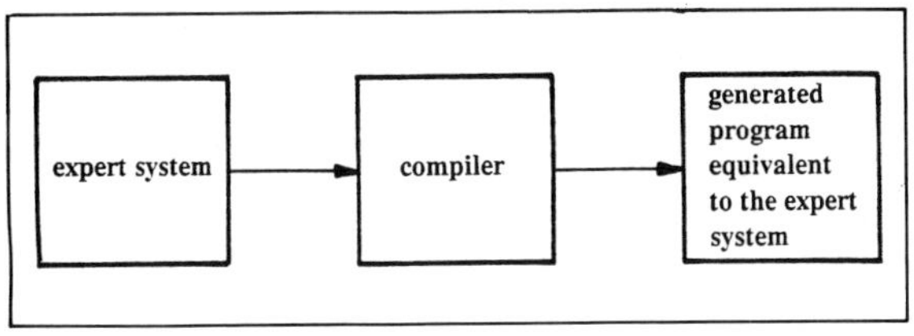

Figure 2: Transformation of expert systems to an equivalent program

The internal design of the generated program is characterized by an explicit control flow. Therefore, there is no need for an interpretative inference engine which always slows down knowledge processing.

Rules are transformed to functions whereas frames and relations are transformed to data structures of C. The objects of the expert system become objects of the programming language C.

The generated program is much smaller than the original expert system because there is no further need for the shell with the inference engine. It is even faster because all available information is transformed in a way that there is no interpretative overhead at run time.

The generated program can be included by this way as a task in an existing real-time software system.

Combining problem solving techniques

Some further advantages are gained by the transformation of expert systems which have not been mentioned yet. For the developer of expert systems it is necessary that he is allowed to mix different paradigms of problem solving because no problem can be solved exclusively by the use of knowledge based techniques. There are always parts of the problem which are solved in a more easy way by the use of conventional programming languages. It is our opinion that the user should be free in choocing an appropriate method of constructing the solution of the problem

For example, to solve the problem of data transfer between some kind of technical process and the process computer we would use predefined solutions in the form of toolboxes or function libraries. If there is no predefined solution available we would realize a little programm which fulfils the required function. For this type of problems conventional programming seems to be the appropriate tool.

For certain applications e.g. diagnosis it seems to be promising to use knowledge based techniques for the realization. For instance, to handle fault diagnosis in a technical process we will build up an expert system.

By this approach it becomes possible to mix conventional techniques with knowledge based techniques because the expert system itself is transformed to the level of a conventional programming language.

By this reasons the expert system can now be fully embedded in a conventional system solution.

Shared objects of the knowledge base

Often it is necessary that two or more expert system tasks are using the same objects of the knowledge base (rules, frames and relations). In the momentary state of our researche rules (functions after the transformation) can be used as shared objects by different expert system tasks. A simple memory lock management is provided to use instances of frames (data after the transformation) in a shared mode.

Example

A little example in a semi formal notation should help us to illustrate the new possibilities for expert systems.

There may be the problem of the supervision of a technical process. The problem can be divided into two parts. The first part is the diagnosis of the continuous operation with the following tuning of a controller. The tuning of the controller depends on the state of the process. The second part of the problem is the diagnosis of the process when a fault happened.

The knowledge base contains some rules to determine the state of the process and the fault. These may be attributes of a frame which represents all important attributes of the technical process.

The two tasks may be defined as follows:

```
task continuous_operation
{
/* reading some data from process */
get_data();

/* use knowledge based technique to */
/* determine the state of the process */
infer (state_of_process);

switch (state_of_process);
{
   case OK:
      /* doing nothing */
      break;
   case TO_LOW:
      /* increasing the value of */
      /* a controller parameter */
      increase (value);
      break;
   case TO_HIGH:
      /* decreasing value of */
      /* a controller parameter */
      decrease (value);
      break;
   }
/* tuning of the controller */
send_to_controller( value )
}
```

The other task for the fault diagnosis of the process may be defined as follows:

```
task fault_diagnosis
{
/* some actions which are always done */
/* when fault is occuring */
...

/* suspending the task continuous_operation */
suspend continuous_operation;

/* use of rules to detect the fault */
infer (fault);

/* actions which must be done */
/* to restore the process */
restore (process);

/* activate the task continuous_operation */
activate continuous_operation;
}
```

There must be a further task for the initialization of the system.

```
task init
{
/* setting up the system */
every 5 seconds activate continuous_operation;
when alarm activate fault_diagnosis;
}
```

The example shows on which way knowledge based techniques and conventional programming languages can be mixed.

Discussion

The suggested method of extending an expert system shell by means of a real-time programming language and its realization by a compiler brings along advantages and disadvantages:

- The method allows a simple integration of knowledge based techniques into conventional software systems. The expert system itself is transformed to the level of conventional programming languages.
- There is no inference engine required. The knowledge processing becomes faster and more problems can be solved without a special strategy of knowledge processing e.g. approximate processing etc.
- The control flow of the generated program contains the strategy of knowledge processing. The size of the generated code depends on the size of the knowledge base.
- A host computer (PC, VAX ...) running an expert system shell is used for the development and testing of the knowledge base but not for the real-time methods. After applying the compiler, the generated equivalent program is loaded down to the target process computer system (micro/mini computers) where the real-time behaviour of the whole system has to be tested in the target environment.

References

Lauber, R.J. and Permantier, G.A.: A knowledge representation language for process automation systems. 10th World Congress on Automatic Control 1987 Preprints Vol 6, pp. 330 - 333.

Wright, L. et al: An Expert System for Real-Time Control. IEEE Software, 1986 March, pp. 16 - 24.

Laffey, Th.J. et al: Real-Time Knowledge-Based Systems. AI Magazine, 1988 Spring, pp. 27 - 45.

Lesser, V.R. and Pavlin, J. and Durfee, E.: Approximate Processing in Real-Time Solving. AI Magazine, 1988 Spring, pp. 49 - 61.

EVOLUTION OF EXPERT SYSTEMS FOR REAL-TIME PROCESS MANAGEMENT: A CASE STUDY ON MOTOR CONTROL

M. P. Lukas*, R. A. Oyen*, M. A. Keyes and A. Kaya*****

**Wisdom Systems, McDermott, Inc., Chagrin Falls, OH 44022, USA*
***Industrial Products and Services Group, McDermott, Inc., Chagrin Falls, OH 44022, USA*
****Industrial Controls Laboratory, M.E. Department, The University of Akron, Akron, OH 44325-3903, USA*

Abstract Expert systems are rapidly moving into real-time process control applications, usually in conjunction with distributed digital control systems. These applications include intelligent alarm management, operator advisories for start-up/shut-down/monitoring functions, and process and equipment diagnostics. In most current systems, the expert systems are implemented using stand-along computer systems, which may be either dedicated LISP processors or conventional computers. This paper discusses the evolution of on-line system implementations from the stand-alone computer approach to imbedded processors within the distributed control architecture. The paper summarizes the benefits that result from this evolution, including a reduction in system hardware and engineering costs, ergonomic benefits in operator interfacing, and a significant improvement in system performance. In addition, those benefits are demonstrated in a case study in the area of motor control. In this case study, an existing set of Boolean logic for motor control is also implemented in expert system production rules. It was found that the production rule approach offers two major advantages: First, the production rules are more understandable; second, production rules are more easily tested because of the features of the expert system shell.

Keywords Expert systems; process management; motor control; computer control; human factors.

INTRODUCTION

The field of expert systems can be defined as the branch of artificial intelligence that attempts to model and retrieve human knowledge about objects, concepts, facts, and their interrelationships. While expert systems are implemented by means of computer programming, this programming differs from conventional procedural programs (e.g., FORTRAN, BASIC, or BOBOL programs) in that the variables being manipulated are symbolic ones instead of numerical ones. Often, the knowledge in expert systems is expressed in terms of "IF-THEN" rules, such as:

"IF the pump has been on for more than 25 seconds, AND its speed is less than 500 rpm, THEN it has failed."

Almost all expert systems that have been developed so far are off-line; that is, they are implemented in a computer that is not connected to a real process. All interactions between the expert system and the outside world are performed through a human being. On the other hand, expert systems for most process control applications must be on-line and real-time. That is, they must gather data from a physical process in real time, make decisions fast enough so that the results are useful, and communicate these results to humans in a simple and meaningful way.

Some example applications of this type of expert system are:

1) "Smart" Control System - The expert system reconfigures the control system changes operating mode (auto/manual), or modifies set points and tuning parameters based on current process conditions.

2) Alarm interpretation expert system - Recognizes the root cause of the set of existing alarms and presents their cause and effect relationships to the operator.

3) Start-up/shut-down advisory system - Walks the operator through a process start-up or shut-down sequence, while reacting in real time to unexpected events such as struck valves or equipment failures.

4) Process diagnostics system - Identifies which of the possible process problems is currently happening, based on the events and trends it observes at the time.

5) Instrument and control diagnostic system - Detects current or impending failures in the field instrumentation and process control equipment.

KNOWLEDGE REPRESENTATION IN EXPERT SYSTEMS

The knowledge in expert systems is usually expressed in one or both of two ways. The most common representation is in terms of "IF-THEN" rules, such as the following rule dealing with pump operation:

If the operation-status of Booster-Pump-A is ON.
And the current-speed of Booster-Pump-A is less than 50 RPM,
Then conclude that the Failure-status of Booster-Pump-A is FAILED.

In any given expert system, there may be hundreds or thousands of such rules that describe the interrelationships among process components and their characteristics.

These rules are chained together as shown in Figure 1, where the conclusion of one rule can be the condition or input for other rules. During execution of the expert system, this rule chain can be traversed from left to right; that is, from data to the resulting conclusions. This is known as "forward-chaining" execution of the rule set. Or, the chain can be traversed from right to left; that is, by postulating possible conclusions, then checking to see if the existing data support the conclusions. This is known as "backward chaining."

The second common way of expressing knowledge in expert systems is by means of object-oriented data structures, such as the one shown in Figure 2 that describes a "generic" pump. The data structure involves an object and its attributes (sometimes known as a frame and its slots), each of which has a given value at each moment in time. The first attribute, "Inherits-from", specifies whether the object "inherits" any of its attributes from other "parent" objects. In this case, the generic pump does not inherit from any other object since it is itself a parent object. This inheritance mechanism in object-oriented programming is a very useful one, since it allows hierarchies or families of similar objects to be constructed and to share common attributes. In these families, changing the attribute value of a "parent" object can affect the values of the "children's" attributes.

Nearly all expert systems implement some form of IF-THEN rule representation of knowledge. Object-oriented structures are used in complex expert systems that require an efficient method of storing large amounts of organized knowledge about a physical object or process. The disadvantage of using object-oriented structures is that they put a greater burden on computer memory and performance capabilities than do rule-based structures.

REAL-TIME EXPERT SYSTEMS

Most of the expert systems that have been implemented to date are off-line ones. Once the knowledge base is entered into the system, all information entering or leaving it flows through the Human Interface by means of interactions with the human user of the system. In a real-time expert system, the "Real-Time Interface" is used to gather data from the outside world and update the knowledge base on a continuous basis. The data might include the current values of process variables or the current operational status of various process components, for example. Also, this interface can be used to transmit the expert system's conclusions to the process - for example, orders to change process set points or to shut off certain motors or valves. When an expert system is used in this real-time, on-line mode, a number of issues arise that were not present in the off-line situation:

1) Representative of time-based information - Real-time expert systems must deal with past and future values of process variables, in addition to present ones. The expert system must provide a way to time-stamp the values of these variables, as well as a mechanism to average and smooth them over time. Also, the system must have the ability to detect patterns in a time series of a variable (e.g., peaks, inflection points, maxima and minima).

2) Ability to keep the knowledge base current - The knowledge base must accurately reflect the current status of the process so that the inference engine arrives at sound conclusions. Any delays in the updating process could lead to erroneous results.

3) Ability to conclude the inferencing process in a timely manner - In a real-time expert system, it is not enough to come up with the right conclusions; they must be achieved soon enough to do some good. In LISP-based expert systems, one impediment to this is "garbage collection" - the recovery of unused memory space by the memory management system. If not scheduled properly. this collection can disturb time-critical expert system functions.

4) Provision of a user interface that is consistent with that of the process control system - From a human factors point of view, it is undesirable to provide the user (generally the process operator) with more than one type of human interface - that is, inconsistent keyboards of CRT displays. It multiplies the need for operator training and increases the chances of human error under stress conditions.

DEDICATED COMPUTER APPROACH

One early approach to implementing real-time expert systems was to dedicate a computer to performing the expert system functions and interfacing it with a real-time distributed data acquisition and control system. (In some cases, data acquisition and control was implemented in a single, centralized computer). The architecture of such a system is shown in Figure 3.

In this architecture, the expert system computer is either a) A LISP machine with a conventional front-end processor to perform the real-time data interfacing functions, or b) a conventional computer with a multi-tasking operating system to run LISP <u>and</u> perform the interfacing functions. The operator or user interface is through the expert system computer console, separate from the human interface for the distributed system.

This approach does provide a way to combine expert system technology with conventional control and process monitoring functions.

However, this approach has the following disadvantages:

1) The expert system shell generally is complex to use, and requires that the knowledge engineer be able to program in LISP or other object-oriented language to enter the knowledge base.

2) A high-end (expensive) computer or work station is needed to run the expert system shell.

3) The operator or user has to learn how to use two types of operator consoles - one to interface with the expert system, and the other to interface with the on-line data acquisition and control system.

4) It is difficult to integrate the functions of the distributed system and the expert system, since the two systems are physically separate and use two different types of hardware and software.

A BETTER APPROACH - IMBEDDED EXPERT SYSTEMS

The above problems point the way to another, better approach shown in Figure 4. In this approach, a Knowledge Engineering work station is used to input the expert knowledge in a dialect familiar to the domain expert (such as English-like IF-THEN rules). After all the rules have been entered, the work station then translates them into code (e.g., function blocks or C-code) that runs in microprocessor-based "expert system" modules within the distributed control system itself. All time-sensitive functions (e.g. data time-tagging or averaging) associated with preparing data for use by the expert system also are executed within the distributed control system. All communications between the user (process operator) and the expert system are handled by the standard human interface consoles and displays in the distributed system.

Some of the advantages of this "imbedded expert system" approach are as follows:

1) An expensive high-level work station or computer is not required to implement the expert system. The KEWS can be implemented in a low-cost personal computer, and the rules are executed in an additional inexpensive module (or modules) in the distributed system. These modules can be added easily to an existing distributed system at minimum incremental cost.

2) The Knowledge Engineering work station allows easy entry of IF-THEN rules through "mouse and menu" or "fill-in-the-blanks" interactions. This eliminates the need for a specially trained LISP programmer or knowledge engineer.

3) The work station is not involved in time-critical on-line functions; these are all performed within the distributed control system. In fact, the work station can be unplugged from the distributed system after the knowledge base has been entered. Therefore, there are no "garbage collection" issues or other problems with running an expert system in a real-time environment, since the compiled on-line code executes on a periodic basis within the distributed system modules.

4) No special training for the operator is required; the operator interacts with both the expert system and the process control system through the same human interfaces.

5) If the expert system becomes large, it can be implemented in multiple modules in the distributed system, thus improving its robustness (tolerance to failures) and real-time performance.

6) The KEWS allows the engineering of both the expert system and the process control system to be performed in an integrated manner.

A MOTOR CONTROL APPLICATION

Let us use an example application to show how a process control solution is implemented as an expert system. The application is motor control logic. Motor control is a common and not unusually difficult use of function blocks.

The authors obtained the Boolean logic and the associated English description of an existing motor controller. We then translated the logic into an equivalent set of rules using the expert system shell. The Boolean logic and the expert system both implement the same set of functions. Requests to either start or stop the motor can come from a manual pushbutton, automatic logic elsewhere in the control system, or protection starts or stops. The protection starts or stops also come from logic elsewhere in the plant but the motor controller lets them override the manual and "automatic" start and stop requests.

Both implementations have start and stop controls which check whether the request to start or stop the motor can be granted. These controls also implement the relative priorities of the request signals. The controls check for evidence that the motor is not responding properly to the signals sent to it by the controller or that the motor has tipped. Finally, both implementations illuminate indicator lamps in flashing and steady patterns to inform the operator of conditions.

Figure 5 shows the schematic of the Boolean motor control logic. The schematic uses AND, OR, NOT, SET-RESET, DELAY, PULSE, and BLINK blocks. Those readers who are control system engineers are most likely familiar with blocks such as these. It should be noted that the control system documentation includes 24 pages (not supplied here) of English description of this motor control logic. This documentation is required to help a control system engineer interpret and understand the logic schematic.

The rule base shown in Figure 6 is the equivalent of the Boolean schematic. We do not describe the grammar in any detail in this paper. We must mention, however that the statements which begin with GET express variables which obtain their values from conventional control blocks. Correspondingly, the statements which begin with PUT cause values of variables in the expert system to be output to conventional control blocks. The rules of the expert system directly describe how the system works so no extra documentation like the aforementioned English description of the Boolean logic is needed.

COMPARISON OF THE TWO APPROACHES

The major difference between the two approaches is in the way the control schemes are expressed. The expert system is expressed in statements which read much like English. For instance, the first IF statement in the expert system is:

IF PROTECTION – START AND FEEDER – AVAILABLE
THEN SET START – COMMAND END

It corresponds to the AND block at the upper left of Figure 5 and parts of the OR and SET-RESET blocks to the right of the AND. The expert system statement shows the intent of the logic. The meaning of the set of function blocks must be interpreted by the engineer. In this case the blocks of Figure 5 are close to each other and the set of blocks begins and ends with English labels. Thus, in this case the engineer's translation task seems effortless. The start and stop command logic is laid out in Figure 5 to be very easily read.

Let us consider a somewhat different case. The motor trip logic is implemented in the following three statements:

IF MOTOR – STARTED
THEN SET MOTOR – SUPPOSED – TO – BE STARTED END

IF STOP – PUSHBUTTON (even if not permitted) OR TRY – to – STOP
THEN FOR 5 SECONDS (CLEAR MOTOR – SUPPOSED – TO – BE – STARTED) END

IF MOTOR – SUPPOSED – TO – BE – STARTED AND MOTOR – STOPPEDTHEN TRIP – MOTOR END

This corresponds to four blocks in the center of Figure 5: the SET-RESET which is labeled "TRIP", the OR and PULSE which reset it, and the AND to which it outputs. The experienced motor control engineers will quickly see the intent of this logic. An engineer less experienced in motor control will need to spend a little time to trace through connecting lines to find the input variables to the logic and to think about how the blocks translate into the design intent.

Let us consider a third case. The experienced motor control engineer expects to see electrical faults handled. He sees the AND block at the upper right of Figure 5 where he expects the fault signal to come into the motor start logic. From there, he can trace connections and blocks until he interprets the intent of the fault logic. The experienced motor control engineer sees the fault logic in a typical position to the right of the center of Figure 6. Some expert engineers may recognize this particular logic design. Some engineers may even recognize the design as one which they either do or do not prefer. This design intent is not expressed in the schematic. It is in the knowledge of the expert motor control engineer.

We are talking about a more and more select group of engineers. Very likely, however, this logic may need to be maintained or re-used by a new and relatively inexperienced engineer.

The corresponding portion of the expert system is the following four statements:

IF FOR 3 SECONDS (START – COMMAND OR STOP – COMMAND) THEN ELECT – FAULT END

IF COMMON – FAULT – SIGNAL AND START – PUSHBUTTON THEN STOP – FAULT – ACK END

IF COMMON – FAULT – SIGNAL AND STOP – PUSHBUTTON THEN START – FAULT – ACK END

IF ELECT – FAULT OR TRIP – MOTOR (summarize the faults)
OR STOP – FAULT – ACK OR START – FAULT – ACK (also keep COMMON – FAULT – SIGNAL asserted until button is released)THEN NEXT COMMON – FAULT – SIGNAL END

These statements show how ELECT – FAULT is determined, how the pushbuttons are used to acknowledge the fault, and the relationship between ELECT – FAULT and COMMON – FAULT – SIGNAL.

One last comment on the expressability of the expert system: much of the meaningfulness of the expert system comes from the application developer's use of meaningful names for variables. The expert system shell promotes the use of meaningful names. The rule editor presents the user with menus of variable names which have been used in the application so that the user does not have to retype them to re-use them. The editor also provides cross-reference menus which show which statements contain a particular variable.

ADVANTAGES IN TESTABILITY

Testing both Boolean logic and expert systems is done by trying sets of input values and observing the outputs. The tester further analyzes the outputs by tracing back through the values of the contributing variables. The person who tests function block logic observes the output of a block and makes an educated guess about which contributing block to observe next. This is another task which requires the engineer to translate from the schematic back to the functional intent of the logic.

Testing of the expert system is done with the viewer (a special CRT display) of the expert system shell. The viewer shows, in expert system, why the variable has its value.

The engineer uses the expert system viewer to display the values of several variables at a certain time. The engineer then asks the viewer why a certain variable has its value at that time. The viewer presents the engineer with the rule or set of rules which determined that value.

The expert system viewer provides an exceptional advantage over the tools available to test Boolean logic. The viewer shows rules which express the intent of the design rather than generic function blocks. The viewer shows the entire computation of the value rather than requiring the tester to individually look at many blocks of Boolean logic. The viewer lets the tester analyze squences of events after they are complete so the tester need not rig the timing of the events for testing, control events and test concurrently, or try to complete testing before further events change the state of the logic.

CONCLUSIONS

As in the case of conventional computer systems, the era of large, stand-alone computers running expert systems is over. The rapid advances of microcomputer technology are allowing expert systems to be imbedded in process control systems in multiple distributed modules. Whether rule-based or object-oriented, these distributed expert systems will make this branch of AI technology available and cost-effective for a large number of applications at a minimum cost to the user.

In addition, implementing control logic and diagnostic systems using expert system technology has major advantages over implementations using conventional Boolean logic or function blocks. For example, expert systems express their application design intent explicitly in their implementation. They can be read without translating from generic function blocks back into a presumption of what the original design intent was. The application developer contributes the major part of the meaningfulness of the expert system by using meaningful variable names. Also, testing the expert system saves the developer from translating from generic function blocks back into a presumption of what the original design intent was. The explanation facility of the expert system gives the same amount of pertinent information in one step as it would take to interrogate several function blocks. Furthermore, the expert system viewer presented by the authors allows the tester to analyze real-time sequences of events after they complete: to take all the time the analysis requires; to move back and forth in time. Finally, because the expert system has been developed and validated in terms of its actual design intent, the developer has much less documentation to write after the application is implemented than a function block implementation would need.

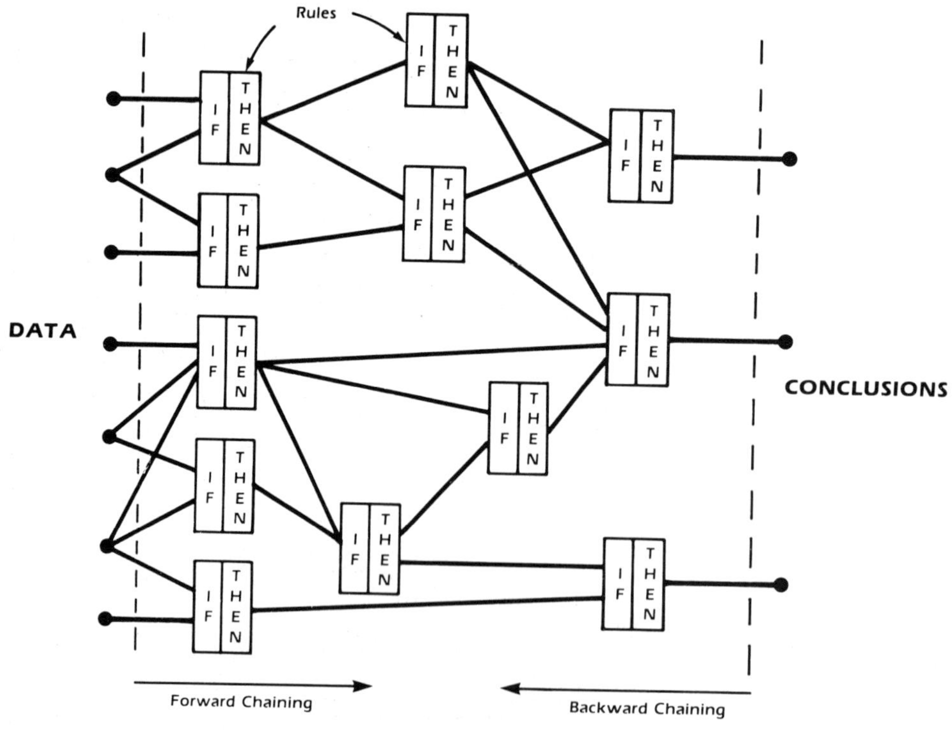

FIGURE 1 — Rule Chains in the Inferencing Process

Object: Pump

Attribute	Value
Inherits — From:	NIL
Pump-Type:	Centrifugal
Max — Head:	?
Max — Capacity:	?
Variable/Fixed — Speed:	Fixed
Operation — Status:	Off
Current — Speed:	?
Failure — Status	OK

FIGURE 2 — Object-Oriented Representation of a Generic Pump

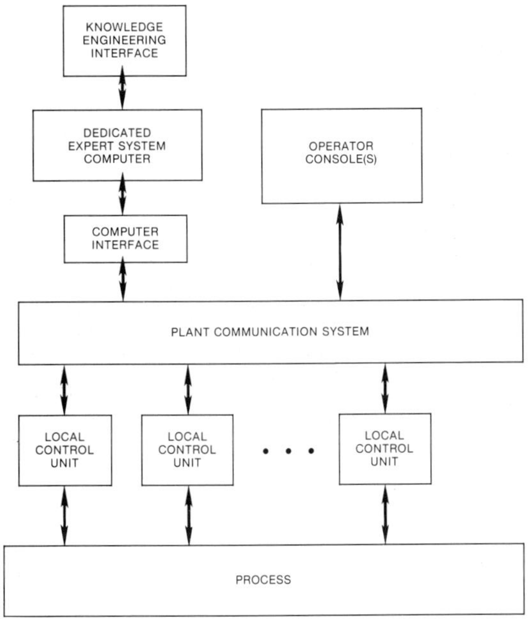

FIGURE 3 — Dedicated Computer Approach

```
{                MOTOR CONTROL LOGIC                }

{Inputs from the controller:}
GET PERMISSION_TO_START BLOCK 101
GET START_PUSHBUTTON BLOCK 102
GET AUTO_START BLOCK 103
GET PROTECTION_START BLOCK 104
GET FEEDER_AVAILABLE BLOCK 105
GET MOTOR_STARTED BLOCK 107
GET MOTOR_STOPPED BLOCK 108
GET PERMISSION_TO_STOP BLOCK 109
GET STOP_PUSHBUTTON BLOCK 110
GET AUTO_STOP BLOCK 111
GET PROTECTION_STOP BLOCK 112

{Outputs from this expert system:}
PUT START BLOCK 214
PUT STOP BLOCK 215
PUT COMMON_FAULT_SIGNAL BLOCK 306
PUT TRIP_MOTOR BLOCK 307
PUT COMMON_PROTECT_ALARM BLOCK 308
PUT PROTECTION BLOCK 341
PUT LIGHT_UP_START_STATUS BLOCK 501
```

FIGURE 6(a) — Motor Control Expert System

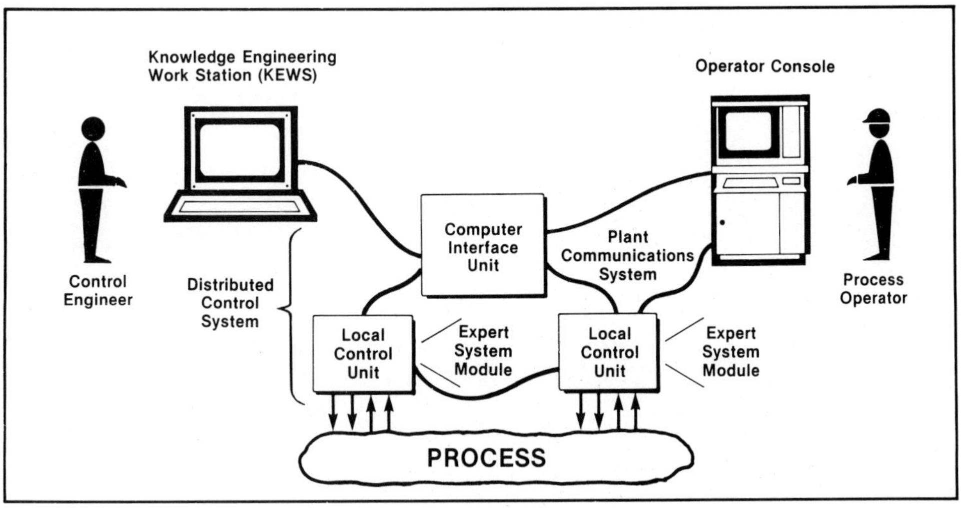

FIGURE 4 — Imbedded Rule-Based System

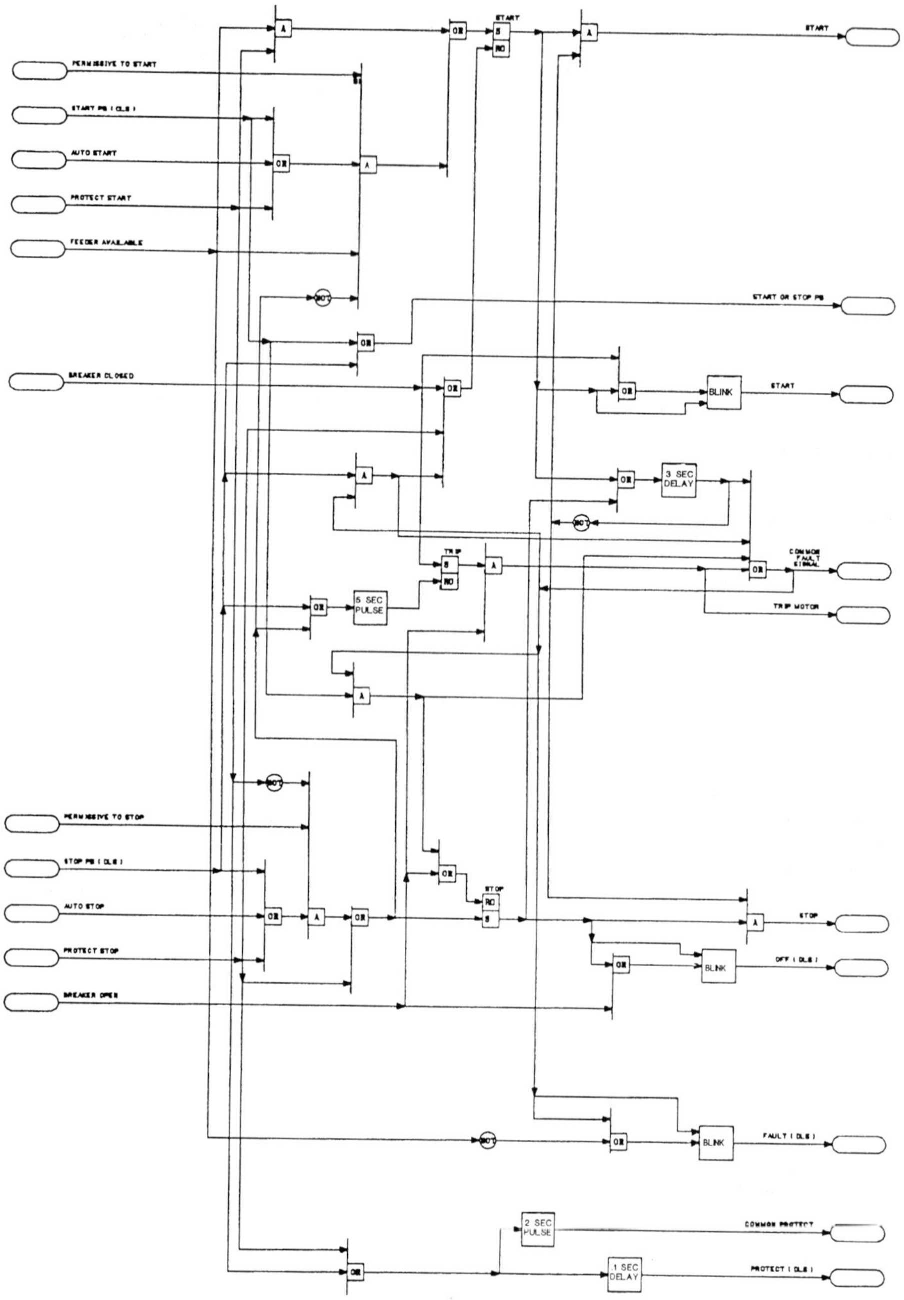

FIGURE 5 — Boolean Motor Control Logic

NEURAL NETWORK BASED REAL-TIME PRODUCTION SCHEDULING FOR INDUSTRIAL PROCESSES[1]

Li-wei Bao and Yong-zai Lu

Research Institute of Industrial Process Control, Zhejiang University, Hangzhou 310013, PRC

ABSTRACT: This paper presents an artificial neural network (ANN) based real-time production scheduling expert system existing in a hierarchical integrated computer control/production management system for some industrial processes with multi-production-stages and discreat event operations. A hierarchical neural network model has been developed to build an expert system to solve the problem under study. According to the real-time information both of status of production facilities and mass/energy flow as well as the long term production scheduling, the expert system makes the real-time production scheduling strategy, supervises the production process, and operats the production process both in normal and abnormal operating conditions. Introducing this real-time production scheduling, a computer simulation for the real-time production scheduling of a steel plate mill shows the satisfactory result.

KEY WORDS: Neural Network, Production Scheduling, Learning, Optimization, Decision Making, Heuristics, Steel Plate Mill, Expert System

INTRODUCTION

As is well known, the real-time computer production scheduling has been playing more and more important role in modern large scale industrial process to increase productivity, reduce energy consumption, and to improve the finishing products quality as well.

The problem of production scheduling could usually be regarded as three important factors (Lenstra, 1984), namely machine environment, characteristics of processing product, and optimal criteria. In other words, when constraints of facilities, raw material, and production processing requirement are given, an arrangement of production processing sequence should be done to make the desired criteria be optimal or suboptimal and to provide a real-time supervision to operation for production process. From the system point of view, real-time production scheduling could be regarded as an real-time information based decision making. It makes a long-term scheduling be production sequence arrangement, based on the production environment. In general, it is a so-called scheduling/rescheduling problem, and the rescheduling can also be worked in abnormal conditions (M. Yamamoto,1985).

An industrial process under consideration can be schematically shown in figure 1, where S_1 and S_2 represent raw material and finishing product inventories respectively, M_i represents a processing link in production chain composed by a group of several sets of facilities, R_i represents buffer joint processing links. The entire production process can be considered as a system, which can then be decomposed to several related subsystems according to the links. The computer control/production management system of the production system is shown in figure 2 (Lu, 1989). Products should go through the relevant production stage of production chain. The processing time is dependent upon the production facilities status, raw materials and products. In order to implement the smooth production rhythm, it is required to reduce two kinds of waiting time: time of raw material waiting for empty facility in buffer, time of facility waiting for works.

In this paper, substance of production scheduling problem has been analizised, and summerized up to be an optimal decision making problem. An idea of building an expert system by using ANN, and an algorithm of step by step heuristic reasoning has been presented. An ANN based expert system (ES) has been built to solve the real-time production scheduling problem. And this method has been introduced to solve a real-time production scheduling problem of a steel plate mill. Computer simulation has been done and shows the satisfactory result.It is obviously that this method could be used in other similar industrial process.

PROBLEM STATEMENT

In order to solve the problem under study, the physical system associated with the production scheduling should be converted into the relevant problem formulation with the following definitions:

Defintion 1

$$M=\{M_1, M_2,\ldots,M_N\} \quad (1)$$

M_n denotes the code of the group facility in the production stage n, n=1, N

$$R=\{R_1, R_2,\ldots,R_L\} \quad (2)$$

is the set of raw materials

$$P=\{P_1, P_2,\ldots,P_M\} \quad (3)$$

is set of the finishing products

Definition 2

[1] This project was partly supported by National Natural Science Foundation of China

$$A=\begin{array}{c} \\ R_1 \\ R_2 \\ \vdots \\ R_L \end{array}\begin{array}{c} P_1 \quad P_2 \quad \cdots \quad P_M \\ \begin{pmatrix} a_{n} & a_{12} & & a_{1M} \\ a_{21} & a_{22} & & a_{2M} \\ \vdots & & & \\ a_{L1} & a_{L2} & \cdots & a_{LM} \end{pmatrix}\end{array} \tag{4}$$

this is the matrix shows the relationship between raw materials and products.

where

$$a_{ij}=\begin{cases} 1 & \text{raw material } R_i \text{ can be used to process product } P_j \\ 0 & \end{cases} \tag{5}$$

Definition 3

$$B=\begin{array}{c} \\ M_1 \\ M_2 \\ \vdots \\ M_N \end{array}\begin{array}{c} P_1 \quad P_2 \quad \quad P_M \\ \begin{pmatrix} b_{n} & b_{12} & \cdots & b_{1M} \\ b_{21} & b_{22} & & b_{2M} \\ \vdots & & & \\ b_{N1} & b_{N2} & & b_{NM} \end{pmatrix}\end{array} \tag{6}$$

this is a matrix shows the dependence of products on facilities, where

$$b_{ij}=\begin{cases} 1 & \text{facility } M_i \text{ can be used to process product } P_j \\ 0 & \end{cases} \tag{7}$$

Definition 4

$$U=(U_1,\ U_2,\ldots,U_L)^T \tag{8}$$

is the quantities of processed work given by long-term scheduling.

$$V=(V_1,\ V_2,\ldots,V_M)^T \tag{9}$$

is the productivities given by long-term scheduling

$$M(t)=(M_1(t),\ M_2(t),\ldots,M_N(t))^T \tag{10}$$

is the productivities of facilities.

Definition 5

$$\mathfrak{D}=\{D\} \tag{11}$$

is the set of scheduling strategies. $D\in\mathfrak{D}$ is a scheduling strategy.

$$D=\{D_\lambda\} \qquad \lambda=1,2,\ldots\Lambda \tag{12}$$

is a production sequence.

$$D_\lambda=\begin{pmatrix} x_{Ri\lambda} \\ y_{Pj\lambda} \\ t_\lambda \end{pmatrix} \tag{13}$$

where $x_{Ri\lambda}$ is quantity of raw material R_i, $y_{Pj\lambda}$ is productivity of product P_j

t_λ is time of producing these products.

and

$$\sum_{\lambda=1}^{\Lambda} t_\lambda=\Delta T_k \tag{14}$$

$$\sum_{k=1}^{K} \Delta T_k=T \tag{15}$$

where T is total processing time given by long-term scheduling, ΔT_k is working time in one day.

Moreover, $T_M(n,\lambda)$ represents time of empty facility n waiting for processed work in scheduling sequence λ. $T_P(n,\lambda)$ represents time of processed work waiting for empty facility n in scheduling sequence.

According to this analyses, the production scheduling optimization problem under consideration can be described as follows:

$$\min_{D\in\mathfrak{D}} J=\sum_{\lambda=1}^{\Lambda}\sum_{n=1}^{N}[T_M(n,\lambda)+T_P(n,\lambda)] \tag{16}$$

Subject to

$$\alpha\le M(t)\le\beta \tag{17}$$

where α,β are constraints vectors

$$\sum_{k=1}^{K}\Delta T_k=T \tag{18}$$

$$\sum_{\lambda=1}^{\Lambda} t_\lambda=\Delta T_k \qquad (k=\overline{1,K}) \tag{19}$$

$$a_{ij}=1 \tag{20}$$

$$b_{jn}=1 \qquad (n=\overline{1,N}) \tag{21}$$

$$\sum_{k=1}^{K}\left(\sum_{\lambda=1}^{\Lambda} y_{Pj\lambda}\right)\Bigg|_{\Delta T_k} \ge V_j \tag{22}$$

Let $\mathfrak{D}^*\subset\mathfrak{D}$ be subset satisfying these constraints, and then the feasible set of the criteria J could be expressed as follows:

$$\min J=\min_{D\in\mathfrak{D}^*}\sum_{\lambda=1}^{\Lambda}\sum_{n=1}^{N}[T_M(n,\lambda)+T_P(n,\lambda)] \tag{23}$$

In addition, when the system works at the abnormal conditions, the maximal productivities of some facilities suddenly decrease even to zero to force the production facilities or whole line shut off. It thus must require to carry out rescheduling based on the updated production environment. It is necessary to make supervision to facilities, estimate status of facilities for predicting abnormal conditions.

ARTIFICIAL NEURAL NETWORK BASED EXPERT SYSTEM

The regular production scheduling of industrial process with discreat event could be solved by using perturbation analysis (Ho, 1983), mathematic programming (Hung, 1985), knowledge based expert system (Dai, 1987) etc. (Wu, 1987), however these methods are hardly possible to be used in real-time production scheduling. Fortunately, optimization based artificial neural network (ANN) with abilities of parallel processing,memory, and learning etc. can effectively be used to solve this problem. An ANN based expert system has been built as schematically shown in figure 3 which is different from the traditional expert system shown in figure 4.

Structure of ANN

There are many studies on ANN (Rumdhart, 1986; Allon, 1988; Hopfield, 1985). Their starting point is to imitate the information processing pattern of neural network of human being. According to the study of neurobiology (Gainer, 1977), the information transmition between neural cells is on synaps by chemical or electrical transmitions. The former neural network models are imitations to the electrical neurons activities and the model structure is shown in figure 5. For example, the learning algorithm of B-P model (Back-Propagation Model) is error back propagate correction, and its learning problem can be transformed to an nonlinear optimization problem, its learning result is weights convergence in network. But its information processing is a nonlinear mapping, not a nonlinear dynamic system. According to the study of neuropeptides, a hierarchical structure neural network model is shown in figure 6. The behavior of elementary network can be governed by high level network via controlling the weights of elementary network. The resulting network has powerful capabilities of memory and information processing, and can become a dynamic system. The learning function is performed by the learnings in two networks coordinatively. The B-P model can be used to construct the ANN. The nonlinear function in the neurons can be characterised as follows

$$f(x)=\frac{1}{1+e^{-x}} \quad (24)$$

The learning algorithm can be described in detail as follows:

Define error function as a criteria:

$$E=\tfrac{1}{2}\sum_{p}\sum_{j}(t_{pj}-O_{pj})^2 \quad (25)$$

where t_{pj} and O_{pj} are desired output and real output of the pth sample respectively. The relevant ANN optimization problem could further be expressed as follows:

$$\underset{wij}{\text{Min}}\ E=\tfrac{1}{2}\sum_{p}\sum_{j}(t_{pj}-O_{pj})^2 \qquad (p=1,P) \quad (26)$$

subject to:

$$O_{pj}=\sum_{i_1=1}^{I_1} w_{i_1 j}\, s_{i_1} \qquad j=1,\ J \quad (27)$$

$$S_{i_1}=f(net(i_1)) \qquad i_1=1,\ I_1 \quad (28)$$

$$net(i_1)=\sum_{i_2=1}^{I_2} w_{i_2 i_1}\, f(x_{i_2}) \quad (29)$$

where J is number of units of output layer
P is number of samples
S_{i_1} is output of unit of hidden layer
I_1 is number of units of hidden layer
$net(i_1)$ $i_1=1,\ I_1$ is input of hidden layer
I_2 is number of units of input layer
x_{i_2} is input of the ANN

Knowledge Representation

Knowledge in the problem under study could be represented by mathematic formulas, rules and ANN learnings. Dynamic models of facilities, optimization criteria, and constraints can be represented by mathematic formulars. The rule base is constructed by rules of judgements of status of facilities, quality of products, whether the optimization criteria is satisfied, whether the constraints are satisfied, etc.. It should be emphasized that the experience of production scheduling could be automatically learnt by ANN learning functions.

The sample rules in the rule-base can be given as follows:

If ($M_i(t)<\alpha$) THEN (LT is abnormal condition)
If ($J>J_o$) THEN (Reschaduling is needed)
If ($p_{m_1}<p_m<p_{m_2}$) THEN (Quality of product P_m is qualified)
⋮

where p_m is a quality function of product P_m, and p_{m_1}, p_{m_2} are constraints of p_m.

A scheduling strategy has been described as a sequence shown in Definition (1). A production scheduling strategy is based on the long-term scheduling and related constraints set Ω. Let LST be the long-term scheduling, then

$$D=G(\Omega,\ LST) \quad (30)$$

where G is a mapping between the original problem and relevant neural network representation. Thus the solution to the production scheduling could be converted into the ANN through finding the mapping G. Obviously, {G} is governed by the weights $\{w_{ij}\}$ in ANN.

Reasoning in Expert System

In fact, the reasoning of the ES/ANN is mainly involving a process of "association-judgement-caculation". The reasoning of the ES/ANN is implemented by heuristic search based on the constraints and learning results. During the heuristic search process, when satisfying the constraints, the search domain turns $\mathfrak{D}^*$ from $\mathfrak{D}$. The learning results being denoted as a set of $\mathfrak{F}$, which could be divided into two subset, namely, the expertise experience learnt by ES/ANN from human being, $\mathfrak{F}_1$; and the experience produced through self-learning via ES/ANN, $\mathfrak{F}_2$, Obviously,

$$\mathfrak{F}=\mathfrak{F}_1+\mathfrak{F}_2 \quad (31)$$

Moreover, the preliminarily solution set $\mathfrak{D}^{**}$ can be obtained from $\mathfrak{D}^*$. At this time, several scheduling sequences are get and an optimal scheduling sequence can be obtained by selecting a $D\in\mathfrak{D}^{**}$ with minimal J. The typical characteristics of scheduling are extracted from long-term scheduling and the relevant constraints.and then these typical characteristics are sent to ANN. According to the learning results memorized in ANN, associative thinking can be performed by ANN. The real-time information can also be processed as noted above, and the processed information then can be sent to high-level network. The operation condition could be classified by associative thinking in high-level network and the thinking results are further used to govern the behavious of elementary network by controling its weights. The output of elementary network are in the domain of $\mathfrak{D}^{**}$.

The other tasks of ES/ANN are real-time supervision and rescheduling, which are based on the production environment and the objective criteria etc..

Rescheduling consists of two parts, one is involving the scheduling in abnormal operation condition, the other is scheduling in the updated normal condition set up from the abnormal condition. The rescheduling strategies are similar to that of the regular scheduling as described above.

Learning Structure

The learning structure of hierarchical ANN can be shown in figure 7 [Bao, 1989], which consists two parts, one is so called "Initial learning" carried out by elementary network ANN_1,and the other is "associative memory" taken by high-level network ANN_2. A production scheduling strategy under a kind of environment can be learnt by ANN_1 as a sample, and this scheduling strategy is represented as the weights of ANN_1. Then the weights of ANN_1 would be sent to ANN_2 to be learnt by ANN_2. The learning result of ANN_2 is the weights of ANN_1 in difference kinds of environment. So the input of $ANN_{1,2}$ is environment factors and long-term scheduling, and the output of $ANN_{1,2}$ is the scheduling strategy under the given environment.

AN INDUSTRIAL APPLICATION CASE STUDY — THE REAL TIME PRODUCTION SCHEDULING OF THE STEEL PLATE MILL

A steel plate mill schematically shown in Figure 8 as a typical example of multi-stage-production process associated with the discreate event operation is considered as an industrial application background in this study. In this production line, there consist of a number of parallel reheating furnaces, roughing mill and finishing mill in series with related buffers between the production facilities.

The major tasks of production scheduling for this production line is to provide a smooth production rhythm with minimal energy consumption and overheated steel losses and maximal productivity for both normal and abnormal production environment, The decision making function is illustratively shown in Figure 9.

The problem of real-time production scheduling of the steel plate mill could be solved by ES/ANN. The simulation software is shown in Figure10, The part of "Information preprocessing system" is used to extract typical characteristics of production scheduling and environment, slab sizes and productivities of facilities are selected as the typical characteristic of production scheduling and environment respectively. Let N=5, L=7 in Definition 1. So in ANN_1,7units are used as input layer, 6 units are used as output layer, and 3 units are used hidden layer, and in ANN_2, 5 units are used as input layer, 39 units are used as output layer, and 4 units are used as hidden layer. A three days long-term scheduling is transformed to a mine-class real-time production scheduling, and during the supervision, two typical accidents take place, one is fault of furnace 2, the other is roller changed. Thus, the rescheduling is done by ES/ANN.

The simulation result is shown in table 1 and Figure 11.

CONCLUSION

An ANN based novel expert system is developed in this paper for solving the problem of real-time production scheduling of industrial process with multi-production-stage and discreat event. The expert system is constructed with hierarchical ANN. The merits of this hierarchical ANN based expert system could be summarized as follows:

- The problem under study could be converted of decision making of ES/ANN, and this method can be used in other similar problem of production scheduling.
- This strategy is different from the traditional method such as operation research etc., and requires less priori-knowledge, particularly, the proposed method can deal with problems with both quantitive and qualitive factors.
- It should be emphasized that it makes the decision making of ES/ANN more practicable with the performance time via learning, memory and associative thinking of ANN.

A simulation example of a steel plate mill shows it practical. But it is just a try to intraduce ANN in industrial process control/production scheduling.

REFERENCE

J.K. Lenstra A.H.G. Rinnoy Kan "New Directions in Scheduling Theory". Operation Research Letter, Vol.2, 255-259, 1984.

M. Yamamoto S.Y. Nof "Scheduling/Rescheduling in the Manufacturing Operating System Environment" Int. Journal of Production Research. Vol.23, No.4, 705-722, 1985.

Ho, Y.C. and Cao, X.R. 1983 "Perturbation Analysis and Optimization of Queueing Networks", Automatica, 19, 439-455.

Y.L. Huang, Y.Z. Lu "Dynamical Model Based Production Scheduling for Ingot Handling Process", Proc. Int. Conf. on Industrial Process Modelling and Control, Hangzhou, China, June, 1985, Vol II, 56-65.

X.D. Dai, Y.Z. Lu "An AI Heuristic Search Based Production Scheduling Strategy". Information and Control (China), Vol.16 (1987).

T.J. Wu, Y.Z. Lu "A Timed Relation Nets Based Novel Strategy for Modelling and Analysis of Dynamic Job Shop Systems", Proc. of Annual Conf. on IEEE, SMC. Alexandria, USA, Oct. 20-23, 1987.

Y.Z. Lu, L.W. Bao "An Integrated Computer Control System for Steel Plate Mill". To appear in Proc. of IFAC Symposium on Automatic of MMM, Argentina, Sept 4-8, 1989.

Hoyes-Roth. F., Waterman, D. and Lenat. D. eds "Building Expert Systems", Addison Wosley, 1983.

D.E. Rumelhart et.al. "Parallel Distribution Processing, Explorations in the Miorostructure of Congnition". MIT Press. Cambridge, MA (1986).

G. Allon, et.al. "Neural Network Architecture for Control". IEEE Control System.April, 1988.

J.J. Hopfield et.al. "Neural Computation of Decisions in Optimization Problem". Biol. Cybern. 52, 1985.

Harold Gainer "Peptides in Neurobiology" Plenum Press, 1977.

Li-wei Bao and Yong-zai Lu "A Novel Structure of Artificial Neural Network with Associate Thinking and Memory". Submitted to IEEE Trans on SMC.

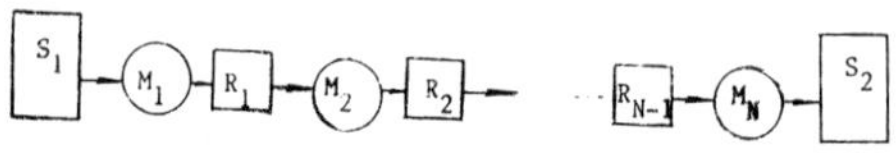

Figure 1 The path of mass flow for system Analysis

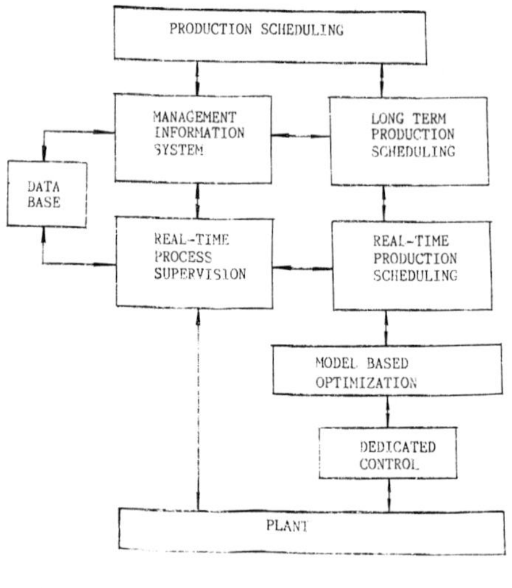

Figure 2 Hierarchical computer system configuration

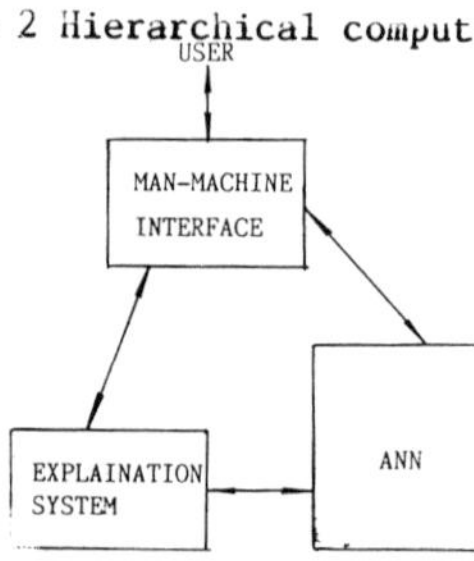

Figure 3.1 Structure of ANN Based Expert System

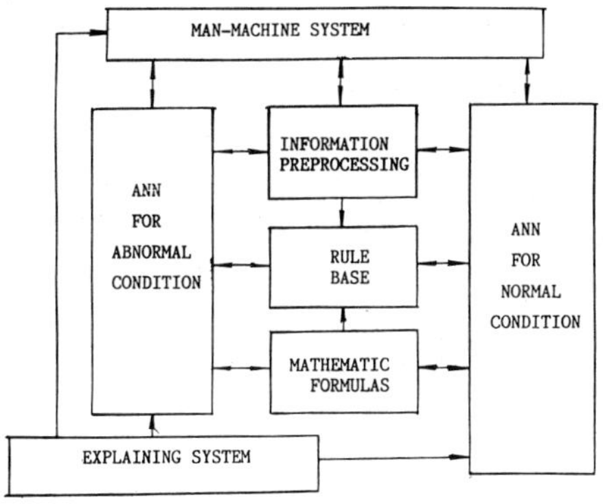

Figure 3.2 System Configuration of ES/ANN

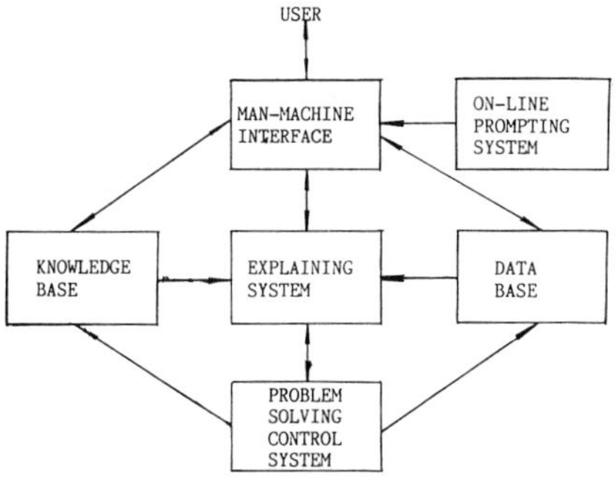

Figure 4. Structure of Traditional Expert System

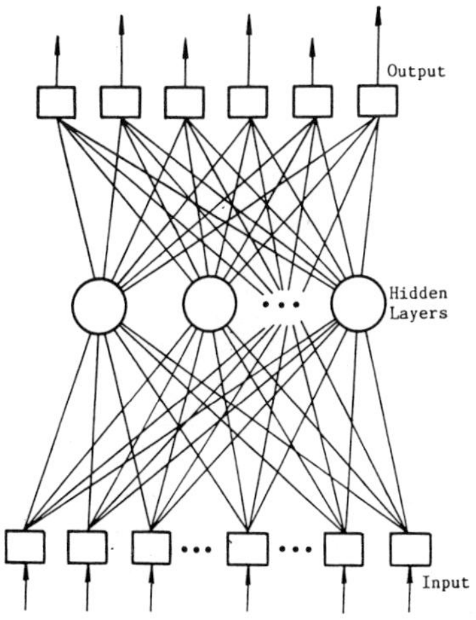

Figure 5 Topology of ANN

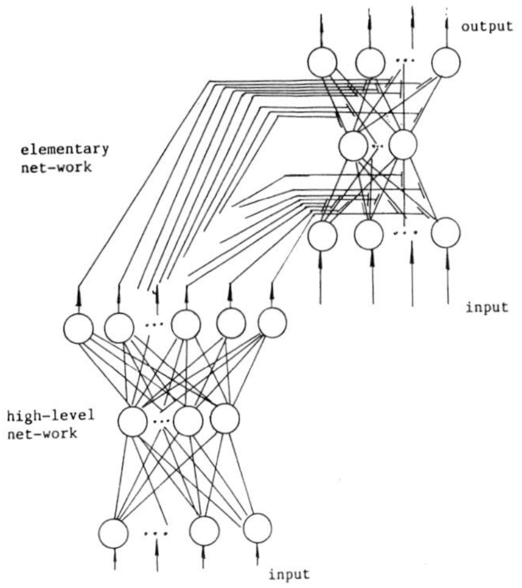

Figure 6 Structure of Hierarchical ANN

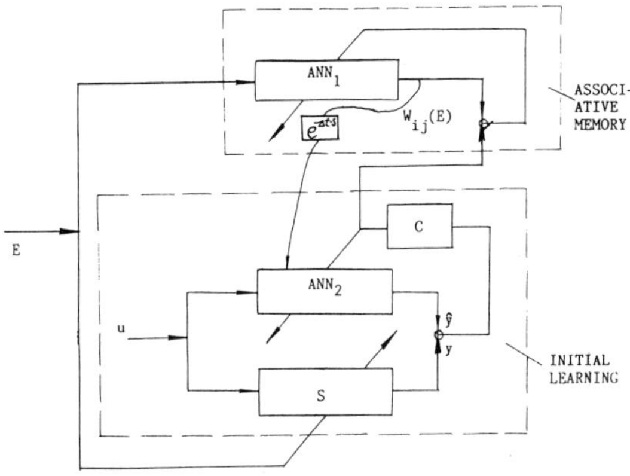

Figure 7 Learning Structure of ANN

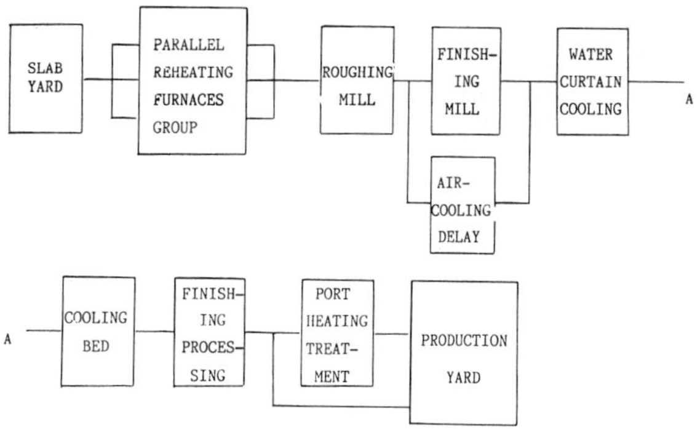

Figure 8 Schematically Production Line of a Typical Steel Plate Mill

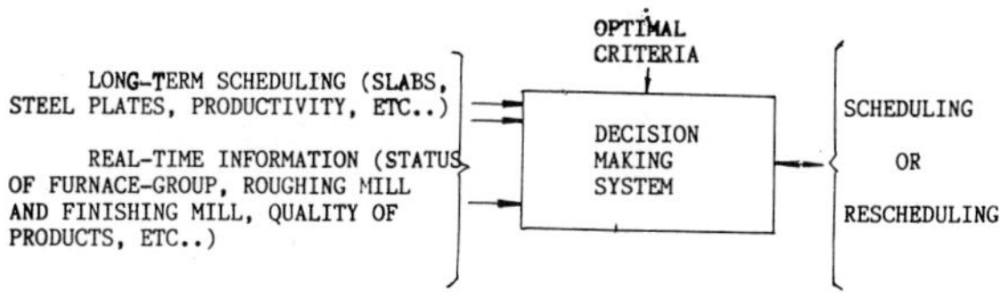

Figure 9 Decision Making Function of ES/ANN

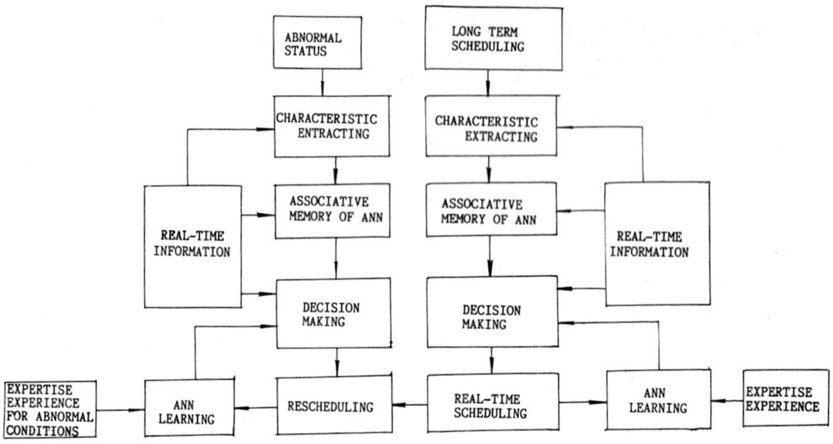

Figure 10 Software Configuration of Simulation

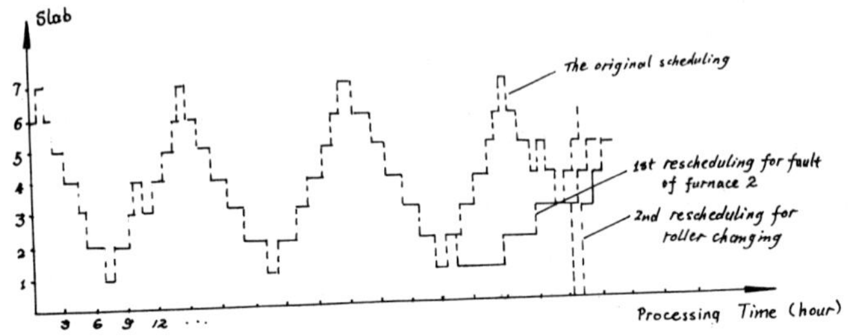

Figure 11 Scheduling and Rescheduling

SLAB	R6	R7	R6	R5		R4		R3		R2
QUANTITY	27	12	27	90		69		16		31
PRODUCT	P10	P11	P10	P9	P8	P7	P6	P5	P4	P3
QUANTITY	27	12	27	31	59	17	52	22	24	31
TIME	0.643	0.324	0.643	0.602	1.018	0.311	0.956	0.394	0.424	1.529
SLAB	R2	R1	R2		R3		R4		R3	
QUANTITY	126	66	157		46		68		29	
PRODUCT	P3	P1	P2	P3	P4	P5	P6	P7	P4	P5
QUANTITY	126	66	63	94	29	17	30	38	19	10
TIME	1.091	1.249	1.051	1.569	0.521	0.297	0.548	0.703	0.341	0.192
SLAB	R3	R4		R5		R6	R7	R6	R5	
QUANTITY	17	68		89		26	12	26	09	
PRODUCT	P5	P6	P7	P8	P9	P10	P11	P10	P9	P8
QUANTITY	16	23	45	29	60	26	12	26	51	38
TIME	0.285	0.420	0.831	0.580	1.212	0.643	0.324	0.643	1.020	0.770

FTable 1 Section of Real-time Production Scheduling

EXPERT SYSTEM FOR SENSOR FAILURE DETECTION OF AIRCRAFT

Shi Zhongke

Department of Control, Northwestern Polytechnical University, Xian, PRC

Abstract. In this paper, an expert system for the sensor failure detection and isolation of flight test system is introduced. In order to detect and locate faults of an aircraft's sensors with sufficient robustness to parameter changes and noises, an accurate discrete-time model is presented and separated-bias algorithm is used for residual sequence generation. The expert system is used for the difficult task of failure isolation and flight decision making. The results of simulation and actual application show that the expert system for the FDI(failure detection and isolation) of flight test instruments can declare the faulty and locate the failures correctly. This expert system is suitable not only to the flight regime of low angle of attack but also to the flight regime of high angle of attack.

Keywords. Expert system; failure detection; flight control; estimation; identification; flight safety; flight testing.

INTRODUCTION

A wide variety of techniques has been proposed in recent years for the detection and isolation of failures in aircraft engine output sensors and airborne flight test systems (de Silva,1982;Patton,1986). In one way or another, all these methods involve the generation of signals that are accentuated by the presence of particular failures if these failures have actually occurred.Looking into the literature on FDI based on analytical redundancy one can see that the wide variety of methods can raughly be devided into two major groups: (i) parameter estimation methods,(ii) state estimation methods. The parameter estimation approach employs on-line identification of the mathematical model in order to determine the physical coefficients of the process, the state estimation approach restricts to the on-line reconstruction of sets or subsets of state or measured variables taking the mathematical model to be given. This is done with the aid of observer or extended Kalman filters whose estimates or innovations are then used for residual generation. In practice, there are two weak points in the parameter estimation approach. First, what is really identified are not the physical coefficients of the process but the parameters of its mathematical model. These actually depend on the choise of the model and there is in general no unique relationship backward from the mathematical parameters to the physical coefficients. Second, though well apt for simple cases, the standard parameter estimation method fail when the process contains nonlinearities. Most of the FDI methods have therefore adopted the state estimation approach. Since biases and unknown scale factors are usually presented in flight test data, these instrumentation errors must also be estimated. The biases and scale factors are usually considered as components of a so-called augmented state vector. Then extended Kalman filter is used for both the state and biases estimation. This approach, however, may be unable to declare the faulty and locate the failures correctly because big modeling errors may often appear when aircraft maneuver especially when high angle-of-attack maneuvers and because it is too difficult for the ordinary approach to achive on-line state estimation (Shi, 1989; Wang, 1988). On the other hand, failure isolation and flight decision are also very difficult taskes. For these reasons an accurate discrete-time model and a robust residual generation method are presented and an expert system for the FDI of flight test system is introduced.

MODEL FOR FLIGHT STATE ESTIMATION

The mathematical model used for flight state estimation is described, in general, by three sets of kinematic equations with the state variables consisting of three linear velocities u, v, and w; three position angles θ, φ, and ψ; and altitude h. The input variables in the equations are the linear accelerations A_x, A_y, and A_z and anglar rates p, q, and r. The kinematic equations are formulated as

$$\left.\begin{aligned}
\dot{u} &= -qw + rv - g\sin\theta + Ax \\
\dot{v} &= -ru + Pw + g\sin\varphi\cos\theta + Ay \\
\dot{w} &= -Pv + qu + g\cos\varphi\cos\theta + Az \\
\dot{\psi} &= (r\cos\varphi + q\sin\varphi)/\cos\theta \\
\dot{\theta} &= q\cos\varphi - r\sin\varphi \\
\dot{\varphi} &= P + q\sin\varphi tg\theta + r\cos\varphi tg\theta \\
\dot{h} &= u\sin\theta - v\sin\varphi\cos\theta - w\cos\varphi\cos\theta
\end{aligned}\right\} \quad (1)$$

Since all variables are sampled, a discrete time filter will be applied to process the measurements. Usually, the nonlinear equations (1) are first linearized and then transformed into discrete-time versions. Big modelling errors may often appear when aircraft maneuvers. In order to decrease modelling errors, this present paper introduces a exact discrete-time model for state estimation.

Integrating equation (1), we obtained the exact discrete-time model.

$$\left.\begin{aligned}
X_{1,k+1} &= X_{1,k} - F^T \int_{KT}^{(K+1)^T} A^T \Phi(t,KT)\, dt\, X_{2,k} - gF^T \int_{KT}^{(K+1)^T} A^T \int_{KT}^{t} \Phi(t,\tau)(u_1+AF)\, d\tau\, dt \\
X_{2,k+1} &= \Phi[(K+1)T,KT]\, X_{2,k} + g\int_{KT}^{(K+1)^T} \Phi[(K+1)T,t](u_1+AF)\, dt \\
\theta_{k+1} &= \theta_k + \int_{KT}^{(K+1)^T} [q,r].\, Bdt.\, C \\
\varphi_{k+1} &= \varphi_k + \int_{KT}^{(K+1)^T} Pdt + \int_{KT}^{(K+1)^T} tg\theta.B.dt.C \\
\psi_{k+1} &= \psi_k + \int_{KT}^{(K+1)^T} B/\cos\theta.dt.\, C
\end{aligned}\right\} \quad (2)$$

$\Phi(t,\tau)$ the state-transition matrix of $\dot{X}=EX$

and

$$E = \begin{bmatrix} 0 & r & -q \\ -r & 0 & p \\ q & -p & 0 \end{bmatrix} \quad X_1 = h, \quad X_2 = [u,v,w]^T \quad X_3 = [\theta, \varphi, \psi]^T$$

$$u_1 = [n_x, n_y, n_z]^T, \quad u_2 = [P, q, r]^T$$

$$F^T = [\cos\theta_k, \sin\theta_k \sin\varphi_k, \sin\theta_k \cos\varphi_k, -\sin\theta_k, \cos\theta_k \sin\varphi_k, \cos\theta_k \cos\varphi_k]$$

$$A = \begin{bmatrix} 1 & 0 \\ 0 & B^T \end{bmatrix} [-I\sin\Delta\theta_k, I\cos\Delta\theta_k]$$

$$B = \begin{bmatrix} \cos\Delta\varphi_k & -\sin\Delta\varphi_k \\ \sin\Delta\varphi_k & \cos\Delta\varphi_k \end{bmatrix}, \quad C = \begin{bmatrix} \cos\varphi_k \\ \sin\varphi_k \end{bmatrix}$$

$$\Delta\theta_k = \theta - \theta_k, \quad \Delta\varphi_k = \varphi - \varphi_k$$

It is considered that the following variables are measured:

(1) The inputs to the system A_x, A_y, A_z ($A_x = gn_x, A_y = gn_y, A_z = gn_z$), p, q, and r;

(2) The airspeed V, two incidenco angles α and β, three position angles θ, φ, and ψ, and altitude h (these variables represent the outputs of the system).

The measured variables are corrupted by systematic and random errors. It is, therefore, assumed that

$$u_1 = (I+\Lambda_1)u_{1,m} + b_{u1} + \eta_1 = \bar{u}_1 + \eta_1$$
$$u_2 = (I+\Lambda_2)u_{2,m} + b_{u2} + \eta_2 = \bar{u}_2 + \eta_2$$

where u_1 and u_2 are the true values of the inputs, Λ_1 and Λ_2 the unknown scale factor matrices, b_{u1} and b_{u2} the constant biases, and η_1 and η_2 the measurement noise vectors, and

$\Lambda_1=\mathrm{diag}[\lambda_x, \lambda_y, \lambda_z]$,

$b_{u1}=[b_x, b_y, b_z]^T$,

$\Lambda_2=\mathrm{diag}[\lambda_p, \lambda_q, \lambda_r]$

$b_{u2}=[b_p, b_q, b_r]^T$

Substitution of equations into equation (2) yields the discrete-time model for the state estimation:

$$X_{k+1}=M_{k+1,k}X+u_x(\bar{u}_1,\bar{u}_2)+B_k b + \Gamma\int_{KT}^{(K+1)T}\begin{bmatrix}\eta_1\\ \eta_2\end{bmatrix}dt \qquad (3)$$

where

$$X^T=[\Delta h, u, v, w, \theta, \varphi]$$

$$M_{k+1,k}=\begin{pmatrix}1 & f_{12} & f_{13}\\ 0 & \Phi[(K+1)T,KT] & f_{23}\\ 0 & 0 & f_{33}\end{pmatrix}$$

$$u_x=[u_{x1}^T(\bar{u}_1), u_{x2}^T(\bar{u}_1,\bar{u}_2), u_{x3}^T(\bar{u}_2)]^T$$

$$b=[b_{u1}^T, b_{u2}^T, \lambda_x, \lambda_y, \lambda_z, \lambda_p, \lambda_q, \lambda_r]^T$$

u_x is not relevant to the states; $f_{12}, f_{13}, f_{23}, f_{33}$ may be carried out from the equation (2).

The output equations take the forms

$$Y_{im}=h_i(X_i,u_1,u_2,b_i)+V_i \quad i=1,2,3 \qquad (4)$$

where $y_1=h$, $y_2=[V_0, \beta, \alpha]^T$ $y_3=[\theta, \varphi, \psi]^T$

$$\bar{b}_1=[b_h, \lambda_h]^T, \quad \bar{b}_3=[b_\theta, b_\varphi, b_\psi]^T$$

$$\bar{b}_2=[b_v, b_\beta, b_\alpha, \lambda_v, \lambda_\beta, \lambda_\alpha]^T$$

and

$$V=[\eta_h, \eta_v, \eta_\beta, \eta_\alpha, \eta_\theta, \eta_\varphi, \eta_\psi]^T$$

Letting $\xi_K=\int_{KT}^{(K+1)T}\begin{bmatrix}\eta_1\\ \eta_2\end{bmatrix}dt$,

and assuming

$$E\{\xi_k\}=0, \quad E\{V_k\}=0, \quad E\{\xi_k V_j^T\}=0$$

$$E\{\xi_k\xi_j^T\}=\delta_{kj}Q_k, \quad E\{V_k V_j^T\}=\delta_{kj}R_k$$

equations (3) and (4) can be used for the state estimation and residual generation.

METHOD FOR ROBUST RESIDUAL GENERATION

Usually, the biases and scale errors are considered as components of a so-called augmented state vector in the most methods of flight state estimation. In the augmented-state implementation the overall process is of the order n_1+n_2, where the number of dynamic state variables (i.e., the dimension of X) is n_1, the number of biases (the dimension of b) is n_2, and the n_1+n_2 variables are all coupled, in the filter and in the covariance matrix propagation. Evidently, it is too difficult for this approach to achieve real-time flight state estimation. In the bias-separated implementation (Friedland, 1983), the maximum dimension one needs to be concerned with is the larger of n_1 or n_2, and errors in the estimation of the biases do not contaminate the estimation of the bias-free estimate of the dynamic state. Theoretical study and actual application show that the bias-separated filter implementation would require fewer numerical operation than the augmented-state one and may be to avoid numerical ill-conditioning. For this reason, separated bias identification and state estimation method would be chosen as the basic algorithm of real-time flight state estimation and residual generation.

Since the matrix $M_{k+1,k}$ of equation (3) is upper trianglar, Hierarchical techniques are used in this present paper to get high computational efficiency.

Letting $b_1=\bar{b}_1$, $b_2=[b_{u1}, \bar{b}_2, \lambda_x, \lambda_y, \lambda_z]^T$

$$b_3=[b_{u2}, \bar{b}_3, \lambda_p, \lambda_q, \lambda_r]^T$$

Expanding the nonlinear equation (4) in Taylor series expansion, we obtained

$$Y_{i,k+1}=H_{i,k+1}X_{i,k+1}+D_{i,k+1}b_i+e_{i,k+1}+V_{i,k+1} \qquad (5)$$

where the matrices $H_{i,k+1}$ and $D_{i,k+1}$ are defined by

$$H_{i,k+1}=\left.\frac{\partial h_i(X_i,u_1,u_2,b_i)}{\partial X_i}\right|_{X_{i,k+1/k},\, b_{i,k}}$$

$$D_{i,k+1}=\left.\frac{\partial h_i(X_i,u_1,u_2,b_i)}{\partial b_i}\right|_{X_{i,k+1/k},\, b_{i,k}}$$

and $i=1,2,3$

$$e_{i,k+1}=h_i(X_i,u_1,u_2,b_i)-H_{i,k+1}X_{i,k+1/k}-D_{i,k+1}b_{i,k}$$

Thus on the basis of stochastic vector difference equation (3) and measurement equation (5), flight state and biases can be estimated by using separated bias identification and state estimation algorithm.

The time update equations are

$$\left.\begin{aligned}&b_{i,k+1/k}=b_{i,k} \qquad i=1,2,3\\&P_{bi,k+1/k}=P_{bi,k/k}\\&X_{k+1/k}=M_{k+1,k}X_{k/k}+u_x(\bar{u}_1,\bar{u}_2)+B_{k+1}b_k\\&P_{o,k+1/k}=M_{k+1,k}P_{o,k/k}M^T_{k+1,k}+\Gamma_k Q_k\Gamma^T_k\end{aligned}\right\} \quad (6)$$

The measurement update of bias-free state estimates

$$\left.\begin{aligned}&X_{0i,k+1/k+1}=X_{i,k+1/k}+K_{0i,k+1}\hat{e}_{i,k+1}\\&K_{0i,k+1}=P_{0i,k+1}H_{i,k+1}R^{-1}_{i,k+1}\\&P_{0i,k+1}=(I-K_{0i,k+1}H_{i,k+1})P_{0i,k+1/k}\end{aligned}\right\} \quad (7)$$

$$i=1,2,3$$

The measurement update of b

$$\left.\begin{aligned}&b_{i,k+1}=b_{i,k}+K_{bi,k+1}\hat{e}_{i,k+1}\\&K_{bi,k+1}=P_{bi,k+1/k+1}(H_{i,k+1}V_{bi,k/k-1}+D_{i,k+1})^T R^{-1}_{k+1}\\&P^{-1}_{bi,k+1/k+1}=P^{-1}_{bi,k/k}+C^T_{i,k+1/k}(H_{i,k+1}P_{0i,k+1/k}H^T_{i,k+1}+R_{k+1})^{-1}C_{i,k+1/k} \qquad i=1,2,3\end{aligned}\right\}$$

where (8)

$$C_{i,k+1}=H_{i,k+1}U_{i,k}+D_{i,k+1}$$

$$U_{i,k}+M_{i,k+1,k}V_{bi,k/k-1}+B_{i,k}$$

$$V_{bi,k+1/k}=U_{i,k}-K_{0i,k+1}C_{i,k+1}$$

$$\hat{e}_{i,k+1}=y_{im,k+1}-h_i(X_{i,k+1/k},\bar{u}_1,\bar{u}_2,b)$$

$$i=1,2,3$$

and

$$M_{1,k+1,k}=1, \quad M_{2,k+1,k}=\Phi[(K+1)T,KT]$$

$$M_{3,k+1,k}=f_{33}$$

The measurement update of X_i

$$X_{i,k+1/k+1}=X_{0,k+1/k+1}+V_{bi,k+1/k}K_{bi,k+1}\hat{e}_{i,k+1} \quad (9)$$

In the equations (6)-(9) subscript '0' represents the 'bias-free' state estimator and subscript 'b' bias estimator; $X_{i,k+1/k}$ can also be calculated by using numerical integration of Runge-Kutta type.

The state estimation error equations can be written as follows

$$E_{i,k+1}=M_{i,k+1,k}E_{i,k}+S_{k+1}-(K_{0i,k+1}+V_{bi,k+1/k})E_{i,k}$$

where

$$S=\mathrm{sign}(E_{i,k+1})\, b^T_{i,k}b_{i,k}$$

BASIC STRUCTURE OF EXPERT SYSTEM

The goal of FDI is to detect and locate failures of the sensors of flight test instruments with sufficient robustness to system parameter changes and noise. Sensor faulty must be distinguished from 'wild' data firstly. Otherwise, what is really detected may not be the sensor failures of flight test system but the effects of the 'wild' data. The output sensor faulty is also distinguished from computed output faulty to get high efficiency of failure isolation. The basic idea of the design of the expert system is as follows. First, the residuals are compared with predetermined thresholds. If the residuals of certain sensors remain below the thresholds the corresponding sensors are declared unfaulty; if the residual surpasses the threshold the expert system first distinguishes the fault from the effects of 'wild' data. If the fault occurs, the inference engine will carry out what kind of the fault may be, the measured output or computed output? If the measured output is fault the corresponding instrument is declared faulty and an alarm is released. If the computed output is fault sensitivity to process parameter or state variations is calculated and the results are given to the expert system. The expert system may accomplish the difficult task of failure isolation and flight decision making. In order to detect the failures of the instruments in various flight test the thresholds may actually be made adaptive to the flight maneuver shapes and to the flight regimes of both low and high angle of attck. Thus the expert system, ES can be structured.

Data base: The data base of the expert system should include the aerodynamic models of aircraft to be test; the experiential threshold values; the inputs of elevator deflection, aileron deflection, rudder deflection, and other control deflections; flight parameters. These data may be used to (1) distinguish sensor failure from 'wild' data; (2) distinguish the fault of measured output and computed output. Knowledge base and inference engine may directly use any of the experimental data in the data base.

Knowledge base: The function of the knowledge base is to provide knowledge sources to the inference engine of the expert system. In general the fault may be one of the following three cases:

(1) Measured output is correct, computed output is fault;

(2) Measured output is fault, computed output is correct;

(3) Both measured output and computed output are all fault.

The knowledge base can provide the knowledge source of distinction between 'wild' data and failures and the knowledge source of distinction measured output error from computed output error. Since the threshold logic is a most simple and common decision strategy, the thresholds should actually be changed in different flight test and flight maneuvers. In the knowledge base the threshold may be made adaptive to the flight maneuvers and to the angle of attack on the basis of the knowledge source of the experiences of many knowledge engineers.

The knowledge base may have the explanation function. When fault occurs, the inference engine will indicate the failures of certain sensors and the commander or aviator can ask 'why the conclusion is carried out' and other questions.

The knowledge base is also of the function of knowledge acquisition. For more experienced users, the engineer will be allowed to enter facts into the knowledge base. In order to make decision for flight, the knowledge source and commander's idea will directly give to inference engine.

The nodes of the knowledge base are the posibilities of the sensor failures of three position angles θ , φ , and ψ; three linear accelerations A_x, A_y, and A_z; three anglar rates p,q, and r; two incidence angles α and β ; airspeed V, and altitude h.

Inference engine: The function of inference engine is to isolate failures and make flight decision on the basis of knowledge base and data base combining the decision of flight commander. In order to judge between measured output fault and computed output fault, the other instrumentation errors should be checked further.

(1) When the residual of airspeed V surpasses the threshold, θ, α, β, φ, and h should be cheked;

(2) When the residual of angle of attack α surpasses the threshold, w,h, θ, φ, and u should be checked;

(3) When the residual of angle of sideslip β surpasses the threshold, u, v, h, θ, φ and ψ should be checked;

(4) When the residual of altitude h surpasses the threshold, u, v, w, θ, and φ should be checked;

(5) When the residual of pitch angle θ surpasses the threshold, q, r, and φ should be checked;

(6) When the residual of roll angle φ surpasses the threshold, p, q, r, and θ should be checked;

(7) When the residual of yaw angle ψ surpasses the threshold, q, r, θ, and φ should be checked;

(8) When the residuals of accelerations surpass the thresholds, V, u, v, w should be checked;

(9) When the residual of roll rate p surpasses the threshold, v, w, and φ should be checked;

(10) When the residual of pitch rate q surpasses the threshold, u, w, θ, φ, and ψ should be checked;

(11) When the residual of yaw rate r surpasses the threshold, u, v, θ, φ, and ψ should be checked.

For example, is the fault of computed pitch angle were caused by the fault of pitch rate, the residuals of φ, u, w, and ψ should all surpass the corresponding thresholds; otherwise the sensor of pitch rate would be unfaulty.

The basic structure of FDI for flight test system is shown in Fig. 1.

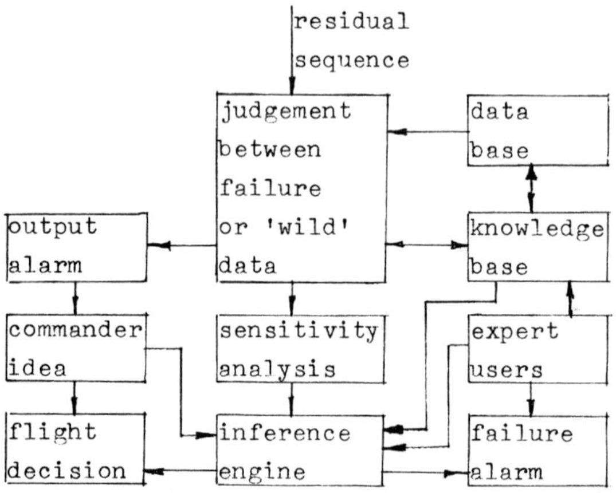

Fig. 1. Basic Structure of Expert System for FDI of Flight.

In Fig. 1 the residual sequece is generated in bias-separated estimator.

SIMULATION AND APPLICATION

The expert system for the FDI of flight test system has been simulated in flight data acquisition system. The results of simulation and actual application show that the estimator of flight state can give robust residual generation and the expert system can declare the faulty and locate failures correctly. Some applications of the flight test of high angle of attack show that this expert system is suitable to the flight regimes of both low and high angle of attack. Fig. 2 shows the results of FDI of the expert system.

CONCLUSION

A expert system for FDI is presented in this paper. The new method has been simulated in Chinese Flight Test Center. Various applications show that the expert system can correctly declare the faulty and locate the failures. For more experienced users this expert system may be improved further.

REFERENCES

Friedland, B. (1983). In C.T. Leondes (Ed.), Control and Dynamic Systems, Vol. 20, 1-45.

Patton, R.J. and others. (1986). AIAA Nav., Gui. and Contr. Conf. Williamsburg.

Shi Zhongke and Wang Peide (1989). Chinese Aero. et astr. sinica. Vol. 10.

de Silva, C.W. (1982). Arabian J. Sci. and Eng. Vol. 7, pp45-53.

Wang P.D. and others (1988). 4TH IFAC Symposium on CADCS, Peijing.

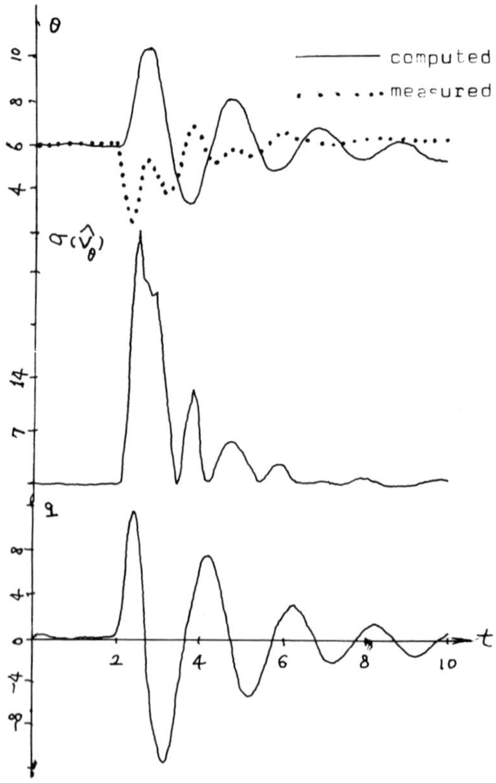

Fig. 2. Result of FDI Of Expert System t=2.3sec, alarm is released.

APPLICATION OF EXPERT FUZZY CONTROLLER IN THE PENICILLIN FERMENTATION PROCESSES

E-hui Xu*, Guo-hua Xu and Shi-liang Zhang****

**Mold High Tech Institute, Zhejiang University, Hangzhou, 310027, PRC*
***Department of Automatic Control, East China Institute of Chemical Technology, Shanghai, 200237, PRC*

Abstract: The expert fuzzy control system of the penicillin fermentation processes is developed in the paper which can recognize different fermentation phases and adopt related control strategies. Feed rates are controlled according to PH value and penicillin productive rate. The fuzzy control models of sugar feed rate are established. Finally, two illustrative examples are given to show that the control strategies developed is feasible and reliable for real plants.

Keywords: penicillin fermentation process, phase recognition, rule base, FLC, expert system, expert fuzzy control, feed rates control

INTRODUCTION

Modelling and control of penicillin fermentation processes is one of the most challenging problems for control engineers. The difficulty is due to the poorly understanding of the underlying processes. To control a fermentation process, one must face to three major problems:

1) measurements are unavailable for some of the critical variables;

2) lack of knowledge of process principles;

3) the fermentation processes are irreversible and very sensitive to environment, and have serious non-linear and time-variant behaviours.

Therefore, it is difficult to describe the process with conventional mathematical model and the related approaches of modern control theory which require accurate process model are not effective in the area. Generally, automatic control is applied only to the subsidiary process variables which can be measured and controlled, e.g. temperatures, pressures and flow rates. The control of the major process variables, such as PH, are still depend on the operators.

Fuzzy Logic Controllers (FLC) simulate the way that a qualified operator makes decision. The control strategy is based on human's experiences and qualitative knowledge. Fuzzy logic controller does not require the accurate mathematical model of the process. It is testified an effective approach to deal with uncertainty. But the structure of FLC is too simple and the rule language of regular FLCs is not expressive enough to capture the heuristic knowledge needed to control complex processes.

Expert System has abundant formats for knowledge expression and a reasonable mechanism for organizing and using knowledge. The approach emphasizes the need for multiple levels and categories of knowledge and flexible computer architectures for reasoning with this knowledge.

If the technique of expert system is introduced into FLC to form the so called Expert Fuzzy Controller (EFC), the new controller may obviously enrich the structure and content of the knowledge that is available to the FLC, while the flexibility of FLC remains. Thus, EFCs are more general in scope and are capable of handling more complex control problems.

In this paper, a Expert Fuzzy Controller will be developed for the penicillin fermentation process. The structure of the system proposed will be discussed in the following sections, and examples will be given to show that the system is feasible and reliable for real plants.

PROBLEM FORMULATION

PH value is a very important condition for mycelial growth and penicillin biosynthesis. The main task of the control system is to keep the PH value in the optimal range in each fermentation phase in order to provide the most suitable condition for penicillin production.

The set of control variables is composed of the following three elements:

. sugar feed rate
. acid feed rate
. alkali feed rate

So, the problem statement of control task can be described below in principle:

$$\min_{x1,x2,x3} \sum_{k=1}^{N} (\hat{PH} - PH)_k^2 \qquad (1)$$

where x1: sugar feed rate
x2: acid feed rate
x3: alkali feed rate
$\hat{PH}$: value given by experts
PH: measurement from real plant

Meanwhile, precursor feed rate is regulated to maintain the stable productive rate of penicillin.

THE STRUCTURE OF THE EFC

Based on the characteristics of the penicillin fermentation process, the structure of the control system is proposed (Fig.1), which can be divided into the following six functional blocks:

- data acquisition
- fermentation phase recognition
- rule base
- reasoning mechanism
- executive mechanism
- man-machine interface

FERMENTATION PHASE RECOGNITION

The period of penicillin fermentation process is normally 140 to 160 hours, and the whole process is generally divided into four phases:

- adaptive phase
- growing phase
- productive phase
- degenerative phase

Because the process states, the needs for nutrient (sugar, PAA, et al) and the control strategies are different in each phase, it is necessary to recognize what fermentation phase the process is in and then the related control strategy may be adopted.

The fermentation phase recognition method used here is the simple pattern match strategy in conventional expert systems.

Suppose that u11, u12, u13 and u14 are the feature subsets of fermentation time (T), and u1=(u11,u12,u13,u14) is the feature set. Similarly, assume that u2=(u21,u22, u23,u24) is the feature set of the percent concentration of mycelial volume (PCV), u3=(u31,u32,u33,u34) is the feature set of penicillin productive rate (HP), then the rules for pattern recognition are given below:

IF < T ∈ u11 and PCV ∈ u21 and HP ∈ u31 >
THEN < control strategy for
adaptive phase >

IF < T ∈ u21 and HP ∈ u32 or PCV ∈ u22 >
THEN < control strategy for
growing phase >

IF < T ∈ u13 and PCV ∈ u23 or HP ∈ u33 >
THEN < control strategy for
productive phase >

IF < T ∈ u14 and PCV ∈ u24 or HP ∈ u34 >
THEN < control strategy for
degenerative phase >

CONSTRUCTION OF RULE BASE

Rule base contains three groups of rules which are used to recognize fermentation phases, select control variables and calculate control actions respectively. PH value and penicillin productive rate HP are the major controlled variables of the fermentation process. In general, PH value is controlled by sugar feed rate. Once PH value is too high or too low, it is regulated by feeding acid or alkali.

Sugar feed rate is the most important control variable of the process. But there is not explicit functional relations between PH value and sugar feed rate. So the fuzzy relations are developed to describe the process.

Suppose D11 and D12 are the fuzzy sets of PH and its variation △PH for feeding sugar respectively. Similarly, D21 and D22 are the fuzzy sets for feeding acid, and D31 and D32 are the fuzzy sets for feeding alkali. The rule set for selecting control variables can be described below:

IF < PH ∈ D11 and △PH ∈ D12 >
THEN < control strategy for
feeding sugar >

ELSE
IF < PH ∈ D21 and △PH ∈ D22 >
THEN < control strategy for
feeding acid >

ELSE
IF < PH ∈ D31 and △PH ∈ D32 >
THEN < control strategy for
feeding alkali >

The penicillin productive rate (HP) determines the feed rate of precursor (PAA). If D41 and D42 are the fuzzy set of HP and its variation △HP, the rule set of control the PAA feed rate is following:

IF < HP ∈ D41 and △HP ∈ D42 >
THEN < control strategy for
feeding PAA >
ELSE < stop feeding PAA >

CONTROL STRATEGY

Sugar feed rate is the major control variable of fermentation process. Based on the experience of the operators and the historical record data of the real plant, a hybrid scheme of reference track prediction and fuzzy feedback regulation is employed. The control algorithm of sugar feed rate is given as following:

$$F(K+1) = F(K) + R(K+1) + \bar{K}_i(PH,\triangle PH) \times F_i \qquad i = 1, 2, 3 \qquad (2)$$

where F(k+1) is the sugar feed rate at the (k+1)th instant, R(k+1) is the predictive increment of sugar feed rate by reference track. $\bar{K}_i(PH,\triangle PH)$ represents the fuzzy regulation factor which is looked up from the fuzzy look-up table of the ith fermentation phase. In (2), i=1,2,3 stands for growing phase, productive phase and degenerative phase respectively. In adaptive phase, the sugar feed rate is constant. The fuzzy look-up tables for different fermentation phases are shown in Appendix.

The control strategies for feed acid and alkali are very simple. If PH > 7.1, acid is feed at the feed rate F1 until PH value drops into the normal range. If PH value is too low, alkali is feed at a feed rate F2 (F1, F2 are experiential values.) until PH value return to the normal range.

Precursor feed rate is calculated according to the following experiential formula.

$$F_{PAA}(A)=\begin{cases} F^{\circ}_{PAA} & \triangle HP > (\triangle HP)_1 \\ F^{\circ}_{PAA} \times \triangle HP/(\triangle HP)_1 & (\triangle HP)_2 \leqslant \triangle HP \leqslant (\triangle HP)_1 \\ F^{\circ}_{PAA} \times (\triangle HP)_2/(\triangle HP)_1 & \triangle HP < (\triangle HP)_2 \end{cases} \quad (3)$$

SIMULATION RESULTS

The system discussed above is developed for a real plant in industry, and it is in the stage of off-line monitor and guide now. The analytic data are inputted to the system in constant period by the operators. Every half an hour, the computer calculates and outputs the new feed rates to the executive mechanism.

To show how the expert fuzzy controller works, the measurements given by real plant about PH values and related sugar feed rates are presented in Fig.2 and Fig.3, where F_{g1} is the sugar feed rate calculated by EFC, and F_{g2} is the sugar feed rate given by the operators. It is obvious that EFC can supervise the process continuously, and the sugar feed rate for the control of the PH value can be regulated quickly and smoothly.

The penicillin productive rates and the corresponding precursor feed rates are illustrated in Fig.4 and Fig.5.

From the simulation results shown above, it can be seen that the control strategy of EFC based on a large quantity of experiences may be more skillful and reliable than any individual operator, and the control accuracy may be improved. It can be expected that the control system may provide significant economic benefits in industry.

CONCLUSIONS

In this paper, a kind of EFC control strategy is developed through introducing the technique of expert system in the conventional fuzzy logic controller for the penicillin fermentation process. The system proposed can recognize different fermentation phases and adopt the proper control strategy. Multiple feed rates such as sugar feed rate, acid and alkali feed rates and precursor feed rate can be calculated automatically. Particularly, a hybrid control scheme of reference track prediction and fuzzy feedback regulation is proposed for sugar feed rate in order to achieve a better and more reliable control performance.

Two illustrative examples show that the EFC designed is feasible and effective for the control of the penicillin fermentation process.

REFERENCES

Curleysmith,S.W., Fox,R.I., Fermentation instrumentation and control, in: Advances in biotechnological Processes, Miznaki,A.,Van Wezel,A.L., Eds., Vol.3, p23, 1984

Mandani,E.H., Application of fuzzy algorithms for the control of a dynamic plant, Computer, vol.C-26, p107, 1977

Tong,R.M., A retrospective view of fuzzy control systems, Fuzzy Sets & syst., vol.14, p199, 1984

Roth,F.H., et al, Building expert systems, Addision-Weisley Publishing Company, Inc., 1983

Xingyan W.,et al, Technology of antibiotic production, Chemical Industry Publishing Company, 1982 (in Chinese)

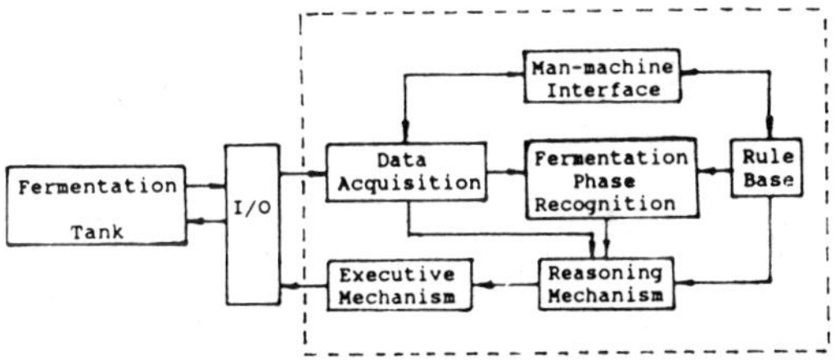

Fig.1 The structure of the EFC

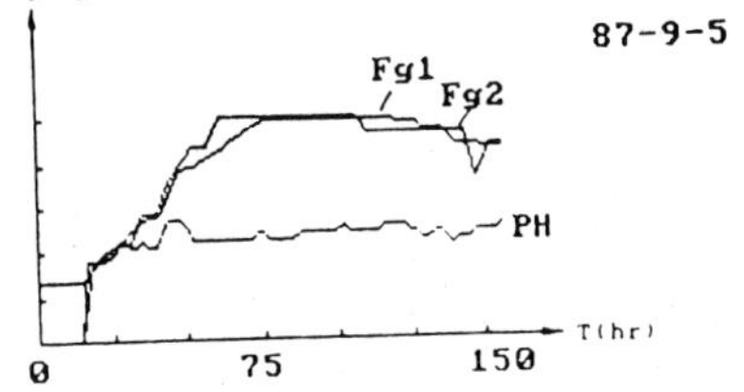

Fig.2 comparison between the control actions computed by the EFC and provided by operator

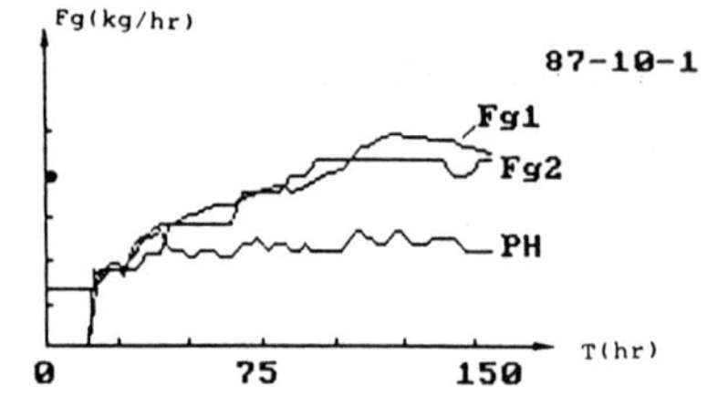

Fig.3 comparison between the control actions computed by the EFC and provided by operator

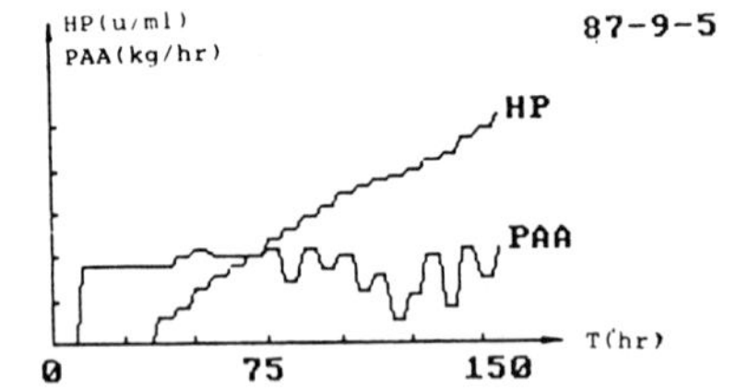

Fig.4 Productive rate of penicillin and corresponding precursor feed rate

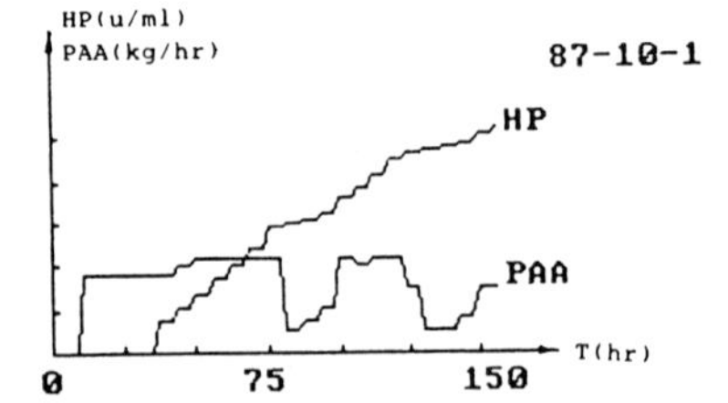

Fig.5 Productive rate of penicillin and corresponding precursor feed rate

APPENDIX

Table 1. Fuzzy look-up table for growing phase $\bar{K}_1$

$\bar{K}_1$ \ E / $\dot{E}$	-5	-4	-3	-2	-1	-0	+0	1	2	3	4	5
5	-2	-1	0	0	0	0	0	1	2	3	5	5
4	-2	-1	0	0	0	0	0	1	2	3	5	5
3	-2	-2	0	0	0	0	0	0	2	3	4	5
2	-3	-2	0	0	0	0	0	0	1	2	4	5
1	-3	-2	-1	0	0	0	0	0	1	2	3	4
0	-4	-3	-1	0	0	0	0	0	1	2	3	4
-1	-5	-3	-1	-1	0	0	0	0	0	1	2	3
-2	-5	-4	-2	-1	-1	0	0	0	0	1	2	3
-3	-5	-4	-2	-2	-1	0	0	0	0	0	1	2
-4	-5	-5	-3	-3	-2	-1	0	0	0	0	1	2
-5	-5	-5	-3	-3	-2	-1	0	0	0	0	1	2

Table 2. Fuzzy look-up table for productive phase $\bar{K}_2$

$\bar{K}_2$ \ E / $\dot{E}$	-5	-4	-3	-2	-1	-0	+0	1	2	3	4	5
5	-5	-4	-3	-1	0	0	1	2	4	4	5	5
4	-5	-4	-3	-1	0	0	1	2	3	4	5	5
3	-5	-5	-3	-2	0	0	0	1	3	4	5	5
2	-5	-5	-3	-2	0	0	0	1	2	4	5	5
1	-5	-5	-4	-2	-1	0	0	0	2	3	4	5
0	-5	-5	-4	-2	-1	0	0	0	1	3	4	5
-1	-5	-5	-4	-3	-1	0	0	0	1	2	3	5
-2	-5	-5	-5	-3	-2	-1	0	0	0	2	3	4
-3	-5	-5	-5	-4	-2	-1	0	0	0	1	2	4
-4	-5	-5	-5	-4	-3	-2	-1	0	0	1	2	3
-5	-5	-5	-5	-4	-3	-2	-1	0	0	0	2	3

Table 3. Fuzzy look-up table for degenerative phase $\bar{K}_3$

$\bar{K}_3$ \ E / $\dot{E}$	-5	-4	-3	-2	-1	-0	+0	1	2	3	4	5
5	-5	-4	-3	-2	-1	0	0	2	3	3	4	5
4	-5	-4	-3	-2	-1	0	0	1	3	3	4	5
3	-5	-5	-3	-2	-1	0	0	1	2	2	3	4
2	-5	-5	-3	-2	-1	0	0	0	2	2	3	4
1	-5	-5	-4	-3	-2	0	0	0	1	1	3	3
0	-5	-5	-4	-3	-2	0	0	0	1	1	2	3
-1	-5	-5	-5	-3	-2	-1	0	0	0	1	2	3
-2	-5	-5	-5	-4	-2	-1	0	0	0	1	2	3
-3	-5	-5	-5	-4	-3	-2	-1	0	0	0	1	2
-4	-5	-5	-5	-4	-3	-2	-1	0	0	0	1	2
-5	-5	-5	-5	-4	-3	-2	-2	0	0	0	1	2

THE RULE-BASED DISTILLATION DECISION AND CONTROL SYSTEM

Z. Song*, J. C. Gao and C. H. Zhou****

**Shanghai Refinery, Shanghai-200137, PRC*
***Research Institute of Industrial Process Control, Zhejiang University, Hangzhou-310027, PRC*

Abstract--After analyzing the basic control system of large-scale crude oil distillation process of a refinery, an intelligente control system RBDDCS (Rule-based Distillation Decision and Control System) is developed for optimization and control of the process. For speeding up the search procedure, an idea of combining the knowledge-based modulization structure and the original cut-branch method has been proposed. The result greatly increases the searching speed and meets the requirment of real-time control. At the same time, the computer memory space is also reduced.

The system is installed with real-time reasoning process. It is found that the system under operating condition can make optimization decision at normal state and reject the fault decision at abnormal state. Therefore the economic benefit of the production of the distillation unit can be increased greatly.

Key words: Expert Systems, Distillation Process, Rule-Based, Modula Structure, Cut-Branch

Introduction

The principles of AI can be applied to almost any field. Expert systems have been developed in the fields of medical diagnosis, finite element analysis as a modeling consultant, design of high-rise building and others. In recent years, expert systems are gradually used in real-time process control. They not only can solve general control problems, but also special problems, which can hardly be solved by conventional control theories. An expert system for reactive power/volage control problem is reported[1]. A PID controller using an expert system approach to self-turning is offered to the process industry[2]. A program ESTRAC-II for railroad traffic control in disturbed situations is reported[3]. The YES/MVS is a continuous real-time expert system that exerts active control over a computing system and provides advice to computer operators[4]. PLANT is a computer-based process control task which may be used to provide opportunities for subjects to control a dynamic system and diagnose, repair, and compensate for system failures[5] [6] [7].

In this paper, an expert control system for distillation process is presented. For a distillation process, the most important objects of control system are safety and stability. Disturbance compensation is considered. A sub-system[9] is applied to distillation process for ensuring the qualities of products and improving light oil yield. Initial and end boiling point temperatures of sidedraws are calculated, and their set points are given as high as posible within bounds for obtaining optimal light oil yield. Another sub-system for increasing recovery rate of energy is developed[10]. Inner reflux of every plate is caculated, and optimal pumparound distribution is given. But it is often conflict for raising yields and energy recovery rate at the same time. How to make both sub-systems run harmonically and stably? It is a very difficult problem if general control method is used. The principles of AI give us an effective way to deal with such kind of problems. An expert system RBDDCS is developed(Fig. 1). It not only can coordinate sub-systems but also detect the fault and make decision to reject it. Moreover, RBDDCS is relatively independent, it can run normally even though other sub-systems does not functioning.

There are two purposes for RBDDCS: (1) Detect the fault and make decision of rejecting it in order to keep the system safe and stable; (2) Coordinate sub-systems so as to ensure the qualities of products, raise light oil yield and increase energy recovery rate.

For meeting the requirment of real-time control, search procedure is speeded up by combing the modulization structure and the original cut-branch method, and the computer memory space is reduced as well.

A real-time expert control system

RBDDCS is a real-time expert control system (Fig. 2). It consists of following components: a global data base, a knowledge base, an inference engine, an explaining system, a knowledge acquisition system(KAS), an user interface and a real-time data communication interface.

Global data base

The system data base contains static and dynamic data. Static data includes alarm level thresholds and operating thresholds, such as constraints of initial and end boiling points, inner reflux, etc. Dynamic data includes mesured values of parameters and their decision values, such as flowrate set points of sidedraws, ASTM overlaps of every two adjacent sidedraws, etc.

Knowledge base

The knowledge base includes rulebase and "fact-making base". Rulebase contains production rules which are typically described as:

IF < situation >
THEN < action >

"Fact-making base" contains a series of test criteria, such as:

IF < something happens >
THEN REMEMBER < situation >

Data are turned into facts by using test criteria.

Inference engine

A method, which combines the knowlege-based modulization structure and the original cut-branch, is used in inference engine(Fig.3). Rules are divided into several modules according to different operation states(Fig.4). After testing operation states, some useless branches are cut off. So the inference process is greatly simplified, the searching procedure is speeded up, and the computer memory space is also reduced. Consequently, the requirment of expert system for real-time control is quite well met.

User interface

User interface is a software package which is provided for users' convenience. Static data can be displayed and modified if the "ststic data window" is "opened". Control process can be monitored if the "decision window" is "opened". Rulebase can be modified too. Of course, reports can be printed easily.

Knowledge acquisition system

Knowledge acquisition system turns operation experience into rules.

Application

RBDDCS system is installed for a distillation process. It is implemented in an IBM-PC and supported by GCLISP. The program storage volume is about 70K bytes. The minimum system requirement to memory space is 640K bytes. More then a hundred rules have been developed. Fig.5 shows the location of system.

Where

UIO is a universal input/ output unit,
UFM is a universal field multiplexer unit,
UCM is unit control modules

Fox-300 is a process control computer. Other sub-systems besides RBDDCS are implemented in Fox-300. Data communication between Fox-300 and IBM-PC is developed.

Decision process is presented as follows:

(i) Decision under normal state

Fig.6 gives a group of recorded curves under stable state. It is found that the temperature values of initial and end boiling points are stable below quality thesholds. Moreover, other parameter values are also stable.

Decision process under stable state is presented as follows:

```
" "
RULE ST-5
DEDUCES (SIDEGRAW 1 IBP IS AFFLUENT)
" "
RULE ST-6
DEDUCES (SIDEDRAW 1 EBP IS AFFLUENT)
" "
RULE ST-7
DEDUCES (SIDEDRAW 2 EBP IS AFFLUENT)
" "
RULE ST-8
DEDUCES (SIDEGRAW 3 EBP IS AFFLUENT)
" "
RULE ST-9
DEDUCES (SIDEDRAW 1 IBP IS STABLE)
" "
RULE ST-1
DEDUCES (SIDEDRAW 1 IBP SP CAN BE INCREASE)
" "
RULE ST-10
DEDUCES (SIDEDRAW 1 EBP IS STABLE)
" "
RULE ST-2
DEDUCES (SIDEDRAW EBP SP CAN BE INCREASED)
" "
RULE ST-11
DEDUCES (SIDEDRAW 2 EBP IS STABLE)
" "
RULE ST-3
DEDUCES (SIDEDRAW 2 EBP CAN BE INCREASED)
" "
RULE ST-12
DEDUCES (SIDEDRAW 3 EBP IS STABLE)
" "
RULE ST-4
DEDUCES (SIDEDRAW 3 EBP CAN BE INCREASED)
```

where

IBP = Initial Boiling Point
EBP = End Boiling Point
SP = Set Point
ST = Stable

It is found that the set points of initial and end boiling point of sidedraws must be increased according to the decision results.

(ii) Decision under abnormal state

Fig.7 shows a group of recorded curves under abnormal state. All parameters are unstable and change greatly.
Fault detection results are given as follows:

||
(PLATE 17 T LOW ALARM)
||
(OVERGAS LOW ALARM)
||
(SIDEDRAW 5 T HIGH ALARM)
||
(TOP T HIGH ALARM)
||
(TOP P HIGH ALARM)
||
(SIDEDRAW 5 P HIGH ALARM)
||
(PLATE 17 F LOW ALARM)
||
(FEED OIL F LOW ALARM)
||
(CIR 2 HIGH ALARM)
||
(CIR 1 F LOW ALARM)
||
(TOP REFLUX LOW ALARM)
||
(SIDEDRAW 5 F HIGH ALARM)
||
(SIDEDRAW 4 F LOW ALARM)
||
(SIDEDRAW 2 F HIGH ALARM)
||
(SIDEDRAW 1 F LOW ALARM)
||
(TOP REFLUX LOW ALARM)

where

T=temperature

The decision process is presented as follows:

" "
RULE HA-12
DEDUCES (SIDEDRAW 5 F MUST BE DECREASED)
" "
RULE HA-15
DEDUCES (SIDEDRAW 2 F MUST BE DECREASED)
" "
RULE HA-28
DEDUCES (TOP REFLUX MUST BE INCREASED)
" "
RULE TL-11
DEDUCES (OVLP 1 SP MUST BE INCREASED)
" "
RULE ST-6
DEDUCES (SIDEDRAW 1 EBP IS AFFLUENT)
" "
RULE ST-7
DEDUCES (SIDEDRAW 2 EBP IS AFFLUENT)
" "
RULE ST-8
DEDUCES (SIDEDRAW 3 EBP IS AFFLUENT)

where

F = Flowrate
HA = High Alarm
TL = Too Low

Results show under abnormal state, RBDDCS can give out alarm immediately and make decisions to reject the fault. Although, the mean values of set points of initial and end boiling points are affluent, they can not be increased because of abnormal state. The same decision as operator will give.

Conclusions

There are two obstacles when expert system approach is applied to real-time control. One is the low search speed, the other is the limitation of computer memory space . As shown in the effective example, RBDDCS overcomes these problems by using a method which combines original cut-branch and modulization structure. At the same time, a knowledge base is developed. The system can make decisions according to diffrent production states. The user interface provides a friendly and effective communication means between operators and computers. It proves that the system has ability to deal with both abnormal and normal production states. Under abnormal state, the system will give alarm immediately and make decisions to rejecting the fault. Under normal state, the system will coordinate sub-systems so as to realize optimal control. Therefore, by introducing RBDDCS to the distillation controll, the economic benefit of the production can be greatly increased.

Acknowledgements

This work has been supported by the Petro-chemical Corporation of China.

The auther thanks Mr.Z.L.Fu for the communication work and Miss.R.Du for part of user interface work.

The auther thanks engineers and operaters of Shanghai Refinery for their suppling expert experience and their supports.

References

[1] C.C.Liu,"An expert system assisting decision-making of reactive power/voltage control ",IEEE Trans. on Power System, Vol.PWrs-1, No.3, aug. 1986

[2] A. Carmon, " Intelligent knowledge-based system for adaptive PID controller turning", Journal A, Vol.27, No.3, 1986

[3] S.Araya and K.Fukumori,"ESTRAC -II: An expert system for train traffic control in disturbed situations", Arti-ficial Intelligence by TIM O'Shea, Proc. of the 6th European Conf. on AI.

[4] R.L.Ennis et al, "A continuous Real-time expert system for computer operations", IBM J. RES. DEVELOP. Vol.30, No.1, Jan. 1986

[5] A.Knaenper and W.B.Rouse,"A rule-based model of human problem-solving behavior in dynamic environments", IEEE Trans. on System, Man and Cybernetics, Vol.SMC-15, No.6, Nov./Dec.1985

[6] N.M.Morris and W.B.Rouse, "The effects of type of knowledge upon human problem solving in a process control task", IEEE Trans. on System, Man and Cybernetics, Vol.SMC-15, No.6, Nov./Dec. 1985

[7] N.M.Morris and W.B.Rouse, "PLANT: An experimental task for the study of human problem solving in process control", IEEE Trans. on System, Man and Cybernetics, Vol.SMC-15, No.6, Nov/Dec. 1985

[8] K.J.Åstrom et al,"Expert control", Automatica, V.22, No.3, pp277-286, 1986

[9] J.P.Gong, et al "Optimal control and decision for large scale oil distillation unit", PhD. Disserts, Zhejiang University, P.R.C. 1988

[10]W.H.Zen, et al, Multi-objective optimization for energy and product ratio in crude distillation process", PhD. Disserts, Zhejiang University, P.R.C. 1988

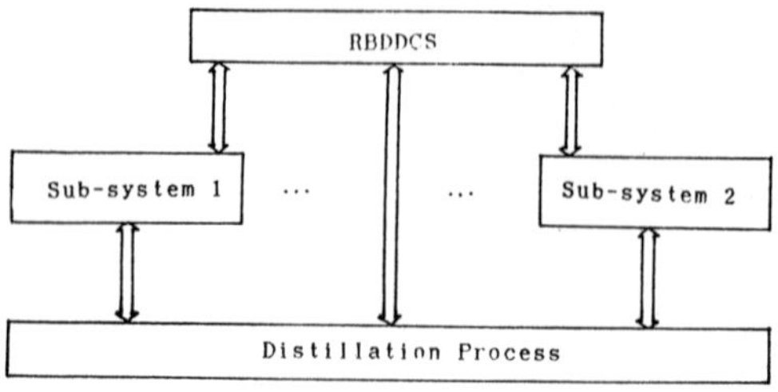

Fig.1. System structure

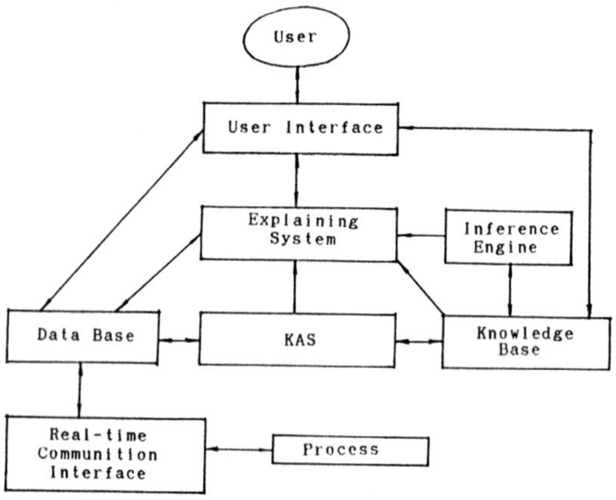

Fig.2 A block diagram of a real-time rule-based expert control system

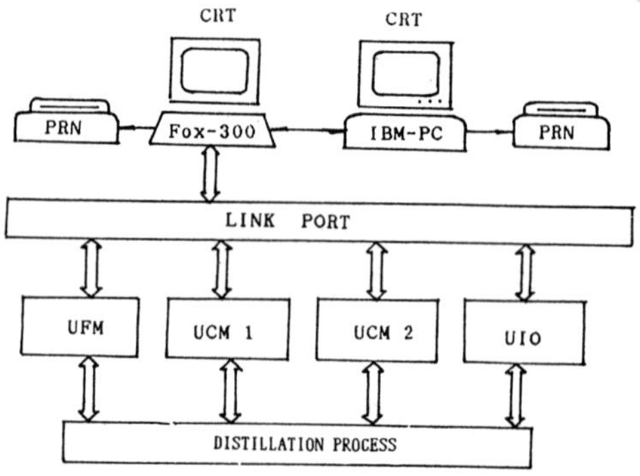

Fig.5. Location of system

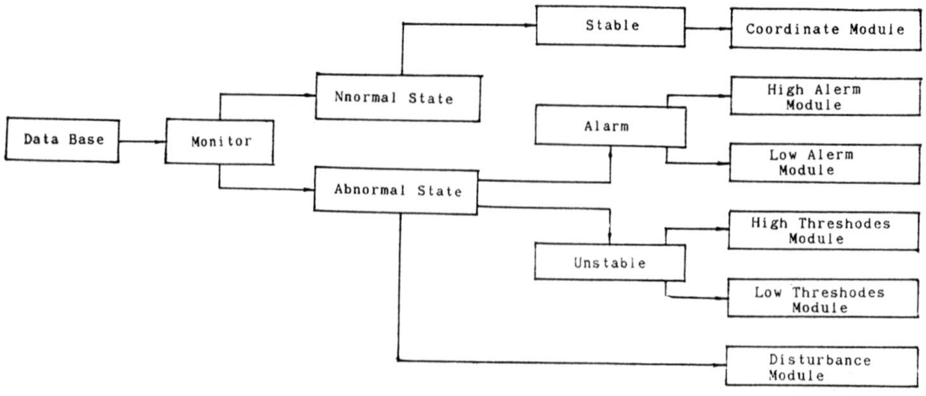

Fig.3. Modula structure

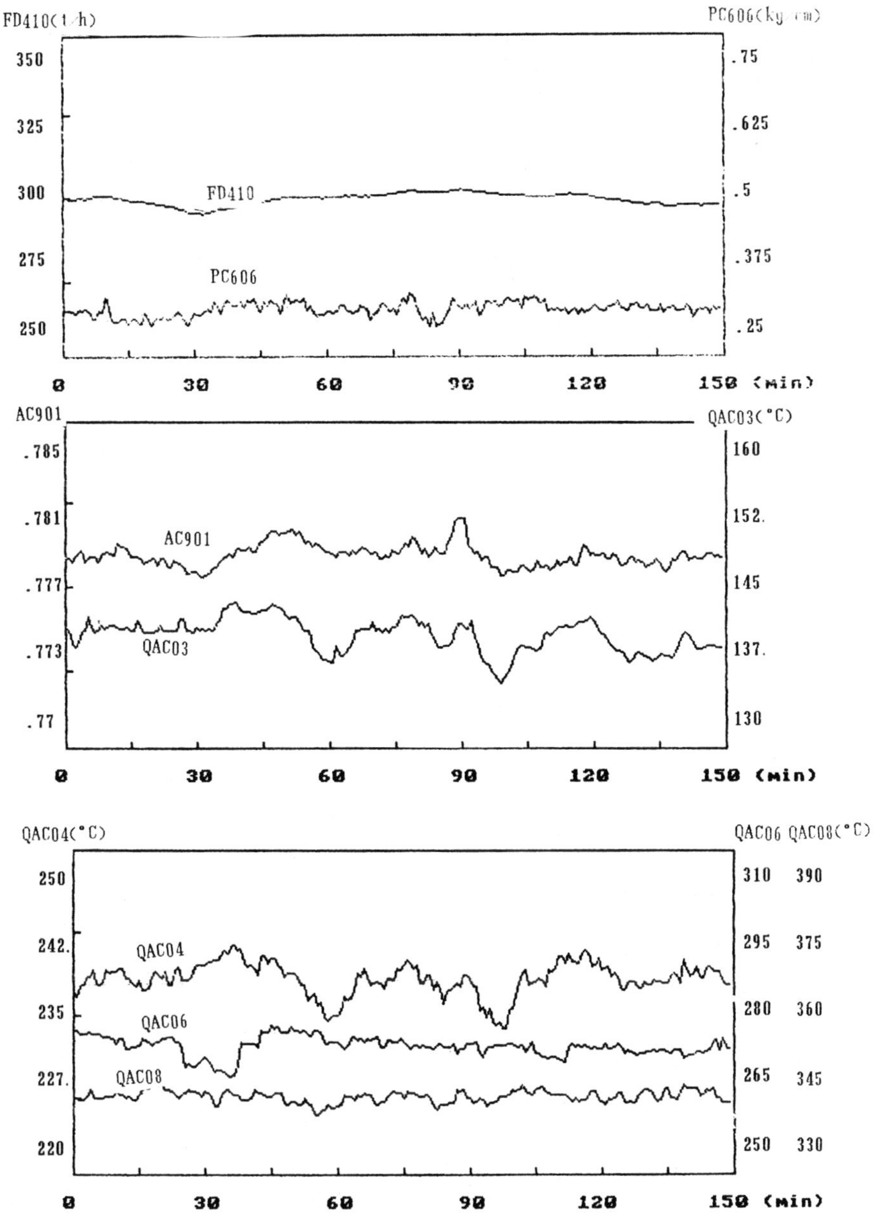

Fig.6. Recorded curves under normal state

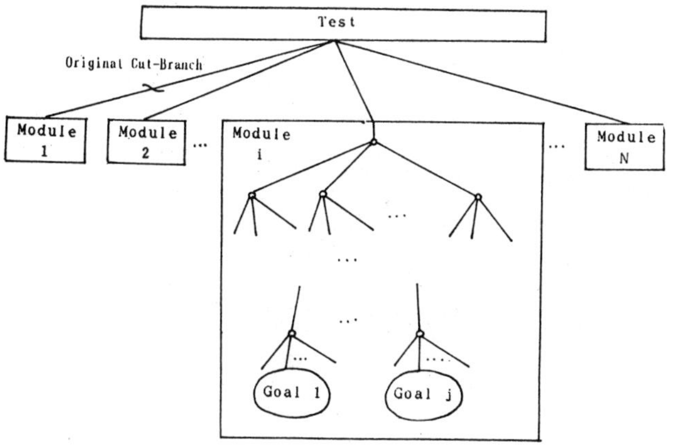

Fig.4. Inference network

Where

FD410=Feed oil flowrate (t/h)
TD175=Feed oil temperature (°C)
PC606=Top preasure (kg/cm)
TC158=Temperature of sidedraw 1 (°C)
AC901=Density of sidedraw 1
QAC03=Initial boiling point of sidedraw 1(°C)
QAC04=End boiling point of sidedraw 1 (°C)
QAC06=End boiling point of sidedraw 2 (°C)
QAC08=End boiling point of sidedraw 3 (°C)
TD175=Feed oil temperature(°C)
TC158=Temperature of sidedraw(°C)

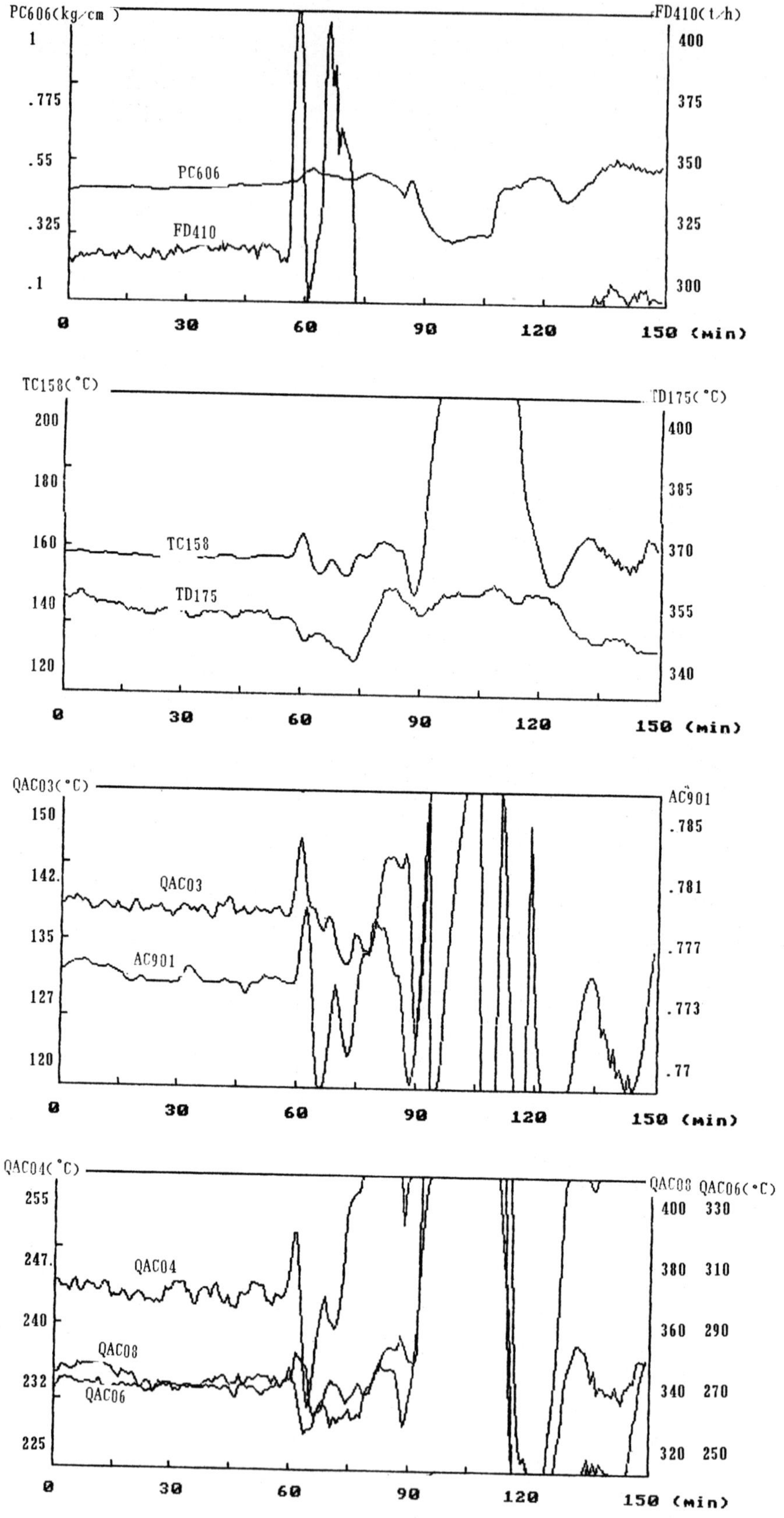

Fig. 7. Recorded curves under abnormal state

APPLICATION OF INTELLIGENT CONTROL OF TIME-DELAY PROCESSES TO THE MIX MOISTURE CONTROL SYSTEM IN SINTERPLANTS

Zhang Huiping*, En Yutian and Zhang Jinliang****

**Department of Electrical-mechanical Engineering, Shenyang Gold College, PRC*
***Department of Automatic Control, Northeast University of Technology, Shenyang, PRC*

ABSTRACT. This paper presents a intelligent controller based on the pole-zero placement self-tuning control strategy, which aims at controlling the mix moisture in sinterplants.

KEYWORDS. Identification; disturbance estimation; self-tuning control; intelligent control.

1. INTRODUCTION

In process control, time delays are always a serious obstacle which complicate the analytical aspects of control system design and make good control very difficult to achieve. Smith (1959) proposed a predicting compensation technique which can eliminate the delay term in the closed-loop characteristic equation (Smith predictor). Among the special control techniques proposed for processes with time delays, the Smith predictor has probably been the one studied most. When applied, however,Smith predictor has some drawback, for example, if processes are subject to disturbances, the predictor cannot predict the output of the process exactly, and the output error cannot decay as fast as desired. If the disturbances happen frequently or vary with time, the output response to disturbances may be sluggish enough to be unacceptable. There have been some attempts to reject disturbance effects (Donoghue 1977, Watanabe et al 1983). These methods, however, only consider the step disturbances. Furthermore, the model used in Smith predictor to design the process controller usually contains many assumptions and simplifications, and consequently the resulting controllers may lead to serious operational problems when they are implemented on real plants. Most often the success of the controller is limited by the magnitude of this model-plant parameter mismatch.

Recently many papers discussed this problem and proposed some adaptive control strategies, which estimate the parameters of a plant based on the inputs and outputs of the process and adjust the parameters of the model and the controller on line to make the control system adapt the change of plant parameters. But if the mathematical model of a plant cannot be obtained, or if the controlled process has unmeasurable disturbances, the parameter estimator in an adaptive controller cannot work well, and the resulting controller and model may be incorrect, consequently the closed-loop system may not be stable.

Considering the case of a controlled process has large time-varying unmeasurable disturbances, this paper presents an intelligent controller which consists of a basic control unit and an intelligent control unit. The former contains an unknown disturbance estimate-predictor and a pole-zero placement self-tuning controller, which can switch-on and switch-off the disturbance estimate-predictor and change the controller output in accordance with the instruction of the latter, the basic control unit, however, does not pay any attention to matters such as the stability or other performance problems; the latter, that is the intelligent control unit, supervises and manages the overall control system, and consists of knowledge base and inference engine. The knowledge base contains the expertise, data from transmitter and information about process state and performance and so on, which are necessary to real-time control and on-line decision. The inference engine employs heuristic rules of the form, "If <Situation> Then <Action>", and uses forward reasoning to deduce the control action.

2. THE BASIC CONTROL UNIT

The system to be considered is a MISO system with delays in control which can be described by the difference equation

$$A(z^{-1})y(t)=B(z^{-1})u(t-k)+B1(z^{-1})v(t-k1)+B2(z^{-1})L(t-k2) \quad (1)$$

where $y(t)$, $u(t)$, $v(t)$ and $L(t)$ are respectively the process output, the input control signal, the measurable disturbance and the unmeasurable disturbance; k, k1 and k2 are respectively the time delays.

The estimation of the unmeasurable disturbance at time t-k2 is

$$L(t-k2)=\frac{1}{b20}\{A(z^{-1})y(t)-B(z^{-1})u(t-k)-B1(z^{-1})v(t-k1)-z[B2(z^{-1})-b20]L(t-k2-1)\} \quad (2)$$

It is assumed that the unmeasurable disturbance satisfies the following model

$$D(z^{-1})L(t)=0 \quad (3)$$

where $D(z^{-1})=1+d1z^{-1}+d2z^{-1}+...+d_l z^{-l}$

As the disturbance is time-varying, the

dynamic model in eq.3 may be time-varying, the value of di (i=1,2,...,l) must be calculated on-line in accordance with the change. A recursive least-square algorithm with a forgetting factor is used to identify the value of di by changing eq.3 into the following form

$$L(t-k2+1)=\phi^T(t-k2)\hat{\theta}+e(t-k2) \quad (4)$$

$\phi(t-k2)$ and $\hat{\theta}$ are respectively the memory vector and the parameter estimates, defined as

$$\phi(t-k2)=[L(t-k2),\ldots,L(t-k2-l+1)]^T$$
$$=[\hat{d}1,\hat{d}2,\ldots,\hat{d}l]^T$$

so, the unmeasurable disturbance model can be written as

$$L(t+1)=\hat{d}1L(t)+\hat{d}2L(t-1)+\ldots+$$
$$+\hat{d}l\,L(t-l+1)+e(t) \quad (5)$$

from it, the prediction value for L(t/t-k2) will be

$$\hat{L}(t/t-k2)=\eta_1^{(k2)}L(t-k2)+\eta_2^{(k2)}L(t-k2-1)+\ldots$$
$$+\eta_l^{(k2)}L(t-k2-l+1) \quad (6)$$

with

$$i=[A^{k2}C]i \quad (7)$$

where, [ ]i denotes the ith component of a vector in the parentheses, and

$$A=\begin{bmatrix}\hat{d}1 & 1 & 0 & \ldots 0\\ \hat{d}2 & 0 & 1 & \ldots 0\\ \vdots & & & \\ \hat{d}l\text{-}1 & 0 & 0 & \ldots 1\\ \hat{d}l & 0 & 0 & \ldots 0\end{bmatrix} \qquad C=[1,0,0,\ldots 0]^T$$

If w(t) is the set-point and $T(z^{-1})$, $G(z^{-1})$, $S(z^{-1})$, $D1(z^{-1})$ and $R(z^{-1})$ are general polynomial in z^{-1}, a general feedback controller may be written as

$$R(z^{-1})u(t)=T(z^{-1})w(t)-G(z^{-1})y(t)-$$
$$S(z^{-1})v(t)-D1(z^{-1})\hat{L}(t/t-k2) \quad (8)$$

From which u(t) can be calculated recursively given w(t) and $\hat{L}(t/t-k2)$ (see eq.6) and measured y(t) and v(t).

Eliminating u(t) by using the plant model (eq.1) gives the closed loop relationship

$$y(t)=\frac{z^{-k}B(z^{-1})T(z^{-1})}{A(z^{-1})R(z^{-1})+z^{-k}B(z^{-1})G(z^{-1})}w(t)+$$

$$+\frac{z^{-k}[z^{-m}B1(z^{-1})R(z^{-1})-B(z^{-1})S(z^{-1})]}{A(z^{-1})R(z^{-1})+z^{-k}B(z^{-1})G(z^{-1})}v(t)+$$

$$+\frac{z^{-k}[z^{-n}B2(z^{-1})R(z^{-1})-B(z^{-1})D1(z^{-1})]}{A(z^{-1})R(z^{-1})+z^{-k}B(z^{-1})G(z^{-1})}\hat{L}(t/t-k2)$$

$$+\frac{z^{-k2}B2(z^{-1})R(z^{-1})}{A(z^{-1})R(z^{-1})+z^{-k}B(z^{-1})G(z^{-1})}\Delta L(t) \quad (9)$$

Where m=k1-k, n=k2-k and $L(t)=\hat{L}(t/t-k2)+\Delta L(t)$. The fourth term on the right side in eq. 9 will tend to zero after the unmeasurable disturbance prediction value have converged to the real value of L(t).

The control objective is as follows

a. Force the close-loop system to follow a reference model

$$Am(z^{-1})y(t)=Bm(z^{-1})w(t-k)$$

b. Reject the effects of v(t) and L(t) to the process output.

These two objectives can be satisfied by choosing properly a group of polynomials of $T(z^{-1})$, $R(z^{-1})$, $G(z^{-1})$, $S(z^{-1})$ and $D1(z^{-1})$ (see [5]). So that the controller output is calculated from eq. 8. If the parameters of the process model are unknown, the self-tuning control strategy is adopted. The step of the self-tuning control may be stated as follows

(a) Identify the parameters of the process

(b) Predict the unmeasurable disturbance

(c) Calculate the parameters of the controller and control signal

It is found that this control method can give a good performance if the unmeasurable disturbance is time-varying slowly. But when the disturbance changes abruptly, the process output may fluctuate as a result of incorrect prediction value $\hat{L}(t/t-k2)$.

3. THE INTELLIGENT CONTROL UNIT

A intelligent control unit is given to detect this changes and make some decisions such as switching-off the disturbance estimate-predictor and adjusting the controller output based on the features of the process output. In this case, the input control signal is modified into the following form

$$u(t)=[T(z^{-1})w(t)-G(z^{-1})y(t)-S(z^{-1})v(t)-$$
$$D'1(z^{-1})\hat{L}(t/t-k2)]/R(z^{-1})+\Delta u(t)$$

Below is the control rules of the intelligent control unit

(1) If $|e(t)|>=e1$ and $e(t)\dot{e}(t)>=0$
Then $\Delta u(t)=k3e(t)$ and $D'1(z^{-1})=0$
(2) If $|e(t)|>=e1$ and $e(t)\dot{e}(t)<0$
Then $\Delta u(t)=k4e(t)$ and $D'1(z^{-1})=0$
(3) If $e2<=|e(t)|<e1$ and $e(t)\dot{e}(t)>=0$
Then $\Delta u(t)=k5e(t)$ and $D'1(z^{-1})=0$
(4) If $e2<=|e(t)|<e1$ and $e(t)\dot{e}(t)<0$
Then $\Delta u(t)=k6e(t)$ and $D'1(z^{-1})=0$
(5) If $|e(t)|<=e2$ and $|\dot{e}(t)|>=ec$
Then $\Delta u(t)=k7e(t)$ and $D'1(z^{-1})=0$
(6) If $|e(t)|<=e2$ and $|\dot{e}(t)|<ec$
Then $\Delta u(t)=0$ and $D'1(z^{-1})=D1(z^{-1})$

Where $e(t)=w(t)-y(t)$, $\dot{e}(t)=e(t)-e(t-1)$. e1, e2, ec and k3--k7 are given by the knowledge base and they can be gained from some actual experiences of process control engineers and the requirements of real industrial processes. This kind of heuristic rules together with the forward reasoning method can do specific work under specific conditions, that is resemble human in control behavior. One obvious advantage of this kind of heuristic rules is that its increasing, decreasing and modifying are easy to realize, which is quite adaptable to process control. Moreover, it is certain that the objective action is searched because that every state of e(t) and $\dot{e}(t)$ has corresponding control rule.

4. APPLICATION TO THE MIX MOISTURE CONTROL SYSTEM IN A SINTERPLANT

In sinterplant production process, the moisture of sintering mixture is one of the main factor effecting the production of a sinterplant (fig.a), and it is very difficult to obtain the accurate mathematical model of the mixing processes due to some uncertainty of the process and various disturbances caused by hot return (In most sinterplants of China, the hot return is fed into mixer directly) and environment. Moreover, there are some problems about the mix moisture measure, especially the moisture measure of the sinter feed which contains hot return is impossible now. That make good control of mix moisture very difficult to achieve by conventional PID control method. Using the intelligent controller given in this paper, the good control performance can be obtained. This is evidenced with the illustrated graphs of fig.b and fig.c.

5. CONCLUSIONS

This paper presents an intelligent controller for the time-delay processes with time-varying unmeasurable disturbance, and gives a method of artificial intelligence as a tool to aid in the implementation of self-tuning controller, the advantages of which is demonstrated by the simulation experiments for the mix moisture control system of a sinterplant.

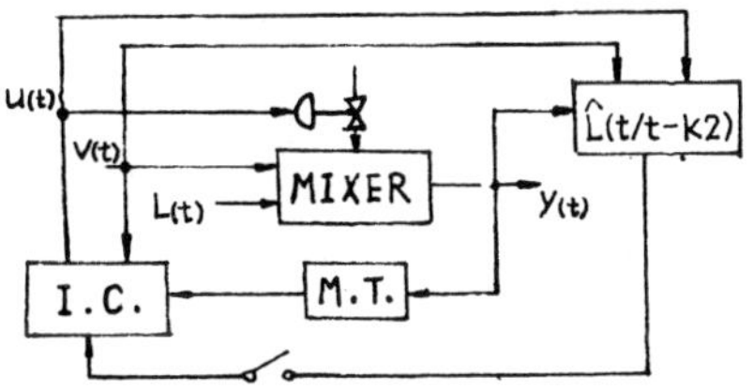

Fig.a Mix moisture control system block diagram
v(t)--measurable disturbance caused by changes of flow of the sinter feed
L(t)--unmeasurable disturbance caused by changes of moisture of the sinter feed
M.T.--the moisture transmitter
I.C.--the intelligent controller

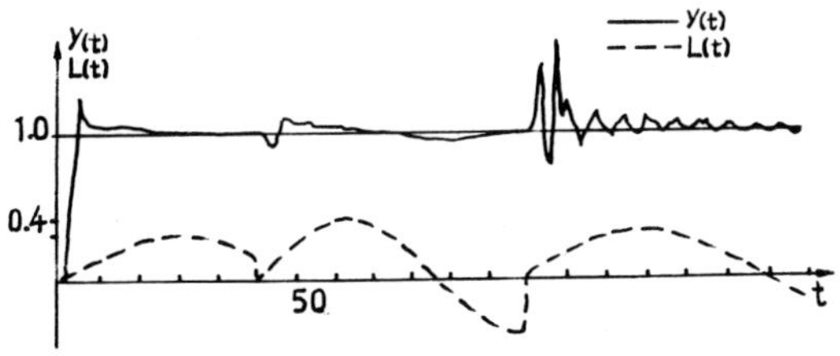

Fig.b The simulation results for the example of a sinterplant mix moisture without the intelligent control unit.

plant: $(1-0.37z^{-1})y(t)=0.57u(t-2)+(-0.01+0.037z^{-1})v(t-2)+(1-0.37z^{-1})L(t-2)$

$$\sum_{i=1}^{150}|ei(t)|=9.460246$$

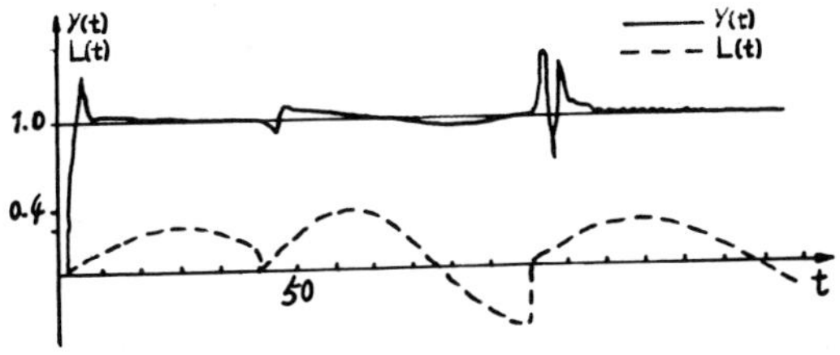

Fig.c The simulation results of the intelligent controller for the same process conditions as in fig. b

$$\sum_{i=1}^{150}|ei(t)|=8.595468$$

REFERENCES

[1] Astrom K.J. and Wittermark B. , "Self-tuning controller based on pole-zero placement", IEE.Proceedings, Vol. 127 pt.d, No.3, 120-130, 1980

[2] Donoghue J.F. ,"A comparison of the smith predictor and optimal design approaches for systems with delay in the control", IEEE. Trans., Ind. Electron. Contr. Instrum. ,Vol. IECI-24, 1977

[3] Smith O.J.M. ,"A controller to overcome dead-time", ISA J. Vol.6, No.2, 28-33, 1959

[4] Watanabe K. , Ishiyama Y. and Ito M. , "Modified smith predictor control for multivariable systems with delays and unmeasurable step disturbance" Int. J.Control, Vol.37, No.5, 959-973, 1983

[5] Zhang H.P., Self-tuning control of the time-delay system with disturbance. M.S. Thesis 1989.1

[6] Zhou Q.J., "The robustness of an intelligent controller and its performance", International Conference -Control,1985.2, 429-434

AUTHOR INDEX

KEYWORD INDEX

SYMPOSIA VOLUMES

ADALI & TUNALI: Microcomputer Application in Process Control
AKASHI: Control Science and Technology for the Progress of Society, 7 Volumes
ALBERTOS & DE LA PUENTE: Components, Instruments and Techniques for Low Cost Automation and Applications
ALONSO-CONCHEIRO: Real Time Digital Control Applications
AMOUROUX & EL JAI: Control of Distributed Parameter Systems (1989)
ATHERTON: Multivariable Technological Systems
BABARY & LE LETTY: Control of Distributed Parameter Systems (1982)
BALCHEN: Automation and Data Processing in Aquaculture
BANKS & PRITCHARD: Control of Distributed Parameter Systems (1977)
BAOSHENG HU: Analysis, Design and Evaluation of Man–Machine Systems (1989)
BARKER & YOUNG: Identification and System Parameter Estimation (1985)
BASANEZ, FERRATE & SARIDIS: Robot Control "SYROCO '85"
BASAR & PAU: Dynamic Modelling and Control of National Economies (1983)
BAYLIS: Safety of Computer Control Systems (1983)
BEKEY & SARIDIS: Identification and System Parameter Estimation (1982)
BINDER & PERRET: Components and Instruments for Distributed Computer Control Systems
CALVAER: Power Systems, Modelling and Control Applications
Van CAUWENBERGHE: Instrumentation and Automation in the Paper, Rubber, Plastics and Polymerisation Industries (1980) (1983)
CHEN HAN-FU: Identification and System Parameter Estimation (1988)
CHEN ZHEN-YU: Computer Aided Design in Control Systems (1988)
CHRETIEN: Automatic Control in Space (1985)
CHRISTODULAKIS: Dynamic Modelling and Control of National Economies (1989)
COBELLI & MARIANI: Modelling and Control in Biomedical Systems
CUENOD: Computer Aided Design of Control Systems†
DA CUNHA: Planning and Operation of Electric Energy Systems
DE CARLI: Low Cost Automation
De GIORGIO & ROVEDA: Criteria for Selecting Appropriate Technologies under Different Cultural, Technical and Social Conditions
DUBUISSON: Information and Systems
EHRENBERGER: Safety of Computer Control Systems (SAFECOMP '88)
ELLIS: Control Problems and Devices in Manufacturing Technology (1980)
FERRATE & PUENTE: Software for Computer Control (1982)
FLEISSNER: Systems Approach to Appropriate Technology Transfer
FLORIAN & HAASE: Software for Computer Control (1986)
GEERING & MANSOUR: Large Scale Systems: Theory and Applications (1986)
GENSER, ETSCHMAIER, HASEGAWA & STROBEL: Control in Transportation Systems (1986)
GERTLER & KEVICZKY: A Bridge Between Control Science and Technology, 6 Volumes
GHONAIMY: Systems Approach for Development (1977)
HAIMES & KINDLER: Water and Related Land Resource Systems
HARDT: Information Control Problems in Manufacturing Technology (1982)
HERBST: Automatic Control in Power Generation Distribution and Protection
HRUZ & CICEL: Automatic Measurement and Control in Woodworking Industry — Lignoautomatica '86
HUSSON: Advanced Information Processing in Automatic Control
ISERMANN: Automatic Control, 10 Volumes
ISERMANN: Identification and System Parameter Estimation (1979)
ISERMANN & KALTENECKER: Digital Computer Applications to Process Control
ISIDORI: Nonlinear Control Systems Design
JANSSEN, PAU & STRASZAK: Dynamic Modelling and Control of National Economies (1980)
JELLALI: Systems Analysis Applied to Management of Water Resources
JOHANNSEN & RIJNSDORP: Analysis, Design, and Evaluation of Man–Machine Systems
JOHNSON: Adaptive Systems in Control and Signal Processing
JOHNSON: Modelling and Control of Biotechnological Processes
KAYA & WILLIAMS: Instrumentation and Automation in the Paper, Rubber, Plastics and Polymerization Industries (1986)
KLAMT & LAUBER: Control in Transportation Systems (1984)
KOPACEK *et al.*: Skill Based Automated Production
KOPACEK, TROCH & DESOYER: Theory of Robots
KOPPEL: Automation in Mining, Mineral and Metal Processing (1989)
KUMMEL: Adaptive Control of Chemical Processes (ADCHEM '88)
LARSEN & HANSEN: Computer Aided Design in Control and Engineering Systems
LEININGER: Computer Aided Design of Multivariable Technological Systems
LEONHARD: Control in Power Electronics and Electrical Drives (1977)
LESKIEWICZ & ZAREMBA: Pneumatic and Hydraulic Components and Instruments in Automatic Control†
LINKENS & ATHERTON: Trends in Control and Measurement Education
MACLEOD & HEHER: Software for Computer Control (SOCOCO '88)
MAHALANABIS: Theory and Application of Digital Control
MANCINI, JOHANNSEN & MARTENSSON: Analysis, Design and Evaluation of Man–Machine Systems (1985)
MARTOS, PAU, ZIERMANN: Dynamic Modelling and Control of National Economies (1986)
McGREAVY: Dynamics and Control of Chemical Reactors and Distillation Columns
MLADENOV: Distributed Intelligence Systems: Methods and Applications
MUNDAY: Automatic Control in Space (1979)
NAJIM & ABDEL-FATTAH: System Approach for Development (1980)
NIEMI: A Link Between Science and Applications of Automatic Control, 4 Volumes
NISHIKAWA & KAYA: Energy Systems, Management and Economics
NISHIMURA: Automatic Control in Aerospace
NORRIE & TURNER: Automation for Mineral Resource Development
NOVAK: Software for Computer Control (1979)
O'SHEA & POLIS: Automation in Mining, Mineral and Metal Processing (1980)
OSHIMA: Information Control Problems in Manufacturing Technology (1977)
PAUL: Digital Computer Applications to Process Control (1985)
PERRIN: Control, Computers, Communications in Transportation
PONOMARYOV: Artificial Intelligence
PUENTE & NEMES: Information Control Problems in Manufacturing Technology (1989)
RAMAMOORTY: Automation and Instrumentation for Power Plants
RANTA: Analysis, Design and Evaluation of Man–Machine Systems (1988)
RAUCH: Applications of Nonlinear Programming to Optimization and Control†
RAUCH: Control of Distributed Parameter Systems (1986)
REINISCH & THOMA: Large Scale Systems: Theory and Applications (1989)
REMBOLD: Robot Control (SYROCO '88)
RIJNSDORP: Case Studies in Automation Related to Humanization of Work
RIJNSDORP *et al.*: Dynamics and Control of Chemical Reactors (DYCORD '89)
RIJNSDORP, PLOMP & MÖLLER: Training for Tomorrow—Educational Aspects of Computerized Automation
ROOS: Economics and Artificial Intelligence
SANCHEZ: Fuzzy Information, Knowledge Representation and Decision Analysis
SAWARAGI & AKASHI: Environmental Systems Planning, Design and Control
SINHA & TELKSNYS: Stochastic Control
SMEDEMA: Real Time Programming (1977)†
STRASZAK: Large Scale Systems: Theory and Applications (1983)
SUBRAMANYAM: Computer Applications in Large Scale Power Systems
TAL': Information Control Problems in Manufacturing Technology (1986)
TITLI & SINGH: Large Scale Systems: Theory and Applications (1980)
TROCH, KOPACEK & BREITENECKER: Simulation of Control Systems
UHI AHN: Power Systems and Power Plant Control (1989)
VALADARES TAVARES & EVARISTO DA SILVA: Systems Analysis Applied to Water and Related Land Resources
van WOERKOM: Automatic Control in Space (1982)
WANG PINGYANG: Power Systems and Power Plant Control

WESTERLUND: Automation in Mining, Mineral and Metal Processing (1983)

YANG JIACHI: Control Science and Technology for Development

YOSHITANI: Automation in Mining, Mineral and Metal Processing (1986)

ZWICKY: Control in Power Electronics and Electrical Drives (1983)

WORKSHOP VOLUMES

ASTROM & WITTENMARK: Adaptive Systems in Control and Signal Processing

BOULLART *et al.*: Industrial Process Control Systems

BRODNER: Skill Based Automated Manufacturing

BULL: Real Time Programming (1983)

BULL & WILLIAMS: Real Time Programming (1985)

CAMPBELL: Control Aspects of Prosthetics and Orthotics

CHESTNUT: Contributions of Technology to International Conflict Resolution (SWIIS)

CHESTNUT *et al.*: International Conflict Resolution using Systems Engineering (SWIIS)

CHESTNUT, GENSER, KOPACEK & WIERZBICKI: Supplemental Ways for Improving International Stability

CICHOCKI & STRASZAK: Systems Analysis Applications to Complex Programs

CRESPO & DE LA PUENTE: Real Time Programming (1988)

CRONHJORT: Real Time Programming (1978)

DI PILLO: Control Applications of Nonlinear Programming and Optimization

ELZER: Experience with the Management of Software Projects

GELLIE & TAVAST: Distributed Computer Control Systems (1982)

GENSER *et al.*: Safety of Computer Control Systems (SAFECOMP '89)

GOODWIN: Robust Adaptive Control

HAASE: Real Time Programming (1980)

HALME: Modelling and Control of Biotechnical Processes

HARRISON: Distributed Computer Control Systems (1979)

HASEGAWA: Real Time Programming (1981)†

HASEGAWA & INOUE: Urban, Regional and National Planning—Environmental Aspects

JANSEN & BOULLART: Reliability of Instrumentation Systems for Safeguarding and Control

KOTOB: Automatic Control in Petroleum, Petrochemical and Desalination Industries

LANDAU, TOMIZUKA & AUSLANDER: Adaptive Systems in Control and Signal Processing

LAUBER: Safety of Computer Control Systems (1979)

LOTOTSKY: Evaluation of Adaptive Control Strategies in Industrial Applications

MAFFEZZONI: Modelling and Control of Electric Power Plants (1984)

MARTIN: Design of Work in Automated Manufacturing Systems

McAVOY: Model Based Process Control

MEYER: Real Time Programming (1989)

MILLER: Distributed Computer Control Systems (1981)

MILOVANOVIC & ELZER: Experience with the Management of Software Projects (1988)

MOWLE: Experience with the Management of Software Projects

NARITA & MOTUS: Distributed Computer Control Systems (1989)

OLLUS: Digital Image Processing in Industrial Applications—Vision Control

QUIRK: Safety of Computer Control Systems (1985) (1986)

RAUCH: Control Applications of Nonlinear Programming

REMBOLD: Information Control Problems in Manufacturing Technology (1979)

RODD: Artificial Intelligence in Real Time Control (1989)

RODD: Distributed Computer Control Systems (1983)

RODD: Distributed Databases in Real Time Control

RODD & LALIVE D'EPINAY: Distributed Computer Control Systems (1988)

RODD & MULLER: Distributed Computer Control Systems (1986)

RODD & SUSKI: Artificial Intelligence in Real Time Control

SIGUERDIDJANE & BERNHARD: Control Applications of Nonlinear Programming and Optimization

SINGH & TITLI: Control and Management of Integrated Industrial Complexes

SKELTON & OWENS: Model Error Concepts and Compensation

SOMMER: Applied Measurements in Mineral and Metallurgical Processing

SUSKI: Distributed Computer Control Systems (1985)

SZLANKO: Real Time Programming (1986)

TAKAMATSU & O'SHIMA: Production Control in Process Industry

UNBEHAUEN: Adaptive Control of Chemical Processes

VILLA & MURARI: Decisional Structures in Automated Manufacturing

†Out of stock—microfiche copies available. Details of prices sent on request from the IFAC Publisher.

IFAC Related Titles

BROADBENT & MASUBUCHI: Multilingual Glossary of Automatic Control Technology

EYKHOFF: Trends and Progress in System Identification

NALECZ: Control Aspects of Biomedical Engineering